I0188272

TESTIMONIALS

"*Steel Soldier* is an important American story about a brave Marine told by a humble family man doing what many did at the time to honor and serve his country. Jim Messina details his time from the steel mills through boot camp, to landing and fighting at Guadalcanal with uncanny detail, raw emotion, and a way of putting the reader right in his boots. Coauthored by Jim Messina's son, Chuck, this book is an important piece of World War II literature, including extensive research, hand-drawn remembrances, and striking historical images. Highly recommended for anyone wanting a better understanding of why these brave men and women have been named 'the Greatest Generation.'"

—Valerie Ormond, Captain, US Navy (Ret.), Chief Executive Officer, Veteran Writing Services, LLC, Multiple Award-Winning Author of the *Believing In Horses* Series

"If you want to learn about a battle or other event in World War II, there are many books and other materials out there for one to read. However, if you want to learn what really happened, read [an account] about an event written by someone who was there and lived through the battle. Such is the case with *Steel Soldier.* Just reading about the challenges and hardships endured by James Messina and his fellow Marines was very inspiring. I highly recommend *Steel Soldier* to anyone who enjoys reading about the Marines in World War II. Semper Fi."

—Lieutenant Colonel Bradley M. Gates, United States Marine Corps (Ret), Author of *Two Good Men*

"James Messina's moving tale of World War II in the South Pacific takes us from a young man growing up in a small steel town in Western Pennsylvania to the terrifying battlefields of Guadalcanal and the many Japanese-occupied islands of the South Pacific. His inspirational tale reads as fiction, being that well written and captivating. I am personally grateful that this story has been preserved and made available for all generations."

—Cindy Murphy, Author of *Images of America: Aliquippa*

"This is an impressive biography in vignette form, featuring naive illustrations by the late author and photos from the family album. If you want to know what it was like to be a working-class boy finding his way in Depression-era West Aliquippa, and eventually to infantry duty during World War II, this is the place."

—*Pittsburgh Post-Gazette*

"Jim Messina was 50 when a back injury he sustained as a Marine at Guadalcanal forced his retirement from J&L Steel's Aliquippa Works.

"But his next avocation is what sets him apart from most who grew up during the Great Depression, fought in World War II and worked in area mills: Messina took up drawing and later wrote his autobiography. And the late Messina's charming illustrations and guilelessly affecting prose have been assembled by his son . . .

"Most of the drawings—whether in pencil, charcoal and ink, watercolors, oil, and tempera—are rendered in simple, even childlike terms. (Some streetscapes are more draftsman-like.) Messina was self-taught; he meant his words and drawings simply as a keepsake for family. "He picked himself up and he found another interest in drawing," says Chuck Messina.

"It's just an amazing gift he left me."

—Bill O'Driscoll, *Pittsburgh City Paper,*

"What makes Jim Messina's life so different is that unlike most of those from that generation, he wrote and made drawings about his life history. To someone who has experienced many of the incidents he wrote and drew about, they bring back vivid memories of West Aliquippa places such as Crow Island, St. Joseph Roman Catholic Church, and the Slovak Club, as well as various businesses and events.

"Jim Messina was a member of the highly decorated 1st Marine Division of the US Marine Corps that on August 7, 1942, invaded

Guadalcanal in our nation's first offensive land operation against the Japanese in World War II. The record of the Marine Corps in the South Pacific is well documented, and Messina was a part of the heroic effort.

"I know his story will be of interest because it reflects the lives of so many from that era."

—Gino Piroli, *The Beaver County Times*

"Reading this first-person account of the beginning of World War II and the author's harrowing experiences at Guadalcanal gave a real insight into what soldiers experienced before and during that historic war. From the opening story of Jim Messina's life in Western Pennsylvania as the son of Italian immigrants—a story that will sound familiar to so many émigrés—to the illustrations that so clearly express the emotions and feelings of the war, this is a fascinating account of what life was really like.

"The layers of detail, so carefully guided by the author's son and coauthor, clearly convey the pride, gratitude, and appreciation he feels. Kudos to Chuck Messina for dedicating the time and effort it took to be able to share this wonderful, descriptive, layered, and personalized history of what it felt like to be a soldier in war."

—Christine Cestello Hinojosa, Director, Communications
and External Relations, School of Architecture, Planning and
Preservation, University of Maryland

"Living in Europe exposes one to daily reminders of the war, yet the Pacific front feels far away. James Messina's memories bring a distant battlefront very near. [Reading his] common American 'lingo' of the time supported by his 'naive' drawings, the reader feels the fear and excitement of a young man trying to do the right thing. The connection with the humanness of his journey is immediate, setting it apart from other narratives. . . . [The] factual details supporting the story enhance the grasp of action and Messina's personal conviction to fight and survive."

—Brad H. Barndt, BHB Creative, Owner, Managing Director,
Amsterdam, Netherlands

"A young, innocent, naive nineteen-year-old enters WWII eager to serve his country, travel some, and break the boredom of his everyday life. He enters the war as a boy and shortly becomes a man, never imagining what he would see and experience.

"This is a must-read because it defines for us what was so 'great' about 'the Greatest Generation.' The freedoms we cherish and enjoy and take for granted were fought for by unsung heroes who did not have a clue what they were getting into.

"This is an easy read that compels you to read on, a sincere and insightful firsthand account of thoughts and feelings expressed by one so brave and so young."

—Linda Ramage, Ret. High School Teacher

"James Messina's *Steel Soldier* account of the Guadalcanal conflict from an insider revealed the personal naivetee and fortitude of a young man coming of age in the worst possible conditions. Messina's diary-type descriptions carry the reader through both the mundane and most horrific scenes of this war. Messina's close friends showed the 'brother' relationships of the Marines and how working together—even with a sergeant no one cared for but [whom they] truly respected—kept the group together and fighting for America. Harsh conditions, horrors of war, and a belief in God and family keeps the reader involved and hopeful. An amazing read."

—Valerie Angeli, BSN, RN

"The journey of James J. Messina's memoir, *Steel Soldier,* immerses the reader intimately into the battle of Guadalcanal. Messina's personable and casual rhetoric takes you by the hand from a quotidian beginning, evolving into a gruesome, historic WWII event that is shown to the world through words and drawings only the experiences of a soldier with his candid storytelling can [offer]."

—Ivys Mary Martinez, Freelance Creative Writer

Cover Photo: Critical Past

Steel Soldier: Guadalcanal Odyssey

by James J Messina with Charles Messina

© Copyright 2023 Charles Messina

ISBN 978-1-64663-890-1

All rights reserved. No part of this publication may be reproduced, stored in a retrieval system, or transmitted in any form or by any means—electronic, mechanical, photocopy, recording, or any other—except for brief quotations in printed reviews, without the prior written permission of the author.

Published by

◤ köehlerbooks™

3705 Shore Drive
Virginia Beach, VA 23455
800-435-4811
www.koehlerbooks.com

STEEL SOLDIER

GUADALCANAL ODYSSEY

JAMES J MESSINA
WITH CHARLES MESSINA

VIRGINIA BEACH
CAPE CHARLES

COAUTHOR'S DEDICATION

To the memory of my parents, James and Kathrine Messina, who instilled in me the fundamental values that I continue to aspire to today.

I dedicate this book with deep gratitude and love to the legacy they both left me and a promise I made to my father before he crossed over into the afterlife.

Acknowledgments

Gino Piroli, Aliquippa, PA, for welcoming me as a complete stranger, providing me with photographs and materials, as well as his insight and passion for West Aliquippa, the town my dad loved so much.

Mandy Yokim, Pittsburgh, PA, for all of her hard work and for having the foresight to photocopy my father's entire manuscript before an unfortunate accident ruined volume two.

Valentine Brkich, Beaver, PA, for his patience and expertise in helping me edit my father's memoir into a coherent narrative.

Susan Nash, James Hebert, Tavis Anderson, National Archives, National Personal Records Center, St. Louis, MO, who assisted with me with the high honor of researching my father's service records and those of his comrades.

Alisa M. Whitley, Kara Newcomer, Annette Amerman, Tom Baughn, Christopher Ellis, Archives Branch, USMC History Division, Quantico, VA, for many years of correspondence and for supplying photographic and informational tools from the battle of Guadalcanal.

Tom McLeod, Historian, 1st Marine Division Association, Texarkana, Texas, for the guidance he provided regarding organizations to consult for imagery and information on Guadalcanal.

LCDR John M. Daniels (Public Affairs Officer), Robert Hanshew (Photo Curator), Laura Wayers (Reference Archivist), Naval History and Heritage Command, Washington, D.C., who assisted me with the usage and copyright issues of photographs, and provided me with information about the composition of Task Forces 61 and 62.

Holly Reed and the Still Picture Reference team at the National Archives and Records Administration in College Park, MD, for sending material useful in enhancing my father's story.

Peter Flahavin, Aberfeldie, Victoria, Australia, who generously mailed me several CDs containing hundreds of images documenting the battle of Guadalcanal.

André B. Sobocinski, Historian, Communications Director, Bureau of Medicine and Surgery (BUMED), Falls Church, VA, for helping me determine the specific locations of the medical units in the South Pacific.

Mary and Bob Closson of Apollo, Pennsylvania, for recognizing my father's talent and the great importance his work is to the people of Aliquippa.

Special thanks to David Stubblebine, James Konicek, Jacob A. Haywood, Tom Palmer, Vito Pisciotta, Joanne Joella, Marilou Regan, Linda Ramage, Carla Lechman, Loretta Pontis, Jamie Messina, and Jack Krick, who all contributed to the creation of this book.

CONTENTS

THE WAR YEARS

Chapter 12: The Matanikau River

About the Author

By Charles Messina

Official USMC Photograph

*Cropped section of group portrait of Company B, 1st Battalion, 5th Marines,
1st Marine Division, taken at New River, North Carolina, April 1942.
PFC James J. Messina (center left)*

Growing up during the Great Depression in West Aliquippa, Pennsylvania, my father was the son of Italian immigrants. At age seventeen, he enlisted with the Civilian Conservation Corps (CCC), a New Deal program enacted by President Franklin Roosevelt to help the country get back on its feet. He was sent to New Mexico to take part in the construction of a new highway, where he got his first taste of the military lifestyle. Shortly after he returned home from the CCCs in 1941, he began working at Jones & Laughlin Steel Corporation's Aliquippa Works, but quickly became bored with the day-to-day routine. At this point, he decided to enlist in the United States Marine Corps because he wanted some excitement in his young life. After a medical discharge from the military, he went to work driving for the Woodlawn & Southern Motor Coach Company, where he met my dear mother. He was rehired by J&L, got married, raised a family, and was forced to retire as a disabled veteran. Following two major back surgeries, he started to dabble in art and basically taught himself how to paint and draw. He also developed a talent for writing, and in the end, he wrote an autobiography that included many colorful illustrations. The project was started in 1985 and he completed it eight years later. A reporter from the local newspaper interviewed my father after I contacted him about his manuscript. Soon after, the *Beaver County Times* featured a two-page article describing his book about growing up in West Aliquippa and fighting as a Marine. The journalist praised my father's work as an outstanding achievement and a valuable contribution to history, urging me to publish it because he believed it had great merit and that many people would be interested in his story.

COAUTHOR'S NOTE

Some people ask, "Why have you spent so many years of your life working on this book?" The answer is my deep gratitude for having been blessed with such loving parents. Also, I'm the last of my family to carry on the name, and since I never married, there are no grandchildren to pass my father's incredible memoir on to. Having this book published is my way of immortalizing both my parents and also my heritage. That's why it means so much to me, and I hope his story will live on for generations. With that said, I'd like to share some of my family history.

My grandfather was a poor immigrant who sailed to the United States in search of the American dream—a dream that has become less and less attainable in this day and age. At the turn of the 20th century, if you had the gumption, it could be accomplished, but it took a great amount of resilience and back-breaking work.

Calogero (Carl) Messina was born on March 19, 1880, in Castelvetrano, Sicily. His parents were peasant farmers, Guiseppe and Antonina Sacco. On May 8, 1907, he emigrated from Palermo, Sicily, to New Orleans, Louisiana, aboard the SS *Il Piemonte*, arriving on May 31, 1907. His older brother, Vincenzo, followed soon after, arriving on October 16, 1907.

Antonina (Anna) Salina, my grandmother, was born in Partinico, Sicily, January 29, 1883. Calogero married her on November 16, 1904, in Castelbianco, a commune in the Province of Savona in the Italian region of Liguria, located about fifty miles southwest of Genoa.

She traveled to New York City, arriving on December 15, 1905, and stayed with relatives in Brooklyn. It's been a mystery within our family as to why our grandmother arrived two years before our grandfather, but it was a time when millions of poor Italian immigrants were fleeing to America. Apparently, Antonina was born into an affluent Italian family, which may have provided her with the opportunity to go to America first.

Calogero eventually made his way to Brooklyn, where he worked as a cook at a hotel in Manhattan, but it didn't pay very well. He had acquired his cooking skills while serving in the Italian Army. After the two were reunited, he and Antonina moved into their own little apartment, and they had two children together, Anna and Joseph.

During the time they lived in New York City, my father told me that my grandfather had a bad gambling habit, and he wasn't very good at it. One time, out of desperation, he traded his wife's expensive jewelry for cash without telling her, then lost everything. Afterwards, she threatened to leave him if he didn't stop gambling. From that day forward, he vowed never to gamble again and to walk a straight line because of his undying love for her.

They lived in Brooklyn for a few years before a friend invited them to move to West Aliquippa, Pennsylvania, where a massive steel plant had been built that was hiring thousands of workers. They decided to relocate, and Calogero was immediately hired in the blast furnace department as a soot blower. Despite the unhealthy conditions and the extreme dangers of the job, he worked there until he retired.

They had five more children, Mary, Grace, Cecilia, James, and John. When Mary was born, Antonina had actually given birth to twins, but the boy didn't survive. She also had another son before her youngest son, John, was born, but he also died. His cause of death was never recorded. Their family would have been much larger, as Antonina attempted to have more children, but they did not survive as well, and no one knows just how many she lost.

There were a lot of mouths to feed, and although Calogero was working in the mill, they were still very poor. They lived in a small house at 315 Main Avenue, which had only one door into the kitchen. In the entranceway, there were steep stairs leading up to two bedrooms and bathroom.

The kitchen was the largest room of the house and had a potbelly stove, which was the only heat source for the entire home. The family would always gather around the stove during the bitterly cold Pennsylvania winters. At night, many handmade afghans and quilts were layered in order to stay warm.

The small front room of the house had an old-style foot-pedal sewing machine where Antonina made most of the children's clothes. A large framed oval photograph hung on the wall of Calogero in uniform when he was in the Italian Army. They also had a big mahogany console Philco radio with a turntable that popped out in front. Everyone sat around in the evening listening to popular radio programs. My father told me that despite being penniless, they were all very happy just being together.

In the past ten years, I've encountered a number of hurdles that have prevented me from completing the rest of my father's autobiography. It's been quite a journey, but I'm happy to report I have kept my promise to publish his entire memoir. There will be a sequel that concludes his life story after this book. My only hope is that I have given him the proper tribute he so justly deserves.

One major obstacle was that volume two of his manuscript was completely ruined due to an accident involving water damage. It was a tragic event, considering my father's drawing style had developed and improved as his story progressed. In this volume, he chronicles his time fighting in Guadalcanal, and his drawings are bursting with color and meticulous detail. After I found out about the mishap, I opened that volume, and found the ink had washed out and bled together, leaving a big puddle of color that looked like an oil slick floating on top of a puddle.

I was devastated, but my dad sat there stoically, as if nothing had happened. My eyes welled up with tears as I asked, "Aren't you upset that all your hard work has been destroyed?"

His smile broadened and he shook his head, "It's all part of God's plan."

Thankfully for us, the first editor I hired, Mandy Yokim, had the foresight to photocopy his entire manuscript before that unfortunate incident occurred, and I will be forever grateful to her. As a result, some of the illustrations used in this book are not direct scans, so they may appear to look somewhat curved or distorted.

In addition to all the drawings my father created for his story, he also cut out newspaper and magazine clippings of articles and photographs relating to WWII and included them throughout his story. As his memoir has gradually become "our" book, I have sought to honor him by consulting the Marines, Navy, and other sources to determine specific facts and choose images he might have utilized, if given the opportunity.

My father's only intention was to leave a casual recollection of his life for his children. He merely reflected on his past experiences, and also referenced *The Old Breed* by George McMillan, to help jog his memory about Guadalcanal. I made it my job to refine, modify, and tweak his story into a cohesive and accurate account of his tour of duty while serving with the United States Marine Corps.

The first action I took was to acquire the muster rolls for his specific unit from the Marine Corps History Division in Quantico, Virginia. Once I had the service numbers of his platoon comrades, I flew to the National Service Records Archives in St. Louis, Missouri, and reviewed each Marine's service record to gain further detailed information. This was one of the highest honors of my life. As I held each member's service record in my hands, I experienced a great deal of emotion. Sadly, three of the service member's service records weren't available due to a devastating fire which took place in 1973.

As part of my research, I reviewed muster rolls, ship war diaries, and final reports of the Guadalcanal Operations, Phases I through V, of the United States Marine Corps, 1st Division, 1942, as well as other official military documents. Several books were also referenced, but my main sources were *Guadalcanal* by Richard B. Frank, *Once a Marine* by General Alexander A. Vandegrift, *The Old Breed* by George McMillan, and *The First Offensive* by Henry I. Shaw, Jr.

Shortly after my father passed away in 2008, I came across a very large trunk filled with books in our attic. All of them were first editions dating back to the 1940s and 1950s, and each was stamped with his name from the same book club. Up to that point, I had no idea how much he enjoyed reading, and it really surprised me. The thing is, I didn't recall my dad reading books that often. It was probably because he was too busy working that he had no time to read. He always said that his family was more important than anything else.

The fact that he had so many books hidden away in the attic really intrigued me. They had a certain mystique to them, and I sat in the rafters for hours examining each one, contemplating my father's dreams. More and more, I began to understand the true scope of why he decided to write a memoir. Aside from the fact that he wanted to leave something for his children, I think he also secretly dreamed of becoming a writer. It makes sense since he enjoyed telling stories from a very early age.

It seems like only yesterday when the local newspaper published a two-page article about his memoir. I'll never forget how proud he was that day, and when he found out I was pursuing the publication of his autobiography. Now more than ever I feel that what I've been doing for the past ten years is precisely what I'm supposed to be doing, since he has departed this earth.

I've said over and over again that getting his book published has been a dream come true. But little did I realize the profound effect this journey would have on me. He has provided me with a better understanding of what's important in life through his writing.

During the entire process, I've been able to get to know him and what he stood for, what motivated him, and his love of life, then just being my plain old dad. In the end, I got to know him all over again, but on a different level from father and son. I now feel a closer connection to him, and what it might have felt like to call him my friend.

PREFACE

By Charles Messina

The first installment of my father's manuscript, *Grit, Smoke, and Steam,* was published back in 2012. Its setting was West Aliquippa, Pennsylvania, during the Great Depression of the 1930s. His entertaining writing and illustrations brought us back to a simpler time when people weren't distracted by all the electronic devices we have today.

In those days, smartphones, computers, and the Internet didn't exist, and people actually interacted with each another. They didn't even have TVs! How did anyone survive? In his world there wasn't any money for toys, or even food at times. Even so, he and his little gang of friends had a lot of fun. They made toys and played many games that enriched their young lives. Those memories, together with his other experiences fighting in the Marine Corps, were so ingrained in his memory that he wrote a memoir about them.

My father didn't have the privilege of higher education. He actually dropped out of high school in 11th grade and got a job to help his parents pay the bills. If he had gone to college, I couldn't even begin to imagine what his future may have looked like.

He was a man who never sat idle. To make ends meet, my dad worked as a steelworker full time and painted houses on the side. Due to an injury he sustained during WWII, he was forced to retire after twenty-eight years of employment at Jones & Laughlin Corporation's Aliquippa Works. At the time, he was fifty years old and in the prime of his life.

As he was working one day, his back gave out in excruciating pain, and he was rushed to the hospital. They discovered a vertebrate in his spine had completely collapsed. After consulting with his doctor, he learned he would never work again and that his lifestyle would be forever altered. This occurred back in the 1970s and required a primitive surgery whereby a part of his hipbone was fused to his spinal cord. It resulted in him having to wear a body cast for fifty-nine days.

After the operation, he had to be rolled over every few hours to keep his spine in alignment. Someone performed this delicate procedure incorrectly, and the surgery had to be repeated, but only after the damaged fusion was fully healed. The whole ordeal was agonizing, and it would take years for him to return to a reasonable quality of life.

Throughout this entire painful experience, he always had a smile on his face. My father was deeply religious, and he often said, "It is in God's hands," shrugging his shoulders. It was this traumatizing event that prompted him to write his life story.

One day, when I was home from college, he brought out two pen-and-ink drawings he had completed depicting scenes from Guadalcanal, where he fought as a Marine. I was majoring in art at the time, so the next time I came home, I brought some drawing supplies and suggested he try to draw again to pass the time.

In no time, he was producing artistic drawings in pencil, ink, and charcoal. A while later, he purchased oil, tempura, and watercolor paints and was creating vibrant compositions. He'd never taken a course in art, but he had a very distinctive style.

Storytelling was another talent he possessed. As a kid, his friends from the Beaver Avenue Gang even nicknamed him, "Jinks the Storyteller." My dad liked to tell stories around our dinner table about his childhood antics in West Aliquippa, as well as fighting as a Marine in the South Pacific. As he recited his favorite anecdotes from these two periods of his life, his face would light up, so I encouraged him to write them down to make sure they wouldn't be forgotten.

Soon after, he began mailing me short essays detailing his experiences as a small boy and as a Marine fighting in the war. A few months later, he presented me with a large black sketchbook in which he had begun hand writing and illustrating his autobiography.

The project took him eight years to complete, and when it was finished, there were five large volumes full of all his stories along with over 160 illustrations. He included full-page color drawings every few pages, representing scenes of his personal experiences, which made it even more interesting.

Everyone who saw his work was fascinated by his vivid memory of his life and the details he remembered. It impressed me so much that I suggested he consider publishing it. But my father was adamant that he was merely leaving a gift for his two sons to remember him by.

This is an American tale about a working-class man who lived an honest life, believed strongly in God, and fought for his country. It's also a compelling story of survival that starts in a gritty Pennsylvania steel town during the Great Depression and then transports the reader into the steaming jungles of Guadalcanal, where a young Marine faces death in one of the most pivotal and bloodiest battles of WWII.

My father's journey begins three months before the bombing of Pearl Harbor, after he quit the steel mill and enlisted in the Marine Corps. Unlike the lighthearted narrative of the first book, the next chapter of his life he is constantly in jeopardy. He had no idea that after joining the Marines he'd be thrown into the middle of a hornet's nest. Despite the horrors and carnage he endures during combat, he never loses faith in God.

A strong bond grows between my father and the other children of his Beaver Avenue Gang in his first book, *Grit, Smoke, and Steam.* Each one of those young boys would defend the other against other neighborhood gangs or anyone who threatened them. This story has a similar relationship that develops between my father and his platoon comrades, but their connection goes a step further. A brotherhood is forged through life-or-death circumstances.

In his own words, he declared, "To this day, I can't forget my buddies from the war. They were all good guys. When I think of my buddies who were killed, tears well up in my eyes. I was proud to serve as a Marine. They might call us jarheads and glory hunters, but that doesn't bother me."

Steel Soldier serves as a testament to the special man my dad was. It's not a gripping mystery that concludes with a thrilling climax. Rather, it is a series of vignettes with some entertaining moments of a bygone era, which have been compiled by a very talented storyteller.

To look at him, you'd never guess this mild-mannered, unassuming, and kind man had once been a fierce warrior. As long as I live, I will always admire and honor my father and all the men and women who have fought for this country. He was loved by everyone who knew him, and to me he is a true American hero.

Author's Dedication

I dedicate this book to my son Kenneth, my son Charles, and to my love, Kathrine.

I can recall most of my experiences throughout my life up to the present day. I am writing these volumes for my two sons. The manuscript will pass into their lives so that they can reminisce about their mom and dad after we've passed into the next life. I hope that as parents we gave our boys everything that was expected of us: our guidance, our deep love, and our devotion to religion. I hope they have learned to love God before family and worldly goods, to respect their family and neighbors, and to always be themselves.

Kathrine and I wish the very best for our two sons, and we hope that someday, at the end of time, to be reunited again in the next world, only if our Creator allows us to do so with His kind and forgiving heart.

INTRODUCTION

BY JAMES J. MESSINA

My manuscript continues in Volume Two. I'm writing the story of my life at the age of sixty-three, some forty odd years after the end of WWII. I served in the United States Marine Corps, as a Private First Class, in the Fleet Marine Force, commonly known as the infantry. When the war was over, the men of our division who survived received a copy of *The Old Breed*. It's a book written by George McMillan, and it tells the history of the 1st Marine Division during WWII. I use this book for the dates, places, and happenings I might have forgotten, as well as a few quotes.

On August 7, 1942, my division invaded the island of Guadalcanal in the British Solomon Islands. The island is located in the south-western Pacific, northeast of Australia. A large mountain range runs through the center of the island, which measures about ninety miles long by thirty miles wide. There were beautiful coconut and pineapple plantations, pecan groves, along with trees bearing long bananas that were cultivated by the British. They also had golden palomino horses and cattle. At that time, it seemed as though the Brits owned property in every corner of the world.

The Guadalcanal campaign marked the beginning of the end for the Japanese expansion in the South Pacific, and ultimately led to their surrender.

Opening quote from *The Old Breed*: *They were the Leathernecks, the old breed of American regular, regarding the service as home and war an occupation, and they transmitted their temper and character and viewpoint to the high-hearted volunteer mass.*

Colonel John W. Thompson

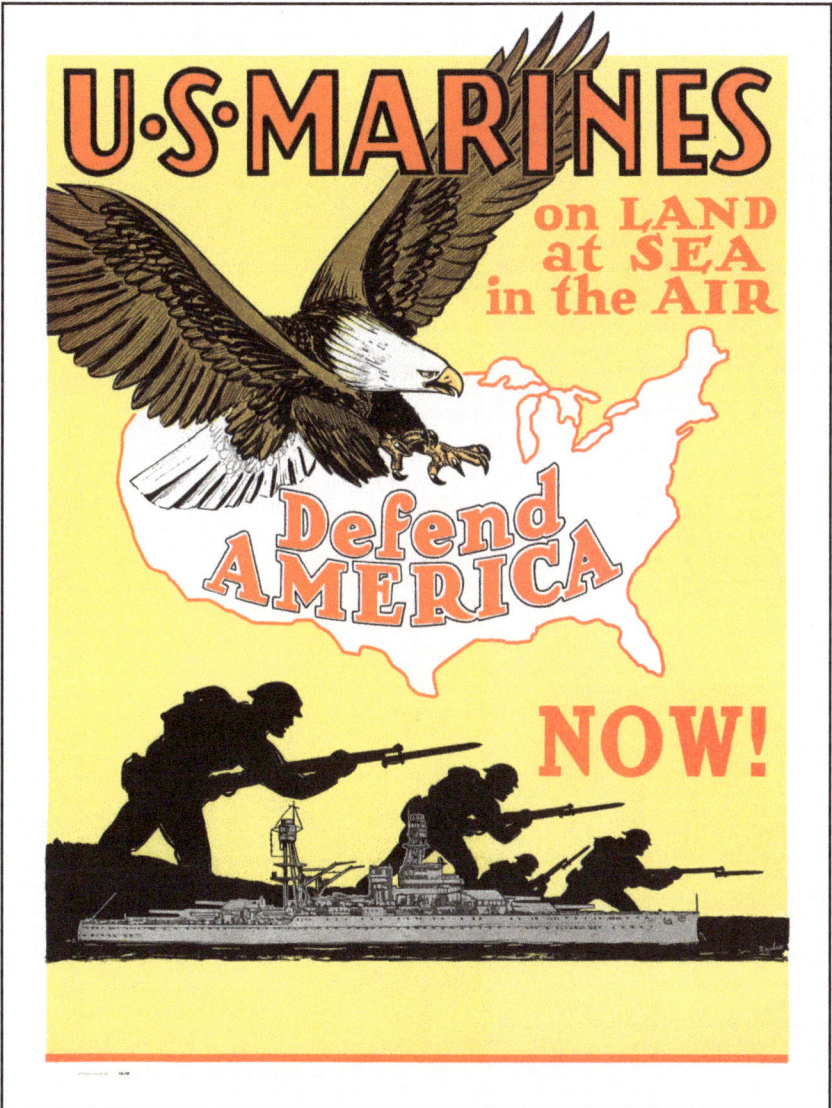

National Archives

World War II Poster, 1942 - 1945

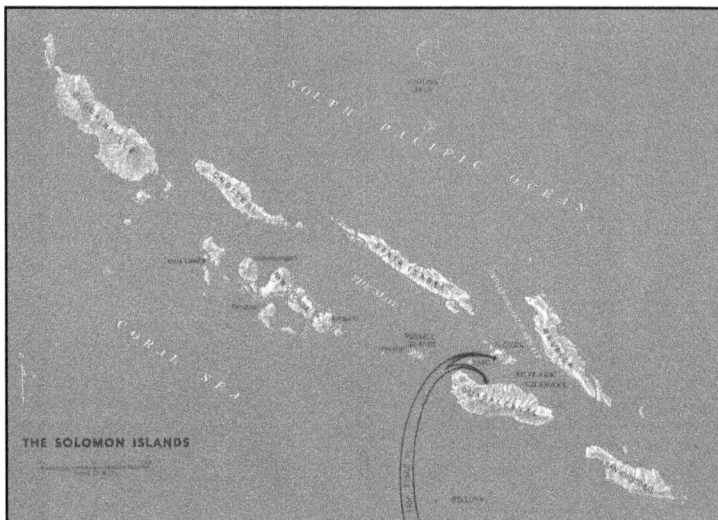

The Old Breed

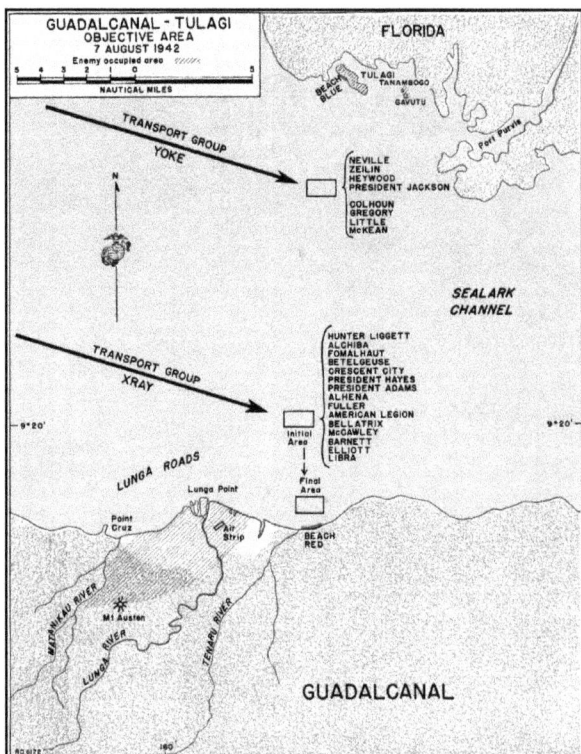

The Guadalcanal Campaign

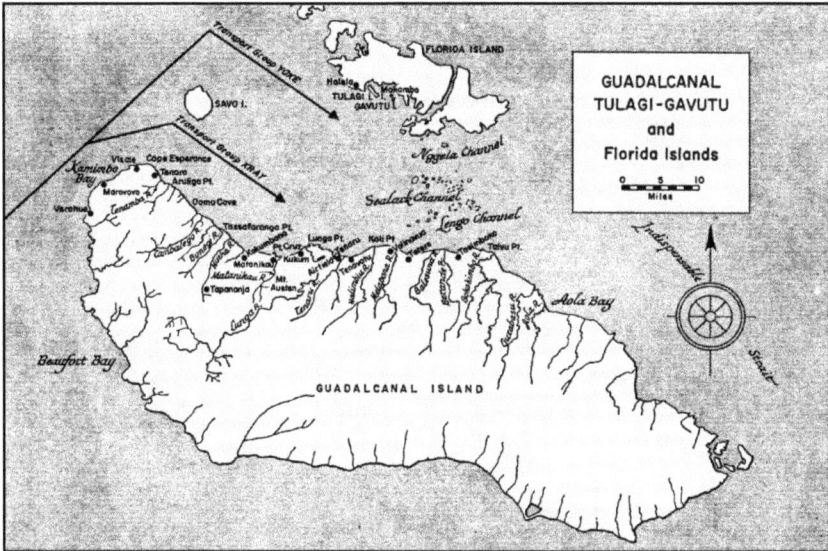

First Offensive: The Marine Campaign For Guadalcanal

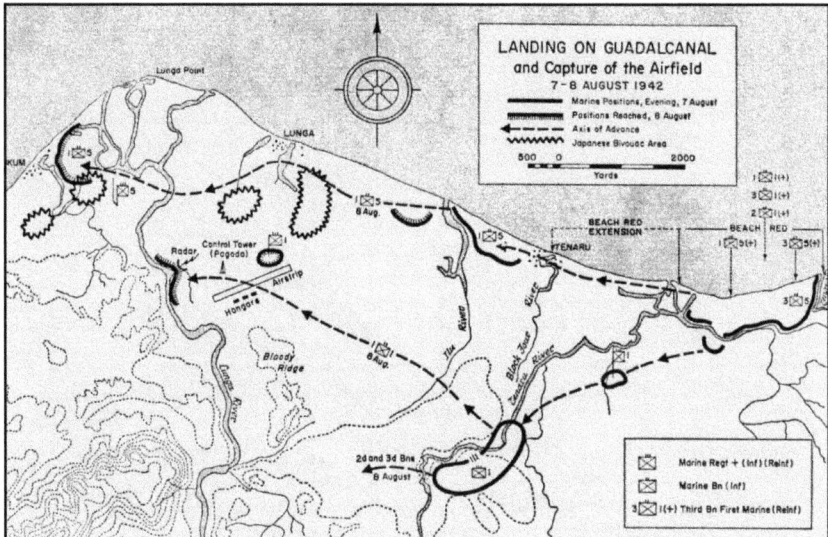

First Offensive: The Marine Campaign For Guadalcanal

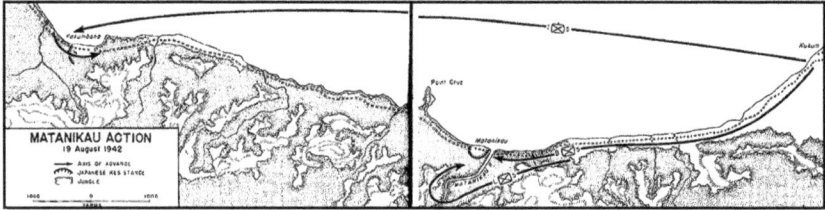

Guadalcanal: The First Offensive

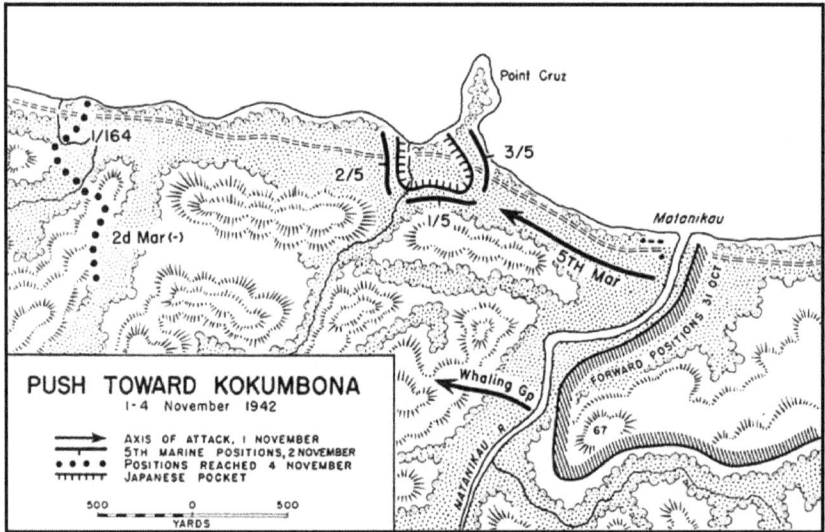

Guadalcanal: The First Offensive

THE WAR YEARS

CHAPTER 1: ENLISTING IN THE MARINE CORPS

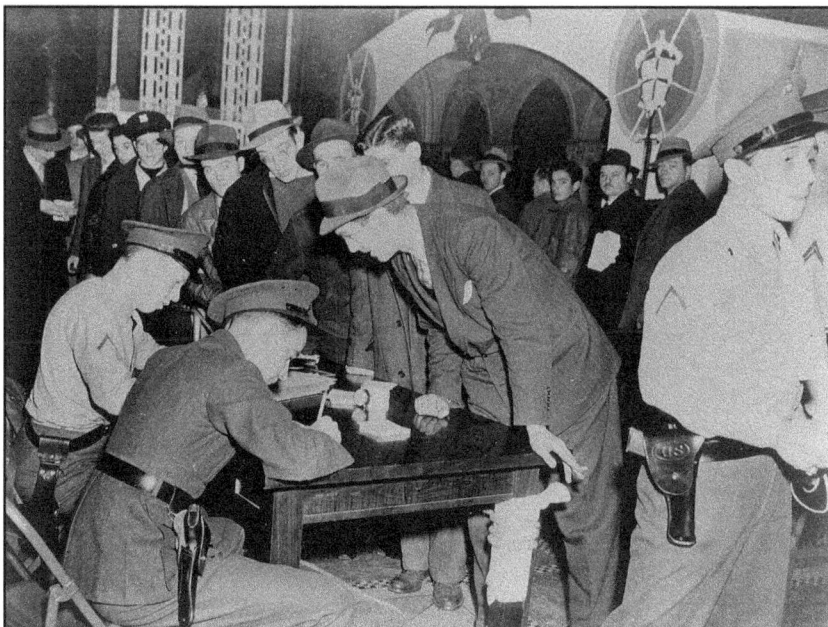

Prints and Photographs Division, Library of Congress

Armed Forces recruiting stations all over the country were overwhelmed by long lines of young men. The total number of enlistments in December exceeded 60,000; fifty percent more than the highest enlistment month the year before. New York, New York, January 1942

1. RECRUITING STATION

My job at the wire mill was going nowhere, so I made my mind up to quit. I wanted some excitement in my life, and I would find it in the Navy.

I asked my friend Granny Markovich for the loan of his '37 Chevy to drive to the Old Post Office Building in Pittsburgh where the recruiting station was located. Granny never refused me the loan of his car since he hardly ever went anywhere and always hung out on the corner with the Redskin Gang. A short, stocky, and soft-spoken man who always had a chew (tobacco) in his mouth, Granny was a tough guy. His four brothers were also my friends. There was Judo, who was thin and short; Stunko, the youngest and the smallest; Mitch, a handsome, tough guy; and Simo, who had an accident around his home and died back in the 1970s.

When Granny married his wife, Stella, I was asked to be an usher in his wedding. His sister was my partner in the bridal group. It was a Serbian wedding, and our priest at St. Joseph's church in West Aliquippa gave us hell about being ushers in a non-Catholic wedding. The church was very strict back then.

I first asked Danny Dinardo to go with me to the recruiting station, but he said no. My best buddy, Dom Sebastian, also declined. "We'll wait for the draft," were their exact words. After I asked a few more guys, I decided to go by myself. I was fed up with the wire mill. Then I asked Dominic Ranieri to go to the recruiting office with me, and he said okay. My brother Joe heard what I was about to do, so he said he would go, too.

Dom Ranieri was a short, heavyset, rugged guy in our Beaver Avenue gang who could speak Italian very well. He had two brothers, Vito and Frank. Dom liked Mary Shomsky a lot and married her after the war. They had a daughter but lost her in an automobile accident. After Mary passed away, he married again. He earned the Silver Star for bravery in WWII and died in the early 1970s.

When the three of us arrived at the Old Post Office Building in Pittsburgh, I was disappointed. At the Navy recruiting office, the chief petty officer (CPO) in charge told us they weren't taking sailors right now.

"We're looking for men with at least two years of college for the Naval Air Force," he said. "In another two months, we'll be recruiting the regular sailors."

I looked at Dom and Joe with regret and said, "C'mon, let's go!" They followed me out into the hall.

Dom and Joe both suggested I join the Army.

"I don't like the Army," I responded. "I'll just wait two more months for the Navy!"

The next thing I knew, as we walked down the hall, Dom disappeared. "Joe," I said, "Where the hell did Dom go?"

Joe shrugged his shoulders. Then I heard my name being called. It was Dom, and he was standing in the doorway of the United States Marine Corps recruiting office.

"Come here, come here!" he urged. Then he disappeared into the office.

Joe and I walked slowly over to the entrance, and we saw Dom fiddling around at the long wooden table in the center of the room. He was wearing the recruiting sergeant's visor cap he found lying on the table. He also had a brochure in his hand and motioned me over to his side. Joe and I looked at each other; we knew what Dom was up to.

"Look at all the opportunities you can have in the Marine Corps!" he said. Then he shoved the brochure in my face. "Join the Marine Corps, Jim. I think it would be better than the Navy!"

He was so excited I came back at him with, "Why don't you join, Dom? Or, better still, we can both join together!"

"Nah," he said. "I'm not ready for the military."

I was about to walk out of the office when the recruiting sergeant started coming towards us. When Dom saw this, he quickly put the sergeant's visor cap back on the table. The sergeant had been eavesdropping.

He approached me directly saying, "Are you interested in the Corps?"

"I don't think so," I replied.

"Why not?"

"I'm too small and don't meet the requirements."

"Let me be the judge of that," he said. "Explain what you mean about not meeting the requirements?"

So, I told him how, a couple of years back, one of my friends from my town enlisted, and he told me in order to get into the Marine Corps, you had to be at least five feet, ten inches tall, weigh at least 160 pounds, and have a good set of teeth.

The sergeant laughed. "Whoa, hold it!" he said. "This is not true. If you pass the physical, you're in."

I looked at him in surprise. "I still think I'm too small for the Corps," I replied. "Besides, I have my heart set on the Navy."

"Go ahead, Jim," Dom urged. "The Marine Corps has a lot of tradition, and you can be part of it."

The sergeant looked at me. "What do you say, son?"

I turned to my brother for encouragement, and he nodded in agreement.

"Well," I said. "I'll give it a try. I don't want to go back to the wire mill, and it's too long a wait for the Navy."

"Follow me to my desk," the sergeant summoned. Then he handed me the enlistment application and told me to fill it out. The application called for three signatures of businessmen besides my father. "Get this all signed up and return it to me in forty-eight hours. Then I'll let you know what day you'll be examined by the doctor."

Dom didn't enlist with me that same day, but he did just two months later.

We went back to West Aliquippa, and I was working the 3 p.m.-to-11 p.m. shift at the mill that week, so I made my rounds in the morning. First off, I had to convince Pop about signing my application to enlist before seeking out the signatures of the businessmen.

Pop didn't refuse to sign, but he did say, "I don't want you to leave home, but I won't stop you from going."

I felt real bad about it. This would be the second time I was leaving home. Pop didn't mind when I enlisted in the Civilian Conservation Corps (CCC) in 1939 and went to New Mexico because, at the time, it was hard getting work in the steel mills.

The first businessman to sign my application was a man who owned the grocery store on the corner of Fifth Street and Beaver Avenue. His name was Nick Mancini. (No relation to my close friend, Henry Mancini, who would grow up to be the famous composer.) The second was a dentist on Main Street named Dr. Slatniske. The third was our Prudential Insurance agent, Joseph Opsatnik. The Marine Corps was always looking for men who could hold up to their traditions and meet their lofty requirements for molding a fighting machine. I guess these signatures were more or less a character reference.

I returned the application, and the sergeant said to report back in two days for the physical at 9 a.m. sharp. I passed the exam, except for one thing: I had to have one bad tooth pulled out at my expense. So, I went to Dr. Slatniske and had it done. He wanted to know why I chose the military. I told him I was looking for travel and adventure. He thought it was a very good idea and wished he was single so he could do as he pleased.

After having my tooth pulled, I returned to Pittsburgh the next day with the receipt from Dr. Slatniske. The doctor, who was a major, was satisfied with my examination. After giving me a physical and a blood test, he said I was accepted into the Marine Corps. It was, Thursday, September 18, 1941, and I was nineteen years old.

There were thirty other men reporting that same day for their physical, and they all passed. When the last man was examined, the major told us to stand in two rows.

"Stand at attention while I swear you into the United States Marine Corps," he said.

Together, we all recited the Oath of Enlistment: "I, James Joseph Messina, do solemnly swear that I will support and defend the Constitution of the United States against all enemies, foreign and domestic; that I will bear true faith and allegiance to the same; and that I will obey the orders of the President of the United States and the orders of the officers appointed over me, according to regulations and the Uniform Code of Military Justice. So help me God."

After we all repeated the oath, the major spoke again. "Come to attention! You will now address me as sir or, major! You are now a United States Marine! You will be sent to Parris Island, South Carolina, for eight weeks of basic training. You are scheduled to leave by train from the Pittsburgh & Lake Erie Railroad Station tomorrow morning at 8 a.m. I want all of you to report here at 7 a.m. sharp. The sergeant will give each of you two chits allowing one overnight stay at the YMCA and breakfast at the restaurant of your choice. Am I clear?"

"Yes, sir!" we all responded.

"One more thing, men." The major looked very serious. "If you're not here tomorrow morning, the Marine MPs will not come looking for you—the FBI agents will. Clear?"

Again, we repeated, "Yes, sir!"

The sergeant handed each of us two slips of paper with a United States Marine Corps heading on it. One read, "A Night's Lodging" and the other, "Restaurant." These slips in Navy and Marine Corps slang were called "chits." Later on in Marine life, whenever you had to get anything through channels, you would have to have an authorized chit.

It was a little scary thinking about what the major had said as I left the recruiting station. "The FBI will come looking for you!" These words stuck in my mind as though we were criminals, not newly sworn-in Marines.

I went home and made my rounds, saying goodbye to my peers. None of them wanted to go with me. The military was a big word, and they didn't want any part of it just yet. Some said they'd wait for the one-year draft, which had been imposed by the government. Others said they would enlist later on.

I quit the wire mill that day without the required ten-day notice.

2. Next Stop, Beaufort, South Carolina

That same afternoon I asked to borrow Granny's Chevy for the last time. About 7 p.m. my brother Joe drove me to the YMCA in Pittsburgh. He would return Granny's car for me. Later on, that night, we went to see a burlesque show. It was the first time I'd ever seen one, and as I watched the gals strip, I must have had a surprised look on my face, because Joe couldn't help but laugh out loud.

Back in 1941 Pittsburgh was known as the "Smoky City," and sometimes it was so bad it looked worse than the heavy fog that hung over London. Visitors from other parts of America always made fun of the city, but this area was the steel giant of the whole world, and it would play a major part in the war effort.

SERVICE RECORD

OF

Name James Joseph MESSINA

Citizenship U.S.

Date of birth 14 JANUARY, 1922

Place of birth Aliquippa, Pa.

Legal residence 515½ Allegheny Ave. Aliquippa, Pa (Beaver)

Name, relationship, and address of person to be notified in case of emergency Anna Messina 515½ Allegheny Ave, Aliquippa, Pa Mother

Accepted for enlistment at D. H. S., PITTSBURGH, PA.

Enlisted as PRIVATE

At D. H. S., PITTSBURGH, PA.

SEP 18 1941, 19___, to serve { FOUR years. during minority.

Foreign shore service last enlistment (months):

From___ to___

Sea service last enlistment (months):

From___ to___

LT. COMDR (MC) USNR ASST Recruiting Officer. ACTING

James Joseph Messina (SIGNATURE OF RECRUIT IN FULL)

Identification tag issued ___, 19.

INSTRUCTIONS

This book is a part of the staff returns of a marine and must accompany him throughout his enlistment.

Entries shall be made to show complete information of the man concerned as indicated on the several pages of this book and in accordance with the provisions of the Marine Corps Manual. No entries shall be made until the man's enlistment is accomplished by the administration of the oath of enlistment.

Neatness, clearness, and strict economy of space must be observed. No blank lines shall be left between entries. Only such forms, letters, or certificates as may be authorized will be pasted in this book.

MESSINA, (322155) James Joseph
Enl 18Sep41
Photo taken 27Sep41

National Archives at St. Louis

Pittsburgh had many busy theaters and nightclubs in those days, and the fun-seekers had their choice of the many nightspots in and around the city. There was one place on Liberty Avenue I favored called Villa Madrid, which was in the cellar of one of the large buildings. There were always at least four of us couples who patronized the club after my years in the military.

The Greyhound bus depot and three train stations were always busy, and the two inclines never stopped running up and down the steep slope of Mount Washington. At the top, on Grandview Avenue, there were many restaurants overlooking the city. I remember this one French restaurant

Prints and Photographs Division, Library of Congress

View of Pittsburgh, Pennsylvania, at dusk, from the top of
Mount Washington, 1941. Photo by Jack Delano

that hung out over the hillside and was the best spot for a panoramic view of the city, when it wasn't too smoky. There were also the many street cars people rode to work or to go shopping, and they are still running today.

In the Oakland section of Pittsburgh there was what was known as hospital row. There were so many hospitals there, I wondered if all of them had a full capacity of patients. The VA Hospital was built in 1950, five years after WWII. Nearby was Pitt Stadium. Many good football players who came out of the University of Pittsburgh made it into professional football. There were also two amusement parks close to the city, Kennywood, and West View. We also had the zoo in Highland Park, which I went to many times.

At the YMCA I told the night clerk I wanted up at 5 a.m. I tried to read that night, but I was nervous about being on time in the morning for the recruiting station. I was afraid the bellhop would forget to call me. It wasn't until midnight when I began to get sleepy, and I finally dropped off into dreamland. I didn't awaken until I heard loud knocks on my door at 5 a.m. I quickly jumped out of bed, opened the door, and thanked the bellhop.

After a quick shower and shave, I was on my way to the Blue Bell Restaurant, which was close to the YMCA. Using my chit, I ordered sausage and pancakes and downed it real quick. Then, I checked my Bulova watch my brother-in-law, Eddie, had given me for my confirmation. It was 6:40 a.m., so I picked up my bag and left the restaurant. It was only two blocks to the Old Post Office Building.

As I walked into the sergeant's office, I noticed all the men were there waiting for orders. The sergeant began calling each name in alphabetical order, and the response was "Here!"

Satisfied everyone was present, he said, "Well, I see I didn't have to call the FBI for anyone who didn't show up!" Then he summoned the tallest man in the group to walk over to his desk. "I'm making you the acting corporal in charge of this group until you reach Parris Island, South Carolina."

"Yes sir, sergeant," the tall one replied. "I'll see to it everyone shows up to our destination."

The sarge marched us to the street in a single-file formation. Then we headed for the train station about five blocks away. As we walked, we looked up at the tall buildings and the hustle and bustle of the streetcars, and the cabs going by. We were all excited just thinking about being in the Marine Corps and trying to live up to all of its traditions.

The Marine Corps motto is Semper Fidelis—Always Faithful. The words were etched in the emblem worn on the cap and the uniform. We were proud to be United States Marines, and we showed it. People smiled at us as they passed by.

As we boarded the train, the sergeant shook hands with each of us and told us to be faithful to the Corps and stay out of trouble. Once we were all on board and seated, we began jabbering about home, Pittsburgh, the sergeant, Parris Island, and whatever else entered our pumped-up, excited minds. We lit up cigarettes, ate candy, looked out the window, and then wondered why the train wasn't moving.

Finally, after about twenty-five minutes, we heard the chug of the engine getting up steam. Then the wheels began to crank slowly as the train started to move. As it left the station, it began picking up speed, leaving a trail of thick, white smoke along the tracks. We just sat there enjoying the scenery, hearing the clickity-clack of the wheels rolling over the steel tracks. Now and then we'd hear the shrill of the whistle as the train rolled about 70 mph.

As I looked out the window, my mind drifted back to West Aliquippa. It had been almost two years since I'd left home for New Mexico, and now I was leaving again. I was sure the Marine Corps would be a lot different from the CCC camps. Mom and Pop didn't want me to leave home again and bless their hearts for not stopping me. There were rumors of the United States going to war in the autumn of 1941, and I knew Mom would be worrying about my safety.

I couldn't believe none of my buddies wanted to enlist when I did. I kind of wished Dom Sebastian would have, but no dice. I remember all the fun we had as kids. The skiing, sled riding, sneaking in the theater, the celebrations, donkey baseball, the homemade scooter. But I wasn't a kid anymore. I had to face reality and get down to brass tacks. The Marine Corps was going to be rough as far as training was concerned. Was I making a mistake? Should I have waited for the one-year draft, which was in progress? No, I didn't make a mistake, because I didn't want the Army. For that matter, I didn't want the Marine Corps. I really wanted to join the Navy. Sure, the Marine Corps was part of the Navy, but the sailors didn't like us. To them, we were known as "glory hunters," "raggedy-ass Marines" (from the East Coast), "Hollywood Marines" (from the West Coast), or "seagoing bellhops." Those swab jockeys had a chip on their shoulder, and they were always looking to fight and belittle the Marines.

"Hey, Jim," a voice called out a couple of seats down from where I was sitting. "Wanna play a little penny ante?" It was one of the guys I talked with back at the recruiting office. He was right from the city and was the same size as I was.

There was six of us in the game. The next coach had seats that faced each other, and three of us sat on each seat. We used one of the suitcases on our knees for a card table. We played a two-cent limit, because I don't think anyone had much more than five or ten dollars in his pocket. Later on when we were broke, we'd play for cigarettes—a two-cigarette limit, so to speak.

We played poker up until someone hollered, "Look, we're approaching Horseshoe Curve!" We all looked out the window, and as the train rounded the bend, we heard the loud sound of the whistle and saw the steam engine bellowing out thick smoke in front of us. We knew Altoona, Pa., would be close by.

After that we broke up the game to look out the window at the scenery. One of the fellows was eating a candy bar, and he had about ten bars in a paper bag.

"Hey, Mac," I said, "Want to sell a bar? I'll give you a dime for one." In the Marine Corps, when you didn't know someone's name, you would always address him as "Mac." In the Army they would use "Joe." Candy was only a nickel a bar, but I offered a dime because I knew he couldn't resist a five-cent profit. I bought a Milky Way bar, and before you knew it, he sold the other nine bars to the other fellows. In the service we call anyone who makes a profit a "BTO," or "Big-Time-Operator." Later on, I'd find a lot of BTOs in our outfit. I finished my pogey bait (candy) after we passed through Altoona, and then leaned back in my seat to take a nap.

I liked riding the train because I could venture from one car to the other. My friend George and I walked through the whole line of cars but couldn't go any further than the baggage car. The dining car had neat square tables that could seat four people. Each table was covered with a clean white cloth, and the waiters wore short white jackets and black pants. It was expensive to eat there. We bought ham sandwiches for fifteen cents each.

It wasn't long before we arrived at Washington, DC. The tall acting corporal told us we'd have a two-hour layover and were allowed to go into the city. He warned us about the FBI if we weren't back on time to continue our journey.

Once we were off the train, George and I went into a newsstand and looked at postcards to send home. I bought about six cards for a penny apiece and sent them out to my family. I kept the note short and told them

I was happy with my new adventure. The cards were too small to write much else.

We also bought three bars of candy each and two packs of cigarettes for sixteen cents a pack. In camp they were a dime; overseas, and aboard ship, they sold for five cents. My brand then was Lucky Strikes in the green pack with a red circle. The green was changed to white in 1942 for the war effort. The war slogan was, "Lucky Strike Green has gone to War!"

We walked around awhile taking in the sights of Washington, D.C. I'd never saw so many limousines go by with VIPs riding in them. The city didn't have real tall buildings like other cities, but the place was beautiful, and we enjoyed our walk. Before we knew it, we had to head back to the train station. The rest of our gang was already aboard. The FBI must have been branded in their brains.

The rest of the train ride seemed to take forever. Finally, the next morning, we arrived at the Yemassee train station near Beaufort, South Carolina. This little town was about a mile or two from our training base on Parris Island. The only view we would ever get of Beaufort would be this train station. The next eight weeks would be rigorous training and gum-beating.

As the train finally came to a stop, through our windows we noticed the Marine Corps trucks waiting for us. The trucks were big, olive-green GMCs made by General Motors. The backs of the trucks were covered with canvas and had long wooden seats on each side. There were four in all, and each carried about twenty men. In Washington, we picked up more enlisted men to make up this total.

As we began to file out of the cars, a loud voice from a buck sergeant boomed out, "Okay, you shitheads, line up in four ranks as your name is called! Clear?" We hastily lined up and waited for further orders. "First twenty men called will climb aboard this truck," the sergeant continued, pointing to the truck on his left side. When everyone was aboard, the first truck moved out, and the remaining three followed in the convoy.

3. PARRIS ISLAND

About two miles down the road, we crossed over the bridge to Parris Island—our first home in the Marine Corps. It was a fairly large island situated away from the surrounding towns. The excitement was building up for me as we got a glimpse of Marines marching in close-order drill and passed the many canvas tents neatly arranged in rows. There were only a few brick buildings; the rest were two-man and six-man tents. The brick buildings were for officer's quarters and those in command of the whole island. It reminded me somewhat of the island off the shore of West Aliquippa.

Part of one building was for those who signed up for Field Music School. Another part was a gym, where a lot of boxing took place. The building in the center of the others was for the high command. One building to the right section was for the quartermaster. Beyond that was the huge mess hall. Living quarters for the enlisted men were all canvas tents.

Each truck went to a different location. Our truck stopped near two long rows of two-man tents. A corporal and a private first class (PFC) were waiting for us.

The corporal was our drill instructor (DI). His first words were, "Let's go, shitheads! Let's go! Down off the trucks! Line up in two rows! Say here when your name is called! Clear?"

We all repeated in unison: "Clear!"

He barked back, "I can't hear you ladies!"

"Clear!" we repeated more loudly.

Again, the corporal bellowed, "I CAN'T HEAR YOU!"

This time we hammered out a thunderous, "CLEAR!"

"Much better, shitheads! You know your ass is mine for the next six weeks. The remaining two weeks, the rifle-range commander will have your ass. You think it's going to be easy here on the island? Think again because I'm either going to make you or break you! If I break you, you can go back to your mommy because you sure don't belong in the Corps! This outfit is for men! I mean real fighting men! By God, I'm going to see to that, or I'm no drill instructor!"

National Archives at St. Louis

Pvt. Albert Donald Palermo

The corporal was a handsome looking guy, around twenty-four years old, and he looked hard as nails with his copper-colored skin. At six feet, four inches, he stood tall and had an athlete's build. He was well-seasoned, having done duty at Guantanamo Bay Naval Base in Cuba, in the Marine Corps since he was eighteen. If you had done duty in Cuba, you were considered an "old salt," a seasoned Marine who had passed the test beyond the call of duty. He was a cocky drill instructor and liked to show his authority. His assistant was a PFC, a little overweight, and he was a more down to earth guy than the DI. Later on, he tried to help us when we didn't grasp a problem or when we didn't exactly make up our field pack correctly.

"Okay," the DI bellowed out, "As I call two names at a time, you will both share the designated tent I assign you to!" When my name was called, and my tent mate also, we walked to our two-man tent. We picked our bunks and sat down. I extended my hand to him and said, "Jim Messina from around Pittsburgh, Pennsylvania."

"Al's my name," he said, as he shook my hand, "I'm from Worcester, Massachusetts. It's a big factory town." Al was little taller than me, had dark brown hair and a big smile on his face.

"You know," I said, "This is great. When I was in the CCC, my close friend's name was Al." I knew from that moment on we would become good friends.

The DI's voice boomed again, "Fall out, you shitheads! Fall out!" We quickly lined up in two ranks and waited for his speech. "Now that you ladies are all settled in your tents, I have this to say to you. You will not get to keep your civilian clothes. You will wrap them up and ship them back home when you're issued Marine clothing and shoes tomorrow morning. Clear?"

Very loudly, we all replied, "Clear!"

"You're catching on, shitheads, but not yet loud enough. I can't hear you!"

This time we all shouted so loudly we could be heard over at headquarters. "CLEAR!"

The DI continued. "Now, you will also be quarantined for your first seven days on this base! If any of you are seen at the post exchange (PX) trying to buy pogey bait, you will answer to me with the shittiest detail I can dream up, and you will not be allowed to leave your tent area. The only exception will be going to the head. [The Navy and Marine Corps called the men's room the "head." The Army called it the "latrine."] There will be no radios, no loud talking at night, smoking only when the smoking lamp is lit, and no horseplay. Lights out will be at 10 p.m., and they better be out!"

This was only our first day, and already no one liked this cocky corporal. He wore a campaign hat like the State Troopers wore, cocked forward down to his nose, and really looked sharp and snappy, the way a Marine should look. But we didn't like him. He was always neatly dressed in a khaki uniform, and had his tie folded and tucked into his shirt. This is the way we wore the tie with khaki attire back then, but not in today's Marine Corps. His sharp commands prickled our skins. The DI wanted everyone to be afraid of him and to look up to him as some kind of god.

As we stood at attention in two ranks, the DI continued. "You will address me as sir, and also my assistant. You will never call me by my name. It's only sir I want to hear!" He then came to the front of the ranks. He asked the first Marine in line, "Where are you from, shithead?" The man looked at him but was immediately corrected. "You will not look at me when I ask a question! You will look straight ahead at attention! Clear?"

"Yes, sir!" the man shouted out.

"Let's try it again—where are you from?"

The Marine did not eyeball him this time and answered, "Washington, D.C., sir!"

"Why are you in the Marine Corps?" the DI demanded.

"I have an older brother in the Corps, and I want to follow in his footsteps!"

The DI laughed. "Do you think you will make a good Marine, shithead?"

"I will try my best, sir!"

"We will see, we will see," the corporal replied.

The next man in ranks was a well-built man who weighed about 190 pounds and was taller than the corporal. The DI looked him over from head to foot, and he liked what he saw, but only as a challenge to intimidate him.

"Where you from, shithead?" the DI's nose practically touched that of the other man.

The big guy's face twitched when he heard the word "shithead." He looked straight ahead as he answered. "Pittsburgh, Pennsylvania, sir!"

"Pittsburgh?" The DI busted out laughing. "You mean Smoky City?"

"Yes, sir!"

"Don't tell me you played football, too!"

"Yes, sir, and track also!"

"Well," the DI sneered. "We have a football hero of a shithead in my ranks!"

The man's face twitched again. He could have torn the DI in half if he wanted to, but he kept his cool.

The DI practically felt what we were all thinking. "Do you think you can take me, football hero?" The man looked straight ahead and did not answer. "I asked you a question," the DI continued, almost touching the man's nose again.

The recruit said, "Sir, I'm not here to fight you! I'm here to learn how to become a good Marine who wants to serve his country!"

"Well, fancy that," the DI said, with a smirky laugh. "Our hero wants to serve his country! The only thing you could serve is a ping-pong ball!"

When the DI saw he couldn't get the tall guy mad, he went on to the next man, and the next. He was satisfied we all were nothing but a bunch of shitheads, who should be in the Army, not in the Marines Corps. He had no more questions as to why we were here.

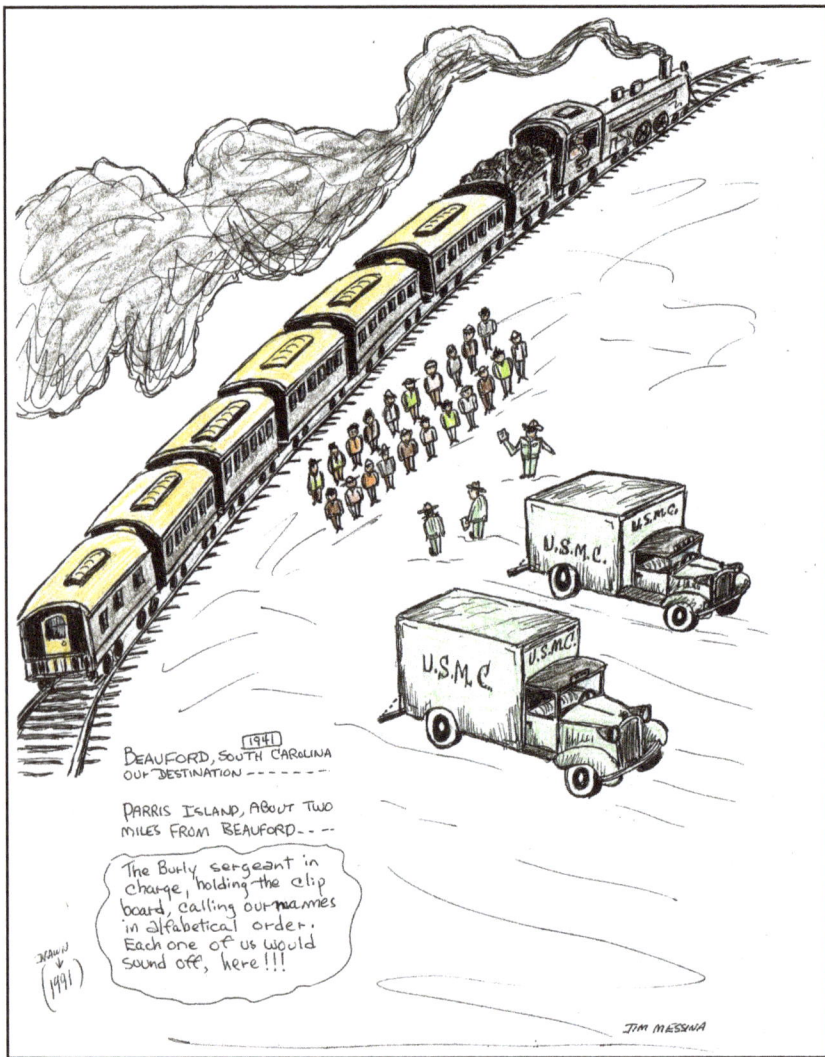

It was dinner time by now, and the chow call blew. The corporal marched us down to the mess hall, walking in front of our platoon while the PFC took up the rear. Upon entering the long mess hall, the aroma was a welcome scent. I was very hungry, as I always was during my whole stay in the Corps. Being young and full of piss and vinegar, I had a healthy appetite.

Inside the mess hall there were many long tables that each held twelve men. As we went through the chow line, we saw the stainless metal trays and the silverware right next to it. There were also thick white cups for coffee or cocoa. The counter was all stainless-steel, and the deep pans in the warming holes held all the steaming food. Even the aroma was delicious, and boy was I hungry! There was a sign behind those who were serving the food, and Al nudged me to read it: "Take all you want but eat all you take!"

Each man got two pork chops, and we also had mashed potatoes, peas, and two slices of white bread with butter. We had strong black coffee and a square piece of white cake. We arrived at our tables but weren't allowed to sit just yet. When everyone was in position at their tables, the rule was to wait until the mess sergeant blew the police whistle, signaling us to sit and eat our meal.

Each table had a jar of peanut butter, a jar of jelly, salt, pepper, sugar, and catsup. Sometimes when I didn't like what they served that day, I would only take the coffee and six slices of bread and then just eat peanut-butter-and-jelly sandwiches.

As I sat there eating, I glanced throughout the mess hall and noticed how spic and span the place looked. You could eat off the floor for how clean it was kept. The rules were very strict on the island. The commander demanded a shipshape code that every man who did KP duty do it well. The outside grounds demanded the same rule.

After we had finished, we marched back to our tent area. The rest of the day was spent hearing the corporal making his demands for discipline. He showed us a little bit of how to stand at attention with our shoes at a forty-five-degree angle. He also showed us how to do a right face, a left face, and an about face. Finally, he briefed us on the schedule for tomorrow's happenings.

4. FALL OUT, SHITHEADS!

I was awakened by the loud sound of the bugle blowing reveille and sat up on my cot with a jolt. It was 5:30 a.m., and it was still dark outside. Al sat up also, and said, "Oh no, it seems like I just closed my eyes a few minutes ago!" We both jumped up and put on our civilian clothes for the last time.

"Fall out you shitheads," a loud voice bellowed. "Fall out!" It was the DI, of course, and in one minute everyone was outside standing at attention.

"Roll call!" the PFC shouted. "Roll call!" He called off all the names in alphabetical order, and each man responded with a loud, "Here!"

It was the DI's turn to speak. "Attention! You will double time around the tent area when I signal with my whistle!" Upon his signal, we began trotting past the two-man tents, and then we had to pick up the pace. We did three complete turns around the tent area when the DI halted us, and said, "March down to the head and get cleaned up for breakfast!"

In the head there was a long, metal trough with many faucets above it. We lined up like cattle and washed up. It's a good thing most of us had brought along a towel from home. There were large cakes of government issue (GI) soap that hardly made any lather. The toilets were in a neat row opposite the long trough. We didn't waste too much time and hurried back to the corporal.

As our platoon got into position (three rows), the DI snapped, "Attention!" After we'd done this, there was a second command: "Right face! Forward march!" We were on our way to the mess hall, where we always went through the same ritual waiting for the police whistle to blow as the signal to sit and eat our meal. After breakfast was over, we had to double time back to our tent area. We weren't in our tents five minutes when we heard the DI's voice crack, "Fall out, shitheads! Fall out!" Again, we were at attention awaiting orders.

After eyeing everyone with disgust, the DI said, "We'll march down to the quartermaster and draw clothing and shoes. This afternoon, we'll be coming back to draw your rifles, packs, canteens, entrenching tools, and whatever else is GI." Our platoon looked sloppy for now, but, in time, we would be as snappy as the platoons we saw marching when we rode in on the trucks from Beaufort.

One by one, we entered the quartermaster's building and named our size as we passed through. Most of us got the sizes just about right; a few got sizes too small or too large. I was lucky to guess the right size when receiving my government issue. We all received combat uniforms with light

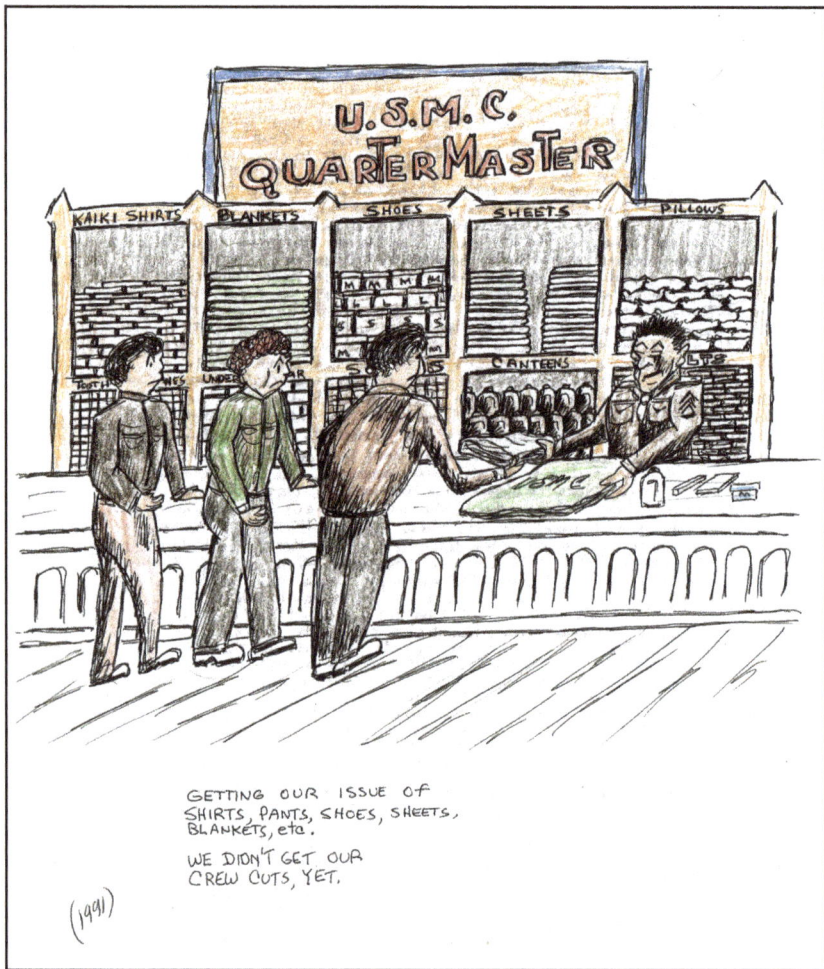

GETTING OUR ISSUE OF
SHIRTS, PANTS, SHOES, SHEETS,
BLANKETS, etc.

WE DIDN'T GET OUR
CREW CUTS, YET.

(1991)

green jackets. Over the pockets were the letters *USMC*. The pants matched, with no cuffs. The combat shoes looked like light suede shoes, and the dress shoes were a purplish black. We received two combat uniforms, three khaki shirts, six pairs of white socks, and light green-colored underwear. We also were issued one set of the green dress uniform, with purplish black emblems for the jacket and matching emblems for our caps. We got one visor cap, two overseas caps, four khaki neckties, and two black belts with shiny brass buckles. We were really loaded down with GI clothes and shoes.

Al and I walked into our tent and unloaded our burden on our cots. Just as we began catching our second breath, we heard the annoying words, "Fall out!" The corporal was never going to let up, and we knew we had better get used to those two words. He said, with a smirk on his face, "Okay, shitheads, what do you say to a nice trim at the barber shop? It's free—on the government!"

There already was a long line outside the building, so our platoon took up the rear behind them. When we saw the first Marine leaving the shop, he had a crew cut. We all looked at each other and just shrugged our shoulders—more government issue. Some of the guys had nice, curly, thick hair, but they would lose it to the floor around the barber's chair. I didn't look too bad, and in about six or eight weeks, it would all grow back.

Between the clothing issue and the haircuts, the time had gone by quickly, and it was close to noon chow. Back at the tent area, we had about a half-hour break. Al and I quickly laid down on the army cots for a short rest. It sure felt good not hearing the DI's voice.

Soon we heard the chow call blow, then the DI's voice cracking, "Fall out, shitheads! Let's go! Move it, move it!" In seconds, we were outside, lined up in ranks. Our noon chow consisted of liver that looked green around the edges, mashed potatoes, peas, beets, butter, and white bread. The liver tasted better than it looked, and besides, I'd liked liver ever since I was a young kid. Al turned his nose up at it and just made peanut butter and jelly sandwiches.

From the mess hall, the DI took us to the quartermaster again. Before we entered the building, he gave a speech. "You will be drawing your rifles and combat gear. Your rifle is vintage WWI, and it's all covered with

Cosmoline. You will also draw buckets and cleaning gear. Your rifles will be issued first, and you will clean them outside at a designated spot near the quartermaster. Your rifle will be spic and span before you are issued the rest of your combat gear!"

All of us were taking everything in stride. We had to accept everything that was dished out to us, whether it was working, drilling, or whatever else was going to make us each a fighting Marine. Al and I picked a spot to clean our rifles. We also were issued rifle rods and cleaning pads, along with a small can of lubricating oil. I opened my can of cleaning fluid and began removing the Cosmoline with the square rags given to us. The quartermaster had bales of these rags, which had to be disposed of after using them. It took us a good hour to clean our rifles.

My .30-06 caliber rifle had a pistol-grip stock. These rifles were M1903 Springfield bolt-action and used five shells in a clip-loading magazine. The first shell of the clip was a tracer bullet, the next three were balls, and the fifth bullet was an armor-piercing one. The first bullet, being a tracer, would let the rifleman know if he was hitting too low, too high, or too far to the right or left of his target. The ball ammunition would flatten out when it hit its target. The last bullet could penetrate metal measuring one-eighth inch thick. These rifles were very accurate in battle, and also made good deer rifles for hunters.

I was very proud of myself when I saw how nice and shiny my rifle looked. I ran the rod through the bore of the rifle and then put a light coat of oil on the inside. Holding the rifle up and looking through the bore, I could see the spiral design inside as a series of curved lines. Al and I returned our buckets to the quartermaster and sat around waiting for the last man to complete his cleaning job.

About fifteen minutes later, we lined up in ranks to have our jobs inspected by the corporal. After he was finished with his inspections, each man had to read off the serial number of his rifle assigned to him. The DI had his clipboard and marked all names and serial numbers. Also, we had to memorize our serial numbers.

Now that this assignment was complete, we had to file into the quartermaster building to draw the rest of our combat gear. Each man got one marching pack, entrenching shovel tool, mess kit, cartridge belt, large seabag, and first-aid kit. We also were issued steel helmets with a fiber helmet insert fit inside to cushion the steel helmet.

Loaded down again, we headed back to our tent area. Once we were in our tent, I began putting my shirts and pants into my seabag. We were doing nicely until, "Fall out!" was heard once again. As we stood at attention, the DI walked back and forth in front of the ranks.

"Shitheads," he began. "Time to send your civilian clothes back to your mamas! You will be issued brown wrapping paper and cord. You will send your clothes back at your own expense! Clear?"

We all responded with a deafening, "CLEAR!"

After our clothes were neatly wrapped and the cord was tightly in place around the package, the DI marched us down to the camp post office to have them weighed. When all of this was taken care of, back to the tent area we went.

Once inside the tents, it wasn't more than ten minutes when we heard the ugly words again, "Fall out, shitheads! Let's move it! Outside, girls!" With his campaign hat cocked forward, the DI gave us a warning. "I want to remind everyone you are in quarantine for six more days! You will not leave the area to buy pogey bait or cigarettes. You will not visit other tents. You will not gamble. You will only smoke when I light the smoking lamp!

"Now, shitheads, I will teach you how to stand at attention, how to make a right face, left face, and about face." We all worked at this for the next two hours. We didn't do too badly, and the next lesson was the manual of arms with our rifles. The corporal showed us how to stand at attention with the rifle resting on the side of our right leg. From this point the next command was port arms, then left shoulder, and right shoulder arms. Present arms (salute with a rifle) was next, then order arms, where the rifle goes back to the right side of your leg, and the butt of the rifle rests up against the toe of your shoe. Chest out, shoulders back, and eyes front was the proper way to stand at attention, with or without the rifle. We spent the rest of the day with this type of drill.

It was now the third day, and after morning chow we were taken to sick bay where we received three shots in the arm—typhoid and two others. There was this one big guy who was about six-four and was acting tough about getting the needle as he saw the scared look on some of the other faces. Looking very tough, he marched up to the corpsman (medic) for his shot. He was smiling at everyone as the needle entered his arm, but the next second he passed out. Big man, each of us thought. The needle didn't bother me, but the serum really hurt.

It was about 10:30 a.m. when we finished up and marched back to our area, where I expected more orders. I was right because we were called to fall in at attention within five minutes.

"Today, shitheads," the DI barked, "You will learn close-order drill on the march! When I give the order to march, you will always start out with your left foot. When I give cadence, I want to see everyone in step. Clear?"

"CLEAR!" was our loud response.

The DI continued. "You will learn the left and right flank on the march, the rear march, and the left oblique on the march. You will learn to be snappy Marines by graduation or stay and rot on this island!" His voice sounded strong, determined, and also a little disgusted at having to train us new recruits.

For the next two days, the DI hammered at us in close-order drill. Left flank, right flank, right and left oblique, and on and on. He shouted, "One, two, three, four, your left! One, two, three, four, your right!" until we began showing signs of well-drilled Marines on the march. The field for marching was always dry and dusty. We were eating our own dust, and the corporal loved it as he watched with a smirk on his face.

Two more days of quarantine before we'd finally be allowed to go to the PX. Meanwhile, some of the other BTO Marines who were stationed on the island would infiltrate into our tent area at night and sell us five-cent pogey bait for a dime and cigarettes for fifteen cents. It was expensive, but we had no choice. We only purchased enough up until the quarantine time ran out.

On the fifth day the corporal passed out gas masks. He marched us to a small building about twenty-five feet long. We entered and the command was given to don our gas masks. The next minute we could see a cloud of gas enveloping us like thick fog. "Remove gas masks!" was the order. Slowly, as we looked at one another, we removed the masks. Instantly, everyone began choking and gagging. This went on for five seconds, then the order to fall out of the building was delivered loud and clear. As we filed out quickly, everyone's eyes were watering, and we felt a burning sensation in our throats.

The DI was laughing and enjoying our predicament. "How does it feel?" he said. "Now you know how the doughboys in WWI felt when they were gassed by the Germans! This lesson is to teach you to never throw your gas masks away if you are in battle. A lot of the WWI boys did just that and were sorry for it. Some died; others suffered the rest of their lives. I'll tell you this: learn now and learn well because you are your own protector of your life. Remember that, shitheads!"

The burning in my throat stayed with me for the rest of the day, and I barely ate my chow at suppertime. It was a very scary experience. Fighting in battle, if the occasion arose, would surely be no picnic whatsoever. When I was a little tyke, around seven, I used to like to hear the WWI vets talk about the trenches in France. I really didn't sit in on their conversations but would sit near enough to overhear them trading experiences. How was I to know someday I would be talking about WWII?

The corporal was satisfied we looked serious enough to grasp this situation, and he marched us back to our area. He let us alone for the next half hour to shake off the effects of the gas. It was really terrible and frightening to us young bucks. We seemed to mature the instant the gas was released. I think I drank a whole canteen of water because I was frightened. We never forgot this incident.

"Fall out, shitheads! Fall out!" Hearing the familiar call, we lined up as our platoon was led out to the drill field for more close-order drill. The DI didn't have pity on us. He constantly hammered away with the duties of a drill instructor.

When we finally sat on our cots before chow, every bone in my body was aching. I never felt this tired, even when I served in the CCC camps in New Mexico. Chow was very good today—spaghetti and meatballs, at last. It sure didn't taste like Mom's sauce, but I was ever so happy to get it. There were also fresh oranges and chocolate cake, my favorite.

It was the seventh day, and tomorrow we'd be allowed to venture down to the PX. Part of this day was spent putting together the heavy marching pack with two rolled-up blankets. We would put it together, then tear it apart until the corporal was satisfied we were doing it right. When the corporal wasn't looking, the PFC would point out the things some of the men were doing wrong. If the DI caught him, he would have to discipline him in front of the men. The PFC was very careful about not being seen doing this.

The next order was about field stripping our .30-06 rifles. After learning how to do this, we also had to do it blindfolded. The reason was, once in battle, you have to know how to handle your weapon in the dark.

We worked with our rifles up until noon chow. Another tradition we learned was to salute when the flag was raised in the morning and also at retreat when the flag was lowered at the end of the day.

After noon chow, we went back out to the drill field. We drilled until we kicked up a cloud of dust. Two hours later, we had to go on a ten-mile hike around the island. In the morning, when reveille blew, we would have to do exercises and run around the area before chow.

The eighth day was spent policing up the area of any papers or cigarette butts lying around. In those days there weren't any filter cigarettes. The DI told us how to strip a cigarette butt before discarding it on the grounds. You take the butt, tear it open, sprinkle the tobacco around, then roll up the paper in a little wad and throw it away.

We went out to the drill field for three hours, showing signs of a snappy, well-drilled platoon. We were proud of ourselves, and we wanted to show off to other well-drilled platoons.

After we were done with the day's duties, Al and I went down to the PX for the first time. It was a fairly large place, about thirty feet by thirty feet. In the showcases we saw campaign ribbons and medals for rifle and pistol qualifications. There were still cameras, movie cameras, wallets, wrist watches, Marine Corps rings, and many other items of interest. On the opposite side of the PX you could see an ice-cream counter, where they had Coke, beer, ice cream, popsicles, cheese crackers, hamburgers, and some other sandwiches.

We purchased a few postcards of South Carolina to send home. Then we bought two Cokes and cheese crackers to take back to the tent area. There was a two-cent deposit on the Coke bottles. We each bought five packs of Lucky Strikes at ten cents a pack. Back at our tent, Al and I ate the cheese crackers and talked about our lives back home growing up until lights out.

The next five weeks were much of the same: always being called "shitheads," each man having to take his turn doing KP, and the ten-mile hikes; standing at attention, fall in, fall out; close-order drill on the dirt field, writing letters home, and learning troop movements; the special care of your rifle, putting a field pack together…and on, and on, until the end of the sixth week had arrived. We were really a snappy, proud platoon on the march now, but we'd worked our butts off to achieve this.

It was now the first day of the seventh week. The corporal had us at attention when he said, "Today, I will march you on a hike out to the rifle range. The range is three miles from here. You will hike with a heavy pack, two rolled-up blankets, rifles, and your mess gear. Your seabags will be loaded on trucks and taken out to the range. Any questions?" No one had anything to ask. We would just follow his orders, and we were all happy to never see him again. We couldn't wait until he delivered our platoon to a new set of instructors, hoping it would be different on the range. But it was a wait-and-see game.

The DI moved us out, full platoon at attention, with rifles on our shoulders and the heavy packs on our backs. The combination heavy marching order and the pack weighed about eighty pounds. As we approached the very first company street, we saw some two-story framed barracks that were very neat and painted white. There were many small-framed panels in each window. The set of steps to get to the second floor was on the outside of the building, and the lawns were well groomed with a rich green color. The rifle range area was really beautiful. Many trees surrounded the barracks and the range area. We didn't see one tent, just all wooden buildings and paved roads. It really felt good not to see any tents.

We were met by two buck sergeants as we approached the designated barracks we'd be living in for the next two weeks. Our DI shook hands with one of the sergeants, then handed him a clipboard with our names on it. He snapped at attention and saluted the sergeant as a gesture of discipline for our eyes. Corporals and sergeants don't usually salute each other, only officers. The DI gave our platoon a stern look, no smile, and climbed aboard a waiting jeep to take him back to the tent area. He'd soon be getting a new bunch of recruits to call "shitheads." He didn't say one word of praise to us for our efforts of becoming a snappy platoon.

As the DI and his assistant drove off, the buck sergeant snapped us to attention, but he didn't call us shitheads. "Men," he said, "Follow me to the first barracks on this street. This will be your new home. Now, the way you see the cleanliness inside is the way you will keep it. Your rifles will always be clean. There are two sets of racks in the middle of the floor, one on each end of the barracks. You will always stand your rifles in the rack. I never want to see your rifle lying around, only standing upright on the rack, understand?"

"YES, SIR!" was our loud response.

We climbed up the steps on the side of the building to the second floor. I couldn't believe how clean it looked inside. It smelled of fresh wax. The floors were hardwood, and they sparkled with cleanliness. There were twenty steel bunks to each side of the large room, and only the mattresses were on the bunks. Later, we'd have to draw sheets at the quartermaster and then learn how to make up a military bunk. We each placed our rifles in position on the racks. Everyone picked their own bunk. My bunk was more to the middle of the barracks. Each bunk had a steel locker to hang our uniforms and a place for our shoes.

The buck sergeant spoke out after we settled in. "The rest of this morning," he began, "You'll not do anything. You'll get acquainted with the barracks, the head, and the outside grounds. We'll get together after noon chow. Clear?"

"YES, SIR!" we replied. Then the sarge walked out of the building.

I said to Al, "Boy, this is nice! I'm going to like the rifle range area. It's a relief not to hear 'shitheads' and also to have the commander talk to us like human beings."

Al agreed with me and said, "Let's walk around the perimeter."

"Okay," I said, and we walked down the steps. As we walked around, admiring the place, I was surprised to see someone I knew coming my way. "Hey, Tommy!" I said. "Of all places to meet somebody from West Aliquippa!" It was Tommy Valiga from Seventh Street.

He gave me a warm handshake and said, "When did you enlist?"

"September 18th," I answered.

"How long have you been on the range?"

"This is my first day," I replied.

Then Tommy said, "I'll be leaving, in two days for advanced training. My basic is complete, but I don't know where I'm going."

We talked awhile, and I introduced him to Al. Then he headed off to his own barracks. I told Al it felt good to see someone from my hometown. "Maybe I'll run into him again somewhere in the future," I said. We covered a lot of the grounds and wondered what it was going to be like for our last two weeks of basic training.

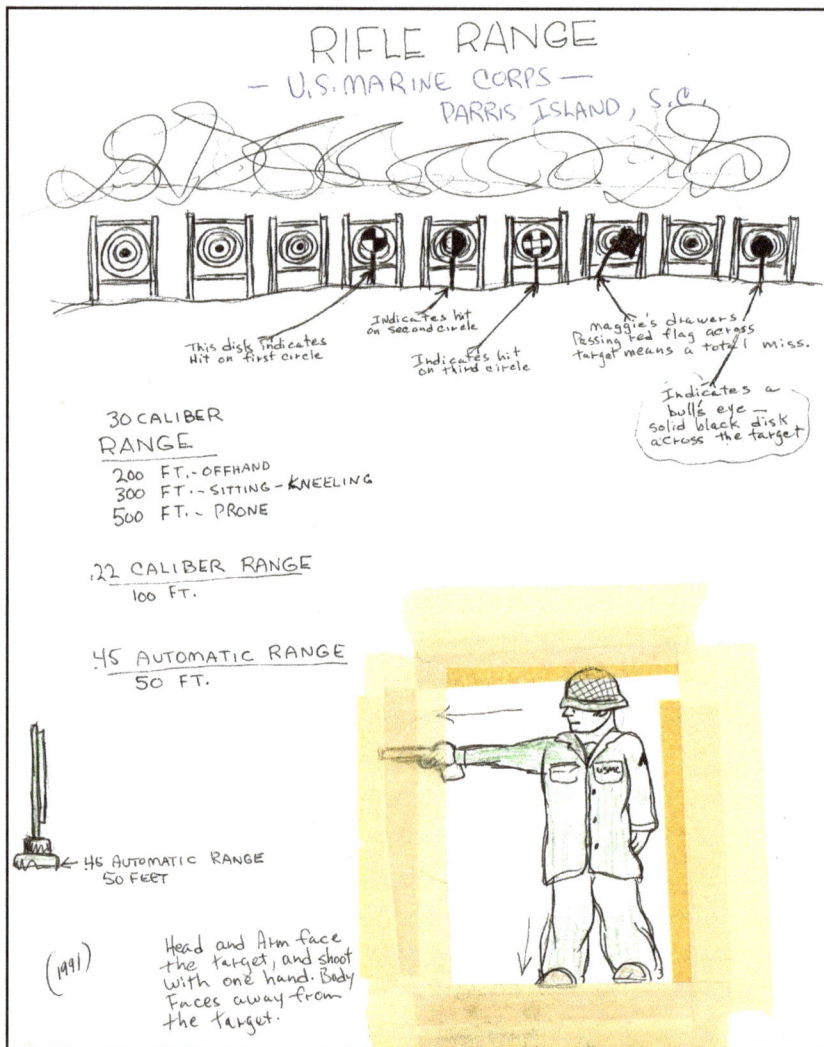

RIFLE RANGE
— U.S. MARINE CORPS —
PARRIS ISLAND, S.C.

This disk indicates
Hit on first circle

Indicates hit
on second circle

Indicates hit
on third circle

maggie's drawers!
Passing red flag across
target means a total miss.

Indicates a
bull's eye —
solid black disk
across the target

30 CALIBER
RANGE
200 FT. - OFFHAND
300 FT. - SITTING - KNEELING
500 FT. - PRONE

.22 CALIBER RANGE
100 FT.

.45 AUTOMATIC RANGE
50 FT.

← .45 AUTOMATIC RANGE
50 FEET

(1991)

Head and Arm face
the target, and shoot
with one hand. Body
Faces away from
the target.

5. PULLING BUTTS

The sarge returned and directed us to the mess hall. We followed in two
ranks, and as we approached the range mess hall, I noticed it was a small
one-story building made of wood. It was about fifty feet long and didn't
look as good as the mess hall back at the main base. I was disappointed upon

entering the building. The rest of the range area was certainly beautiful, but this mess hall was the only sore spot. The walls were a faded, greenish color, and it was badly in need of a new paint job. Also, the tables looked like picnic tables, and I even noticed a cockroach walking across the floor.

"I can't believe it," I told Al, as I looked at the place in disbelief.

He countered, "Well, Jim, look at it this way, we're only going to be here for two weeks."

"Right," I grudgingly agreed. We were directed to the metal serving trays and noticed we didn't have to wait for a signal to sit down and eat, like at the first mess hall. The tables also had ketchup, salt, pepper, peanut butter, and jelly on them. The sign behind the serving counter was the same as the other mess hall but with a few more words added: "If you come up for seconds, eat all that you take!"

Following noon chow, the sarge took us out to the .30-caliber range to watch the other Marines firing in different positions. The firing position at two hundred feet was standing and the position for the three-hundred-foot target was sitting and kneeling. The last position was at five hundred feet, lying flat on your belly, with your legs spread apart, also known as the prone position.

Another thing we had to do on the range was take turns "pulling butts" behind the huge black-and-white targets with the bullseyes on them. In back of the targets, you're protected from the flying bullets because there is a trench dug lower than the targets. When five rounds of a clip are fired, the men behind the targets get a call to pull down the targets and check the bullet holes. There's a disk on a long pole with different patterns to indicate what position of the bullseye the bullet hit. You'd pass the proper disk on a long pole across the target. A red flag indicating a total miss, aka "Maggie's drawers," was the most frequent among the Marines.

When checking for holes on the target, we'd use small square stickers of paper to patch the holes for either the black or the white part of the target. The targets were rigged on little roller wheels on each side of the supports and a rope hung to pull them down. Once they were pulled down, you locked the target until you patched up the holes. When you released the lock, the target would automatically snap back into the firing position because it had a set of springs to bring it back up. It sure was scary crouched down behind the targets and hearing the crack of the bullets penetrating the canvas targets.

After we watched the other Marines firing for about a half hour, the sarge motioned us to follow him to the .22-caliber range. The purpose of the .22 range was when you came from practice on the .30 caliber, you could find out a lot of your mistakes on this range.

The third range was the .45-caliber range, where you would fire one-handed at a target fifty feet away. On this range, when you fired, your right shoulder would be facing the target, and your body would be facing away. The way they teach you how to fire your hand weapon today is with your full body facing the target, using both hands to grip the pistol.

The whole afternoon was spent visiting all three of the ranges. The sarge told us we would start tomorrow morning on the .30-caliber range.

The next morning found us scrambling out of the barracks, down the steps, and falling in for roll call. It was good to hear the sarge say, "Okay, Marines, today you'll learn the military way of firing a weapon! You'll get into positions that will make your muscles sore, and you'll be using muscles in your body you thought you'd never use. I'm going to make you an expert shot when I'm through with you. Those who don't pass the range at the end of two weeks will be punished, and you'll be kept here on the island until you do. Am I clear?"

"YES, SIR!" we loudly responded. The sarge didn't call us shitheads, but he was very strict and commanding.

After breakfast, we were marched out to the rifle range in platoon formation. Upon arriving at the .30-caliber range, the sarge gathered us in a circle and said, "Now, I'm going to pick half of the platoon to fire first, and the other half will pull butts behind the targets." He explained about the different disks and Maggie's drawers, which would be passed across the target to indicate your score. "You will patch each hole every time you pull the target down, and when you are finished, you'll come out to take your turn at firing. Clear?"

"YES, SIR!" we shouted in unison.

I was picked in the half that would pull butts first. Behind the targets it sure was nerve-racking. If it wasn't for the big mound in front of us for protection, you'd think you were participating in a battle. Every time the bullets hit the canvas target, there was a loud, whacking sound and then a ring when the bullets passed through. For about two hours we were behind the targets doing what we had to do marking scores with the disks. Then we got the signal to come out to the firing line. As we watched the first half walk towards the targets, the sarge approached us to give the order for the firing line.

The sarge was a big guy—blond, blue-eyed, with a strong square jaw protruding forward from his face. He was well-built and looked like a weightlifter. He was also a cool speaking person who had been in the Corps for two hitches, according to the hash marks on his sleeve. Each hash mark represents four years of service in the Marine Corps. His khaki pants were ever so neat with the military creases and well-polished shoes. He had done duty in Cuba for two years and was picked to train the Marines on Parris Island. He liked his job, molding new recruits into weapons experts. And he did make experts out of a lot of men, but not all.

The sarge called each name off of his clipboard and told us where to take up our position on the firing line. I was on the left flank, and our first target was two hundred feet away, in the off-hand position, which is standing. We had to slip our left arm into the sling of the rifle and keep our elbow in close to our body, which caused the muscle in my shoulder to pull. The right arm and elbow extended out even with the right shoulder, and in this position, I felt my ribs pull.

6. Bullseye

"When you aim your rifle at the bullseye," the sarge began, "Remember to squeeze the trigger and not flinch! Take your time and don't pull the trigger until your eye is square on the bullseye. Clear?"

Again, we responded, "YES, SIR!"

I fired my five rounds of ammunition then had to wait for my score. I got three disks on the outer circles and two misses, or Maggie's drawers.

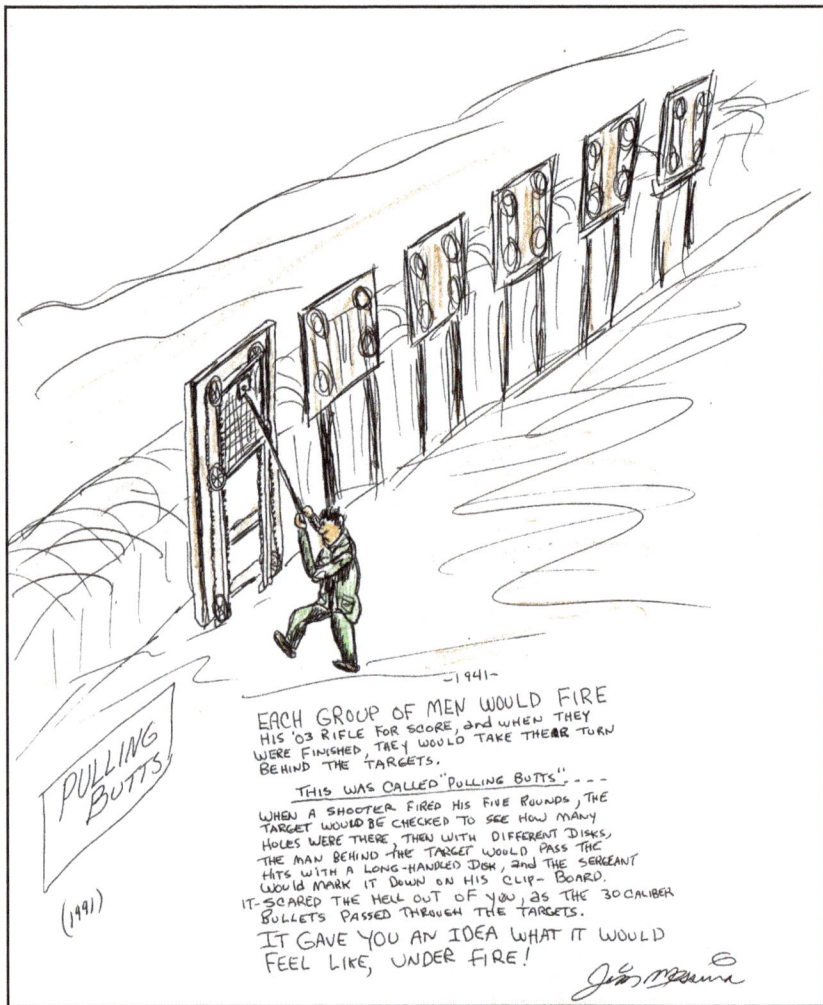

PULLING BUTTS

(1941)

-1941-

EACH GROUP OF MEN WOULD FIRE HIS '03 RIFLE FOR SCORE, and when they were finished, they would take their turn behind the targets.

THIS WAS CALLED "PULLING BUTTS".---
WHEN A SHOOTER FIRED HIS FIVE ROUNDS, THE TARGET WOULD BE CHECKED TO SEE HOW MANY HOLES WERE THERE, THEN WITH DIFFERENT DISKS, THE MAN BEHIND THE TARGET WOULD PASS THE HITS WITH A LONG-HANDLED DISK, and THE SERGEANT WOULD MARK IT DOWN ON HIS CLIP-BOARD.
IT-SCARED THE HELL OUT OF YOU, as THE 30 CALIBER BULLETS PASSED THROUGH THE TARGETS.

IT GAVE YOU AN IDEA WHAT IT WOULD FEEL LIKE, UNDER FIRE!

This was the very first time I fired a .30 caliber rifle. The only other rifle I ever fired was the .22 I'd won in a craps game back in New Mexico when I was in the CCC. The sarge warned me he better not see too many Maggie's drawers, or I would be on extra duty in the mess hall.

It was really tough in the standing position. I swayed as I aimed at my target and wasn't steady at all, but I did cut down on Maggie's drawers. I never hit the bullseye while standing, but I did get a marksman score. The best score is expert, the second highest is sharpshooter, and last is marksman.

When every man had taken his turn pulling butts and firing their rifles, the sarge took us over to the .22-caliber range. Upon firing the .22, we realized our mistakes. It was much easier hitting the target on the .22 range.

The last thing we did was to go over to the .45-automatic range. The sarge split us up in twos for each target. The Marine I was with fired the range, and he made a sharpshooter's score. When it was my turn, the instructor asked me if I had ever fired a hand weapon. I told him no, not even growing up in West Aliquippa.

The instructor, a corporal, said, "Now, when you aim at this target, which is fifty feet away, I want you to do as I instruct you. First off, when the front sight of your weapon comes into view of the top of the bullseye, you squeeze not jerk, okay?"

"Yes, sir!" I confirmed.

He told me to raise my weapon straight up, then slowly come down in sight of the black bullseye. I did exactly as he instructed, squeezed, and, lo and behold, hit a bullseye! I couldn't believe it.

"Marine," the corporal asked, "are you sure you never fired this weapon?"

"No sir, Corporal, never did."

"How did you manage a bullseye on your very first shot?"

"I followed your instructions, sir!" I replied.

"Okay, continue your next nine shots," the corporal commanded.

I can't believe what happened next, and until this day, I don't know how I did it. The next nine bullets were all bullseyes! The corporal questioned me again about not ever firing a pistol before, and he took it as beginner's luck. I scored as expert with the .45 automatic!

Prints and Photographs Division, Library of Congress

Target practice, "On the firing line," 1942.

In the following week, we learned to shoot the .30-caliber rifle in the sitting position, kneeling position, and then the prone position. Sitting and kneeling were very tough for the target at three hundred feet. I fired best in the prone position at five hundred feet, and even made a bullseye. I guess I just felt more relaxed lying down.

On Saturday Al and I were taking a walk down the company street when I ran into another fellow from West Aliquippa, Buddy Dolnak, who was in our Main Street gang when we were eight years old. I greeted him with, "Buddy, you old son of a gun! Imagine running into you on Parris Island!"

"Same goes here, Jim!" he replied. "When did you decide on the Marine Corps?"

"On September 18th," I answered.

"I'm here for another day, and then I'll be leaving," Buddy said. "But I don't know where."

I told Buddy I'd also seen Tommy Valiga. Buddy also saw him, and Tommy had said so long to him before he left.

"I won't be finished with basic until the end of next week, Bud."

"Well, Jim, nice seeing you again. I hope they send you to the same base where I'm going to be stationed."

"I hope so, too, Bud," I replied. Then I introduced Buddy to Al, and Bud told him I was the storyteller of the gang when we were kids. After that Bud was on his way. I never did see Buddy or Tommy for the rest of my hitch in the Marine Corps.

On the final week, it was the .30-caliber, .22-caliber, and the .45-caliber range up until Friday, which would be the final day on the range, and then graduation. About the middle of the week, we were called into the sarge's office one at a time. When it was my turn, I came in and stood at attention in front of his desk.

"At ease," he commanded. "I would like to know if you want to sign up for Field Music School here on the island. We need buglers for different Marine bases."

I hesitated. "I don't know, Sarge. I never thought about it. I was thinking of communications or artillery."

"If you sign up," he said, "you'll be here on the island until you learn the bugle, then they'll assign you to a permanent base. After your ten-day recruit furlough, you'll report back here. It's not so bad."

I thought it over for a couple of minutes. Maybe it would be better than the infantry if I didn't pass for communications or the artillery batteries company. "Okay," I told him. "I'll give it a try!"

"Fine," he replied. "Report to me after graduation."

When Friday came, we all took our final stand at the different caliber ranges; we would have to wait until after evening chow for the results. One other thing we did, after we completed the firing range, was to take turns firing a .30-caliber machine gun on a tripod. It felt good firing this weapon. Boy, what a lot of firepower in this gun! You could really mow down the enemy. Someday one of us might have to take over on a machine gun if the gunner was killed.

After evening chow, the sarge came to our barracks with his clipboard and read off the names of each man who had graduated basic training. I was one of them, and I was ever so happy there were only two Marines who didn't pass. They would have to complete the whole firing course on the range again and remain there for two more weeks. For their punishment, the sarge had two full buckets of water on one end of the barracks and two empty buckets on the other end. He told the two men to carry a tablespoon of water to the empty buckets, a spoonful at a time, until they completed the task of filling them up. He sat in our barracks for the next three hours reading a novel, making sure they didn't goof off. After that he got up and started walking towards the door.

He told the two men he would keep checking up on them, but he didn't. Faithfully, and fearing the sarge, they completed their punishment, but not until it was nearly midnight. The sarge came through about 0030 hours for bed check, but he never approached the two men. He was satisfied to see the full buckets were now empty. The following morning, as their final phase of punishment, the sergeant ordered the two Marines to scrub the entire floor of our barracks from end to end on their hands and knees.

7. Recruit Furlough

The next day was Saturday, and we had to report to headquarters for our furlough papers. We got a ten-day recruit furlough for completing basic training. It was now the middle of November. I had saved money for my train fare to Pittsburgh because we knew we'd be getting this furlough.

When I approached the desk of the sergeant major in charge of the furlough papers, he said to me, "Messina, I see you signed up for Field Music School. Am I right?"

"Yes, sir," I answered.

"Upon completion of your furlough, Messina, you are to report back here to me so I can assign you to Field Music School. Are you sure you want to go into music?"

I replied, "So far, Sarge, but I'll see when I start the course."

"Okay, here are your papers. You'll be able to leave anytime this coming Monday morning. You can make arrangements by bus or train. These are the phone numbers for your transportation. Whichever mode of travel you choose, transportation will be furnished for you to pick up your train or bus. Is everything clear, Messina?"

"Yes, sir!" I responded.

"Okay, fine. Have a good time on your furlough." He closed with, "Semper Fi," the shortened version of the Marine Corps motto, *Semper Fidelis.*

On Monday I decided to take the train. There were two Marine Corps trucks taking a bunch of us to the station, and I said goodbye to Al. He was leaving later that day to go back to New Jersey. This would be the last time I'd see him, since I'd be starting Field Music School when I returned from the ten-day furlough, and he'd be going to advanced training with another unit.

Going back to Pittsburgh didn't seem as long as it was traveling down to Parris Island. It was nice seeing the city again, smoke and all. It seemed like I was away for ages. I guess it was a little homesickness that made me feel this way. Standing on the corner across from the train station, I noticed the Ohio River Motor Coach approaching my stop. We had two different bus lines from Aliquippa to Pittsburgh. The other was the Shafer Coach Line. The Shafer coaches were light green and white. The Ohio River coaches were dark green, and the fare from Aliquippa was thirty-five cents. The Ohio River Motor Coach would travel through Ambridge, then follow Ohio River Boulevard to the North Side, cross over the Manchester Bridge, and come out on Liberty Avenue. The Shafer Coach Line would leave Aliquippa, go through South Heights and Glenwillard, then through Coraopolis, Neville Island, and McKees Rocks, and wind up on Liberty Avenue from the side where Horne's department store was situated.

I stepped onto the bus and took my seat in the rear because I wanted to be by myself. As I sat there, looking out onto the street, I kept wondering about Field Music School. Did I make a mistake? Do I really want to go back to Parris Island? I wondered where my platoon would be sent. Would I ever see the guys I went through basic training with again? I hope to make

Mom and Pop proud of me by being in one of the finest branches of the service in our United States. I will try my damnedest to be a good person in the military and not have any bad marks in the service of my country.

As the bus rolled down Liberty Avenue, it made a right turn on a side street and crossed over to the North Side. This is the same route we took to the produce market in the Strip District when I used to work for Benny Gorman, the fruit huckster, a few years before. I looked in the direction of the river as the bus proceeded down the Ohio River Boulevard, and there was so much thick smoke blocking the view of the hills in the background. It was coming from the mills on Neville Island. Gulf Oil Company was also on the island, and this is where tank trucks loaded up gasoline for delivery to local service stations in our region. The old slogan was, "That's good Gulf gasoline!"

Halfway down the Boulevard, the bus swung into a right turn and onto the road going through Sewickley. After passing through Sewickley, we entered Merchant Street in the next town of Ambridge. Then there was a left turn onto the Ambridge-Aliquippa Bridge across the Ohio River. We reached a "T" on the other side of the bridge and turned right following the two-lane highway, which led to Aliquippa. The bus went under the overhead walking bridge at the south mills section of Jones and Laughlin Steel Corporation, continued another mile, then stopped on Franklin Avenue across from the Joseph building to unload its passengers.

I stepped off the bus with my seabag, crossed the street in front of the Joseph Building, and waited for the Woodlawn and Southern orange bus that would take me to West Aliquippa. These buses charged ten cents a ride or three tokens for a quarter. A few of the people waiting for the bus just stared at me and smiled. They didn't see too many servicemen in the Aliquippa area. While I was waiting for the bus, a car stopped in front of me and someone called out, "Want a ride home, Jim?"

I said, "Yeah," and noticed it was my buddy Dom Sebastian. I shouted out, "How are you doing, Dom?"

"Okay," he replied with a smile. "How about yourself?"

"Never felt better," I answered as I climbed into his car.

Dom asked, "How do you like the Marines, Jim?"

"Okay so far, but I was a little homesick for West Aliquippa!" I confessed. Dom asked many questions: How long would I be home? Was I going to go roller skating? Did I have a steady girlfriend? There were so many I didn't know which to answer first. I guess it was because Dom was so happy to see me.

When he dropped me off in the alley in front of my house, he said, "Come over later, and we'll talk, okay?"

"Sure, Dom," I replied. "See you later, after supper maybe."

Mom and Pop's faces lit up when they saw me, crew cut and all. The first thing Mom wanted to know was did I eat anything?

"Hai fame (Are you hungry)?" she asked, speaking in Italian. "Cosa vorresti (what would you like)?" I hugged Mom very tightly. I loved her so much. Then I put my arms around Pop and hugged him, too. I noticed a small tear in the corner of his eye. He was happy to see me home, even though it was for only ten days. I guess Pop at this moment thought of the many times he would ask, "Jimmy, you wanna go pick blackberries, mushrooms, or apples?" He was in deep thought as he stared at me. Pop was usually asleep around this time, after working the graveyard shift as a soot blower in the blast furnace department of J&L Steel. But he knew I would be home today, so he made sure he was up to welcome me home.

"Mum," I said, "do you have any leftover spaghetti and meatballs?"

"Yes!" she answered happily. She knew I loved her meatballs and began warming some up. After I ate, Mom wanted to wash some of my soiled shirts I had in my seabag. After she ironed them, I would then press in the three military creases in back and two in the front of the shirt. My sisters were all happy to see me, and they had so many questions to ask. They didn't like what they were hearing about Germany and Japan on the radio, and everyone was worried about my future in the military.

Pop talked a little about the time he was in the Italian army when he was younger. He had been a cook in the army, and he was a very good cook at home, too. I ate Mom's homemade bread with the meatballs, and what a difference from the white sliced bread we got in the Marine Corps!

I sure was happy to be home for ten days enjoying Mom's home cooking.

Later in the evening, I went over to Dom Sebastian's house, and we went out onto the street and met a couple of the guys from our Beaver Avenue gang. I got more questions. They were happy to see me, but they weren't enthused about enlisting in any military branch just yet.

Next, Dom and I drove to the Monaca Roller Rink in his 1938 Buick Sedan. I didn't skate that night and instead just talked with a lot of the old skating gang who patronized the place faithfully. We talked to a couple of girls but didn't take any of them out. Dom had to work the next morning at the mill and didn't want to be out late.

During my leave, I visited with my sisters. First, I went to see Mary and her husband Eddie, who lived in Plan 11. Then it was over to Ann and Vic's house on Cherry Street in New Sheffield. Finally, I went to see Grace and her husband Charlie, who lived above Ann and Vic's place.

Our whole family worked for the Jones and Laughlin Steel Corporation. Charlie was a machinist down at the mill, and he worked steady daylight. Vic worked at the open-hearth furnace, running the hot ladle crane. My other sister, Cecelia (Cis), worked in the seamless tube mill, running an overhead crane. Eddie worked in the welded tube mill. Fred Ross, who would marry Cis, worked as a pipe fitter at the north mills and sometimes at the south mills. Before enlisting, I worked at the south mills as a wire drawer.

Dom and I went out together four days of my ten-day furlough. The other days I spent with the family. I wondered to myself if I'd see them again soon, but I didn't know what the future would bring. The family didn't think I'd like being a bugler, but it was a wait-and-see situation.

8. Field Music School

Ten days at home seemed to fly by, and before I knew it, it was time to return to Parris Island. It felt like I was going back to another eight weeks of basic training. That day was a lonely ride back for me because already I was missing the guys I trained with. Suddenly I heard the conductor call out "Beaufort!" I knew I was back in South Carolina, and I didn't like it.

When I thought about being on the island again, all I could see was the face of the corporal, my instructor, and his dumb name for us— "shitheads."

There were about twenty new recruits who got off the train for basic training. I walked over to one of the non-coms, showed him my furlough papers, and he told me to hop on one of the trucks. We pulled up to headquarters and they left me off, then they continued on with the new recruits to the tent area, where they would begin their eight weeks of basic training.

I entered the office to report back to the sergeant major. He had three hash marks on his sleeve, which meant twelve years' service already. He was from the "Old Breed" Marine Corps; a big, burly Marine with a long mustache and very hairy arms. He also had kinky hair and a deep voice. He looked like a bull.

The sergeant major glanced at my papers, got up from his desk, and said, "Okay, Messina, follow me!" I walked out behind him, and he led me over to the brick barracks that housed the Field Music School. He handed my papers over to a corporal and said to him, "Here's a new student for you. Treat him good and make him a number one bugler!"

"Right, sarge," the corporal answered. Then the non-com directed me to my steel bunk. There were about twenty other Marines here who also signed up for the school. Already, I didn't like it. There seemed to be something missing. Maybe it was my warm-hearted buddy, Al. Maybe I was homesick. I seemed a little confused. When it came to the military life, I wasn't sure where I was going to fit in. Well, let's give the music school a try, and if I don't like it, I'll have to talk to the man in charge.

For two days I went to music school. I talked to my bunkmates on the right and left, but I didn't feel at home with them like I did with Al. I wondered where they sent him. On the third day, I didn't seem to catch on about reading music. I wasn't interested, and I knew I had made a big mistake. I thought I'd be better off being a foot soldier. Well, I got up enough nerve to go and see the captain who was in charge and one of our teachers.

"Sir, can I speak to you?"

"Sure, son," the captain answered. "Do you have a problem?"

"Yes, I do," I replied.

"Well, let's hear it."

"Sir, I don't fit in as a bugler. I'd like to know if I can get a transfer to advanced training?"

"Are you sure, Messina?"

"Yes, sir," I answered.

The captain then said, "Well, if you don't think you can cut it, we'll just have to transfer you. Come and see me in about two hours so I can get your papers ready for transfer."

I walked out of his office with much relief because I thought he would say no, but I was surprised.

When I went back to him a little later, my papers were ready. He said, "Messina, you'll be transferred to New River, North Carolina, for advanced training. Here are your papers and your ticket for the Greyhound bus. The bus will leave Parris Island, Monday, December 8th, at 0600 hours, and you'll be on it with eight other Marines. Now, I warn you, don't be changing your mind too often. You may not meet someone who understands like I do. Clear?"

"Yes, sir," I replied. "It won't happen again; I made a mistake!"

"Remember," the captain said, "sometimes mistakes can cost you your life, especially on the battlefield!"

"I'll remember that sir! Thank you!" When I walked out of the office, I went straight to the PX and was in the mood for a can of beer. At the PX, there wasn't any place to sit; you had to stand and drink your beer. As I drank the can of beer, I walked around looking at the items for sale on the shelf to pass time.

I stayed at the PX until closing time, which was 2100 hours. I had two beers and two bars of candy and purchased five packs of Lucky Strikes. Back then I smoked a pack a day. I returned to the barracks and my two bunkmates were sorry to hear I was leaving; they both told me they had begun to like me. But I didn't really get too close to them because I knew the Field Music School wasn't for me.

National Archives

The USS Shaw *explodes during the Japanese attack on Pearl Harbor,*
December 7, 1941.

9. DAY OF INFAMY

It was December 7, 1941, and I'd just left the mess hall. Heading back to my tent, I heard the shocking news from the blare of a loud radio coming out of another tent. A big band music program was interrupted with the words, "The Empire of Japan has just bombed Pearl Harbor!"

I was dumbfounded and didn't know whether to run and shout the news or just go quietly back to my tent. Just then some boot came running up behind me.

"Did you hear about those Jap bastards bombing Pearl Harbor?"

"Yes, I did. That means we'll be getting ready to go over and fight them."

He said, "Oh, I don't know. We have to get organized to go over first."

"You're right," I replied. "I hope we get a furlough to go home before we leave for overseas."

"I'm sure we will," he replied, and rushed off. The very next day the United States declared war on Japan.

December to May were very busy days in our camp. The twenty-mile hikes were stepped up, the working parties were busier, and the drilling on the field more intense. The fighting machine was real mad and wanted to grind the Jap bastards into hamburgers. It was going to be a long war, though; the Japanese had wiped out many of our battleships. You wouldn't believe how busy the recruiting stations were with enlistments who wanted to fight for their beloved country.

The steel mills stepped up production for arms, and the weapons companies began working overtime to supply all our armed forces. The airplane factories were working twenty-four hours a day. We were building tanks, making shells and bombs, and selling war bonds. Women went to work in the factories and steel mills to replace the men who enlisted for military service. It took some time to build up our country's military to make it ready to retaliate against our enemy who dared to declare war on the United States of America.

To quote Japanese Admiral Isoroku Yamamoto: "I fear all we have done is to awaken a sleeping giant and fill him with a terrible resolve."[1] No truer words were spoken. We pledged the Japanese would regret the day they bombed Pearl Harbor!

The next day I boarded the bus along with the eight other Marines. I liked riding the Greyhound bus better than the train. As we left Parris Island, I looked back but not with sadness. I was happy I'd never see this island again. I sure wouldn't want to spend my time in the Marine Corps here.

As the bus went along, it stopped a few times to pick up passengers. There was a pretty, freckled-face girl who got on and sat right next to me. I was sitting by the window, and I asked her, "Would you like to change seats for a better view?"

"Sure, Marine," she smiled. Upon switching seats, she began with, "What's your name? Where are you headed?"

"New River," I answered, "Jim's my name. What's yours?"

"Mary," she answered.

"Where are you headed to, Mary?" "I'm going to spend a week with grandma on her farm. Her and grandpa are alone there. All her children are married and live in different states. I try to visit her at least twice a year. She lives in Kinston about forty miles from your new base!"

"Well, Mary, who knows? Maybe sometime I may run into you again in the future." I was flirting with her.

"That would be nice, Jim."

We talked about many things. Did I have a girlfriend back in Pennsylvania? Did she have a boyfriend in Kinston? I took down Mary's address, but I never wrote to her. It was just a friendly gesture at the time.

It was an all-day trip before we arrived at my new camp about twenty-five miles from Jacksonville, North Carolina. It was called "Tent City" because there were rows and rows of six-man pyramid tents all over the place. The only wooden buildings were the mess hall, headquarters, quartermaster, and the heads. It wasn't any better than Parris Island!

The Old Breed

A platoon sergeant leads the men to Tent City, Camp Lejeune, 1942.

10. ADVANCED TRAINING

Looking at the camp as the bus drove through the front entrance, I couldn't believe I'd be stuck in another stinking tent again! Well, I guess the Army was the only branch of service with all wooden barracks. I stepped down from the bus and lifted my seabag onto my right shoulder and headed for the headquarters building, which was made of red brick. I left my seabag near the clerk's desk as I reported to the Sergeant in Charge (SIC), who announced my arrival to the commanding officer. I was then told to enter the CO's office. I walked in, stood at attention, and waited for him to speak.

The CO was a tall, thin Marine, about six foot two. His skin was a pale white, like he had no blood in his veins. He was soft-spoken with whitish blond hair and penetrating blue eyes. He looked me in the eye and said, "Jim Messina?"

"Yes, sir," I answered.

"I see here on your report sheet you have given up Field Music School before you even got started."

"Yes, sir," I replied, getting red in the face, thinking he was going to comment on my situation.

"Okay, Messina, I'm assigning you to, Fox Company, 2d Battalion, of the 5th Regiment (2/5). When you leave this building, make a left and go straight up the company street until you come to a marker designation for F Company. Is that clear?"

"Yes, sir!"

The CO called in one of his clerks to stamp "Arrival" on my transfer papers from Parris Island. The clerk stamped my papers and told me to take them to the company clerk of F Company. I followed the directions of the CO and went to the company headquarters located in a huge pyramid tent at the end of the company street. The December chill in the air made me shiver.

As I walked into the headquarters, the clerk sat to the left of the entrance. I was surprised to see how neat and orderly the place looked. There was a kerosene burner in the center near the middle support pole holding up the tent. The whole tent stunk of kerosene, and it burned my eyes a little. A lone lightbulb hung down in the center of the tent, and there was a small lamp on the clerk's desk. He had one stripe and was neatly dressed in khakis.

The PFC said, "Let's see your papers." I handed them to him, he read them, and then said, "Follow me." We walked past a long row of pyramid tents, then he pointed to mine. It was about thirty feet from the CO's tent. I walked in, but there wasn't anyone inside. The men of F Company were out on the drill field and wouldn't be back until chow. I sat down on the steel bunk assigned to me and lit up a cigarette. This tent, like all others, had a smelly kerosene burner. The light hanging in the tent had a dim, soot-covered bulb.

With all the men at the drill field, the company street was very quiet. There was a radio near one of the bunks, but I didn't turn it on.

The only noise I heard were trucks passing by on the company street. I reached in my seabag and took out the *Saturday Evening Post*, which I had purchased in the PX back at Parris Island. I wanted something to read on the Greyhound bus to Camp Lejeune.

Glancing at my wristwatch, I saw the time was 1430 hours, so I lay back on my bunk, and looked at the hanging uniforms near the heads of the bunks. Some of the uniforms had three and four stripes, one had PFC stripes, and one didn't have any stripes. I was tired from the long bus ride and dozed off.

Sometime later, I was awakened by the clamor of rifles and shuffling feet. I opened my eyes and one of the Marines said, "Well, looky here, we have a boot from Parris Island!"

I just smiled, "Jim's my name. I'm from Pennsylvania!"

"Big deal!" he scoffed. And already I didn't like him. He was a rebel from South Carolina and a buck sergeant with two hash-marks on his sleeve. He was an old salt with over eight years in the Marine Corps. It seemed like most of the Marines who saw duty at Guantanamo Bay in Cuba were always full of themselves, especially the diehard rebels. They forgot they started out in the Marine Corps as boots. Those guys did duty in Cuba for two years, like it was the only place in the world. They thought they were the elite troops, and no one could match their past duty at Guantanamo Bay.

I ignored this rebel and spoke to the next man who didn't have any stripes on his sleeve. I asked him, "Are you a boot?"

"Yes, I am," he replied. "You have to ignore these old salts. They always ride any new boots assigned to their company." I was glad to hear this because they also rode him when he first arrived.

I walked out of the pyramid tent and reported to the CO. He was a New Yorker who spoke with a husky voice of authority. He was a huge frame of a man with bright red hair. He said, "Right now you're assigned to my company, and it may be only temporary." Later on, I found out he was right.

The chow whistle blew, so I headed for the mess hall two streets over from the CO's office. When I sat down, the fellow next to me introduced himself as John and told me he was from New Jersey. We talked a bit, and he told me he didn't know what was in store for us either.

On the third day, all of us recruits were called into the CO's headquarters. One by one we went into the office as our name was called out. When it was my turn to enter, I walked in and stood at attention with my garrison hat in my left hand and said, "James Messina reporting, sir!"

His first question was, "What did you do in civilian life?"

"I was a wire drawer in a steel mill back in Pennsylvania, sir!"

He mumbled to himself as his fingers searched through the big book of civilian jobs, looking for the meaning of a "wire drawer." He found it and read aloud, "Put rods through a set of dyes, reducing to a finished gauge ordered by the customer. Well, Messina, as you can see, we don't need any wire drawers in the Marine Corps. I'm going to assign you to the Fleet Marine Force known as the infantry—the backbone of this man's Army!"

"Yes sir!" I replied.

"One more thing, Messina," he said. "You are temporarily assigned to Fox Company. Next February you will be assigned to Baker Company, 1st Battalion, of the 5th Regiment (1/5), as a rifleman. B Company is being newly formed to fill the ranks of the 1st Marine Division. We're picking men from different companies, plus the new boots coming in from Parris Island. Understand?"

"Yes, sir," I replied. "I understand." I then did an about-face and walked out of his office.

In one way, I was very happy. I didn't care for F Company with all those salty rebels who thought they were king shit. B Company also had wooden barracks. I could hardly wait to be living in the warm barracks, rather than those stinky pyramid tents eight men had to share.

11. Holiday Furlough

Two weeks before the holidays, we were told half of our division would be able to go home for Christmas; the other half would be going home for New Year's. For some this would be the last time they would see their sweethearts, wives, parents, and friends. I was real lucky when I saw the roster posted and my name was listed for a one-week furlough at Christmas time. I didn't have enough money for the train or bus fare to Pennsylvania, so a buddy of mine named George and I decided to hitchhike home.

George lived in Youngstown, Ohio. He was a big guy, about six foot one, and he was built like a weightlifter. He had big powerful arms; I looked like a little peanut next to him. He had blondish hair, pale skin, and always wore his garrison hat tilted to the right. It was nice to have him along as sort of a bodyguard.

George and I went to the B Company office and picked up our furlough papers. We both carried seabags slung over our shoulders. When we walked out to the highway, there were already many Marines waiting for a ride. Some had four men in their party. George and I walked past all the Marines to the other end of the line, about two-hundred feet away from them. We only waited twenty-five minutes until a civilian driving a 1937 Plymouth picked us up.

"Where are you heading, Marines?" asked the driver. We both answered him at the same time.

"Pennsylvania!"

"Ohio!"

He smiled and said, "Hop in, I'm going as far as Kinston."

Kinston was about forty miles from Camp Lejeune. When he let us off, there wasn't anyone else hitchhiking along the road. It wasn't too long before we got a ride to the next town of Wilson. There, a businessman and his secretary picked us up on their way to Washington, D.C. The man had a blue, pin-striped suit on, slick, wet-combed hair, and drove a 1941 black Studebaker with whitewall tires. He was very good looking, and his secretary had long, red hair—and boy, was she a knockout. She didn't have much to say, though.

The man asked us about President Roosevelt declaring war on Japan after the attack on Pearl Harbor, and if we thought we would be going overseas soon. We told him we didn't know. He laughed and said, "I guess you Marines have to keep tight-lipped, because you really don't know who you're talking to, right?" Neither of us answered, and he said, "That's okay, I'm on your side. I'm not a Communist." Then he laughed again.

The man did all the talking; we mostly just listened. We only answered some of his questions, like, "How do you like the Marine Corps?" and "What's your hometown?" and so forth.

Upon arriving in D.C., the man asked George and I if we'd like to join them for dinner. We accepted and went to a nice restaurant downtown with big round tables and high-back chairs, many Tiffany lamps hanging, and clean white tablecloths with a single rose in a vase on each table. "Order anything you want, Marines!" he said. "It's the least I could do for our fighting men."

I ordered a steak dinner with mashed potatoes, gravy, and red beets. We all had hot biscuits, butter, and coffee.

As we were eating our dinner, a cigarette girl with her tray came to our table. "Cigarettes, gum, candy, cigars?" she asked. The salesman bought four packs of Lucky Strikes and handed George and I two packs apiece. We didn't know how to thank him for his kindness and generosity, and he could see we felt uneasy, "Enjoy, Marines, and don't let your guard down. Mow down a couple of those little Jap bastards for me, okay?"

"Yes, sir!" we answered in unison.

Before parting company, we asked him where the best place in Washington would be to hitchhike a ride to Pittsburgh. He told us to go down this one street about two blocks, make a left, and hitchhike from there, because that street led to the highway towards Pittsburgh. We thanked him at least three times and started walking in that direction.

As George and I walked along, we both lit up a cigarette. About twenty steps later, this Army Captain was heading towards us, walking in the opposite direction. We didn't realize as we saluted him that our cigarettes were dangling from our lips. Two steps past us he turned and ordered us to halt. "Do you Marines always salute with a cigarette in your mouth?"

"No, sir," we answered. I began explaining to the officer, "Sir, we were caught off guard to salute you. It wasn't intentional."

He said, "Okay, then, I understand. Just don't let it happen again!"

At the same time, we both replied, "No, sir! It won't, Captain." Satisfied with our explanation, he let us continue on our way.

We were really lucky when we approached the left turn onto the next street. This civilian was traveling alone, and he stopped and asked us where we were headed to.

We both said, "Pittsburgh, sir."

He smiled. "Okay, hop in. That's where I live."

In about four or five hours, we arrived on Liberty Avenue in Pittsburgh. We thanked the man, and then George and I walked toward the bus stops.

"I'm going to walk over to the Greyhound bus depot," said George. "It shouldn't cost too much to get to Youngstown from here."

"Okay," I answered. "I'll see you back at Camp Lejeune."

I headed for the stop where the Ohio River Motor Coach would be waiting. Back then, it was only about forty-five cents to Aliquippa. When I boarded the bus, I noticed "Skip" Hanich was the driver. "Hi, Skip," I said. "How you doin'?"

"Okay," he replied, but he looked at me like, *who are you?*

I paid the forty-five cents and said, "Don't you remember me, Skip?"

"The face looks familiar, but I still can't place you."

"I'm your brother Chuck's friend, Jim Messina. I live in the alley behind Frankovich's house."

Suddenly he remembered. "Okay, now I know why I didn't recognize you. The last time I saw you, you were a lot younger."

I sat in the side seat behind him as we talked about West Aliquippa and the Marine Corps.

Arriving in Aliquippa, I couldn't help but wonder if I would ever see this town again. Would my number be up in the battles to come? I had a prickly feeling in the back of my head, thinking about getting shot by those Japanese weasels. Many things raced through my mind as I crossed the street to catch the Woodlawn and Southern Motor Coach to West Aliquippa. I had a blank stare when a voice rang out, breaking me out of my thoughts.

"Hey, Jim, nice to have you home!" It was Guido "Gigi" Sebastion.

Prints & Photographs Division, Library of Congress

J&L Steel plant, Aliquippa, Pennsylvania, January 1941. Photo by Arthur Rothstein

His brother Dom, who had enlisted in the Navy and was a yeoman, was one of my best friends back home.

Gigi was on the shorter side, a little fat, and had freckles on his reddish face. He had several brothers: Dom, Eddie, Bernard, Billy, and Paul. He also had three sisters: Pauline, Emma, and Eleanor. Their mother had died in 1931 from childbirth. Both she and the baby died, and they were laid side by side in one casket. In those days, a person wasn't laid out in a funeral home. They were either laid out in their home, or at the Sons of Italy (S.O.I.) hall. Because of this their father had all the responsibilities of a large family. Dom was the oldest who watched over them. Pauline was the oldest girl and did all the cooking.

"How long are you home?" Gigi asked.

"One week, then back to camp."

"Will you be goin' overseas?"

"I suppose so," I replied, then changed the subject because we weren't supposed to talk about any plans the military had, especially on our furlough.

Prints & Photographs Division, Library of Congress

Houses in West Aliquippa, Pennsylvania, January 1941. Photo by Jack Delano

Gigi and I sat together on the bus, and I asked him if he'd be going into the service. He told me no because he had a few things wrong that the Army wouldn't accept.

As I stepped off the bus across from Nick Mancini's grocery store, I swung the seabag over my shoulder and headed for the alley to my house. I could see the lone star hanging on the living room door. During WWII, each star hanging in a window represented the number of persons that family had serving in the military. I sort of felt proud seeing the star, knowing I was doing my part to bring this war to an end.

I don't know why I knocked on the door; I usually walked right in like the rest of my family. After I knocked, I heard someone fumbling with the lock. It took a little time, but Pop finally got it open. Well, I was very happy to have one arm around each of my parents. They both hung on tightly, so happy to see me home. Tears began to swell in my eyes.

Pop let go after a while, but Mom hung on. "Figlio mio (son of mine)," she said in Italian, "possa Dio vegliare su di te sempre e portarti a casa sano e salvo (may God watch over you always and bring you home safe)!"

I had a choking feeling, in my throat, as Mom said these words. I loved Mom and Pop very much, and I wanted them to be proud of me. That's why I made sure I walked a straight line during my military life.

After everyone settled down, the conversation was about the Marine Corps. I did tell Mom and Pop I'd most likely be shoving off somewhere, and I told them and the rest of my family not to repeat it to the neighbors or friends, or I would be in trouble. My parents had a right to know, although I was breaking a rule. I could see the tears on Mom and Pop's faces, because they figured I'd be going up against our enemy in some far-off land, sometime in the future. Mom tried to be brave, but I could see the fear on her face. I told them I am in God's hands, and He would protect me.

My furlough seemed to go by very fast. I hardly did anything except go to the skating rink to see my buddies and spend time with the rest of my family. Before I knew it, the time had come to head back to Camp Lejeune. This time, I took the train back to North Carolina, with help from Pop paying for my fare. Departing was difficult, with my parents hanging on saying, "Torna a casa sano e salvo (come home safe)." I really took it hard on my bus ride back. All the way to North Carolina, Mom and Pop were constantly on my mind, and their words were ringing in my ears. God, I thought, watch over me in battle. I asked this of Him many, many more times throughout the whole campaign.

12. A New Alliance

When I arrived back at Camp Lejeune, I still had Mom and Pop on my mind and couldn't seem to shake it. But when we got busy with exercises, the pain eased up. I got sucked up in the frenzy of preparations for the upcoming battles.

The first of January was approaching, and the rest of our company had gone home on furlough. I had one more month to go with all the salty rebels in F Company. Each day seemed to drag on, listening to them brag about their time in Cuba. I wanted to remind them they were once boots, but decided to keep quiet, knowing I'd be transferred to B Company in a month.

February couldn't have come sooner. I had my transfer papers signed by the F Company commander and said goodbye to this group of glory-hunter rebels. B Company was located on the other end of camp, maybe 2,000 yards from F Company's location. It was on a nice clean street and had small wooden barracks, each housing a whole platoon of men.

Camp Lejeune was named in honor of Lieutenant General John Archer Lejeune, former Commandant of the Marine Corps,[1] and was tagged "Tent City" because there were more tents than small barracks. I was really lucky to be transferred to B Company, 1st Battalion, of the 5th Regiment, with its newly built, small barracks. There were only two platoons in B Company, and new men were needed to fill the rest of the ranks.

As I entered B Company headquarters, I saw a red-headed company clerk sitting behind his desk. He eyed me from head to toe, then he asked, "Where are you coming from?"

I promptly responded, "F Company, 2d Battalion," as I handed him my papers.

"Well, Messina," he said, Glancing over my file, "we're glad to have you in B Company." He told me to call him "Red" and said they needed a lot more men to make up two more platoons.

Already I liked him. It seemed like a different atmosphere here. I said, "I'm glad to be here, Red. I didn't like F Company."

He smiled, "Well, I think you'll like it here in B Company." He filed my papers then told me to report to Captain William L. Hawkins, commander of B Company, 1st Battalion, 5th Marines.

Later, I found out Robert James Johnson was everyone's friend in our company. He took care of all the paperwork in B Company and was the sergeant's right arm. He was tall and lanky, had dark red hair, and many freckles on his face. Red was from Roselle, New Jersey.[2] He was a great kidder, always fooling around with the guys. You couldn't get him mad, no matter what you said to him. He had a million-dollar smile and kept his nose to the grindstone. Red had served with B Company since he had first arrived in Camp Lejeune.

B Company's commander was down the company street, in another building. I was ordered to report back to Red, afterwards. Then I'd be assigned to the wooden barracks. I walked into the CO's office, and the clerk at the desk announced me over the intercom. Upon entering the CO's office, I stood at attention but didn't salute. If you don't have your cap on, you don't have to salute; you can just stand at attention.

Capt. Hawkins was a short, stocky man, around five foot six, about two-hundred pounds and slightly balding. He had been a schoolteacher in Long Hill, Connecticut.[3] His black hair was combed back with a small part on the left side. He had a round face with a reddish complexion, and spoke softly, as though he was talking to one of his former students. His size and manners didn't seem to fit a Marine commander. He didn't look like a gung-ho Marine at all; he really had that schoolteacher look.

He was always concerned about the welfare of his men. Whenever Capt. Hawkins talked with one man alone, it was like a father-and-son conversation. He never seemed to get mad at any Marine. The only time he ever raised his voice was when he addressed his company on the drill field. Whenever he inspected the troops while standing in ranks, he always asked the usual questions: Where you from? Are you married? Have any sisters and brothers? Are your parents living? Why did you join the Marine Corps? Are you homesick? etc. Capt. Hawkins wanted to know the backgrounds of all the men who were under his command. Even though his voice lacked authority, the men of B Company had a lot of respect for him and enjoyed serving under him. He knew the rules and regulations about the Corps, was a very smart man in his knowledge of troop movements, and all the other officers paid him much respect.

When we were finished with the conversation on my background, the captain told me to report back to Red Johnson.

I returned and Red directed me to one of the small wooden barracks on our company's street at the far end. As we walked in, most of the men were sitting on their steel bunks, and a few were lying down. All eyes were on me as Red showed me to one of the bunks with only a rolled-up mattress on it. Red told me to see him later, and he would give me a chit to draw sheets and blankets from the quartermaster.

I put my seabag down between the bunks and leaned it up against the wall. Then I sat on the bare springs of my bunk and lit up a Lucky Strike. The guy sitting on the next bunk was named Cosimo Angelo Negri from East Orange, New Jersey.[4] Cosimo was a powerful, dark-skinned "dago" with a hooked nose. He was a very strong and wiry type of man, and slightly bow-legged, too. The fellow on my left side was from Little Falls, New York; his name was Andrew John Yanno.[5] He was a six-foot-tall Marine who spoke Italian and shuffled when he walked. Yanno had curly brown hair and was always bragging about his hometown.

Everyone was called by their last names in the Marine Corps. If anyone had the same last name, you'd say their initials to distinguish them from one another. Negri and I introduced ourselves, and I did the same with Yanno. Most of the men had arrived here about eight days ago from Parris Island. In ten minutes, we were talking like we all grew up together. All three of us were Italian, and we felt a strong bond with each other.

The next guy I met was a Messina—Salvatore. He hailed from Brooklyn, New York,[6] and had a thick accent. The Italians seemed to outnumber other nationalities throughout the entire military forces. Salvatore Anthony Messina was a huge man with thick, kinky black hair, thick eyebrows, and a large round head. He was the spitting image of Maxey Baer, the prizefighter from back in the 1930s. Salvatore told me New York was loaded with Messina's. I already knew that because my Pop told me the same thing. Salvatore grew up in a tough neighborhood, and he showed it. He'd talk to us roughly and was always ready for a fight. You had to watch what you said to him most of the time. He sure made a typical gung-ho Marine. Eventually, he would call me his little brother.

Then I met Davie Warren Shuford, a rebel from Bishopville, South Carolina.[7] He never brought up the Civil War like the other rebels in our company. Shuford was smaller than I was but was a well-built, sturdy little fellow with a lot of strength. He had wavy, dark blond hair and a small, pointy chin with big, round, dark blue eyes. Most of the rebels would say the reason they had joined the Marine Corps was to make a career out of it, so they wouldn't have to wind up working in the cotton fields. I liked Shuford right off the bat, but I couldn't say the same for some of the other rebels in our platoon.

The next introduction was George Felton Jones from Macon, Georgia.[8] We called him Jonsey. He was about three inches taller than me and spoke with a southern drawl. This guy was skinny, had curly black hair, and a very pimply complexion. It sure seemed like he lacked something in his diet. One thing I liked about Jonsey is he never got mad and was always smiling, showing his big front teeth. You couldn't help but like him. He always wanted to help someone if they were having problems.

Next was Gerrit Edward Heidema from up around Grand Rapids, Michigan.[9] "Hennigan" is the nickname we gave him. He was medium height, had kinky dark hair, and a large head for his body. He was slow in everything he did, even eating chow. He reminded me a lot of Stepin Fetchit in the movies, a slow-moving black man. An independent guy, Hennigan liked being in his own little corner. He didn't have any close buddies, and never asked anyone for favors. He was sloppy with his dress uniform, didn't take orders very well, and was always defiant. He'd always crack jokes and bad-mouthed everyone, even if something serious happened to someone.

I also met Robert Julius Johnson. He was about my size and had curly, dark red hair. He came from Lake Orion, Michigan,[10] and he made friends easily like I did. He'd also worked in a steel mill and had it rough during the Great Depression. Johnson outweighed me by twenty pounds but didn't look it. We had this Robert Johnson, and our company clerk, Robert "Red" Johnson in our barracks, and both of these guys had red hair. Talk about a coincidence.

Another fellow by the name of Robert Joseph Hilsky, was from the Woodside section of Queens in the Big Apple. He would be awarded the Navy Cross for valor in combat later on.[11] Hilsky was heavy-set and very strong. He reminded me of my brother-in-law Charlie Trone. He had

National Archives at St. Louis

Top, left to right: PFC Gerrit Edward Heidema, "Hennigan," PFC Robert Joseph Hilsky, PFC Robert James Johnson "Red;" Middle, left to right: PFC Robert Julius Johnson, PFC George Felton Jones "Jonsey," PFC Salvatore Anthony Messina; Bottom left to right: PVT Austin Windell Pollock, Jr., PFC Davie Warren Shuford, PFC Andrew John Yanno jet-black, wavy hair, broad shoulders, and always acted like a lamb. But don't get Robert mad!

There were a couple of other men who, at first, were very quiet and kept to themselves. Austin Windell Pollock, Jr., from Louisville, Kentucky,[12] was tall and lanky with heavy scruff on his face, even though he shaved every day. His complexion was pimply, and he walked forward with a lean, like he was going to fall on his face. Pollock would turn out to be one of our bravest Marines. Lawrence Ray Cokley grew up in the farm country of Waynesburg, Indiana.[13] He had an oblong, freckled-face, ruddy complexion, and wavy black hair. He always confided in me about his personal matters. Larry would become one of my close buddies.

After all the introductions were made, I was satisfied this would be my permanent company with no more transfers. I had at least ten good buddies I would be sharing my Marine life with. We'd be going out on liberty together, living together, fighting together, and would become very close, just like we were all brothers.

Then there was our platoon sergeant, Eugene Breeding—a gung-ho rebel Marine from Dwarf, Kentucky,[14] who hated all the "Yankees" in his company. Us Yankees always got hollered at and had the shittiest details handed out to us. He was a man alone and had no friends. He didn't associate with anyone and was always in a bad mood.

Sgt. Breeding was tall, weighed about 190 pounds, and had an average build. There were funny marks on his face and his hair was scraggly. He had a Southern drawl, chewed tobacco, and smoked cigarettes. He would constantly be on guard for one of us Yankees to make a mistake, so he could shove extra duty or shit details on us. Sgt. Breeding was a career man making the Marine Corps his life, so he wouldn't have to work in the tobacco or cotton fields. He had one hash mark, but he acted like he was a high-ranking officer. He was our platoon sergeant, and he made it known he wasn't taking any crap from anyone.

The Marine Corps has many stories to tell. All its traditions go back to 1775. In *The Old Breed*, George McMillan states:

Left: Sergeant Eugene
Breeding

Right: Corporal Albert
Steve Podracky

National Archives at St. Louis   National Archives at St. Louis

When the first Marine in history was recruited at Tun Tavern in 1775, he was ordered to report aboard a ship then lying in the Philadelphia yard. "What the hell is a Marine?" barked the bewildered officer-of-the-deck, "You go aft there and sit down until I find out!" A few minutes later, the second Marine reported aboard, and the still confused OD told him to go aft and stand by the first. How did the first man greet the second? "Listen boy," he snarled, "You shoulda been in the old Corps!"[5]

This was the folklore handed down by some of the Marines. The longer you're in the Marine Corps, the more you'll brag to the new boots.

I swear Sgt. Breeding thought the same way as this story from *The Old Breed*. As the days went by, I learned he was worse than the DI on Parris Island. Among the men the talk always was if we were ever in battle and he was leading us, he would be the prime target. Ultimately, this wasn't to be, because Sgt. Breeding was the one who led us to safety and saved a lot of lives.

Another officer in B Company was Second Lieutenant George H. Guyer, Jr., a ninety-day wonder out of officers' training school, who didn't know very much about combat. He learned later, in battle, who the real leaders were from our seasoned sergeants. Secretly, 2nd Lt. Guyer would rather have been an enlisted man. He came from a well-to-do family that wanted him to follow in the footsteps of his father. His dad, an officer in the old Marine Corps for twelve years, was also a good businessman and a great success with many assets.

The lieutenant hung around us as often as he could because, to him, someone who needed to learn the ways of the military, the enlisted men were of great value. A first lieutenant is two steps above a warrant officer, and most men in the military didn't think much of first lieutenants, but us guys thought different. We liked him for what he was, a good Joe. When we were alone with him, he would say, "Knock off the 'sir' shit. Just talk or cuss like you do among yourselves." He was smiling when he said this, so we obliged. Our two best officers in B Company were 2nd Lt. Guyer and Capt. Hawkins.

The winters in North Carolina were bitter cold, and we suffered many a day trying to keep warm. Those kerosene burners always left a sooty residue inside the tents or small barracks. What made it worse, we used newspapers and magazines to patch up a lot of the air holes that allowed the smoke to seep out but let the biting cold still seep in.

New River was a mile or two from our base—far from the mainline railroads. Bus service into the Jacksonville area was scant; it barely served the townspeople and the servicemen always had to hitchhike. In those days hitchhiking was common, especially for young military recruits. You wouldn't have to wait very long before someone would offer you a ride.

The PX on the base sold beer, but there was no place to sit. It was a very small building, and you had to stand to drink your beer. Canned beer was very popular in the South and was your only choice.

There wasn't any entertainment like the USO shows. It seemed like the show-business people avoided Camp Lejeune. The Marines made their own entertainment because a lot of the fellows had talent and would display it in this huge circus tent we called the "Big Top," where they also showed movies regularly. But there was this constant, strong wind always blowing the big tent down.

Among the men was the usual gum-beating and many complaints about the conditions at New River. The circus tent was from an old carnival, and at least 1,500 men could be seated under it. We constantly had to patch the tent, and the sagging ropes were old and barely able to support it, as the wind played havoc. We tried to rig it up umpteen times, but the wind would constantly blow it down. There were always at least four Marines to stand guard over the tent to make sure it didn't collapse.

13. TWENTY-MILE HIKE

When I first entered the barracks, I didn't know the guys had just come off of a ten-mile hike. Negri assured me there were many more hikes to come with heavy marching packs.

As we sat around asking each other questions, in walked Sgt. Breeding. "Okay, you knuckleheads," he began, "today was a ten-mile hike, but tomorrow morning after chow, we'll be doing twenty with full marching order. You will hike fifty minutes and rest ten! We will be going out to the M1 (rifle) area on maneuvers using live ammunition. Any knucklehead who doesn't keep his head down will certainly have it blown off, understand?"

"Yeah, Breeding," we responded. It was good not having to say "sir" anymore to a non-commissioned officer; we always used "sarge" or "Breeding" when speaking to him.

The next morning after chow, we were all busy in the barracks loading our packs. Our equipment, including a rifle, weighed about eighty pounds, and we had to lug it for twenty miles. The hike was ten miles out and ten miles back. Our hiking shoes were made of a hard tan suede and looked like work shoes. We all acquired some lard from the mess hall and rubbed down the suede to soften it, making it more comfortable to walk with, but we still got a lot of blisters on our feet during the hike.

We followed an old railroad track out to the M1 area, and it took all morning to get to our destination. The government owned a lot of the swamp surrounding the New River area; most of it was the boondocks. Marching along I felt a nudge on my back. I turned around and saw my buddy Al with a big smile on his face. He was also transferred to B Company but assigned to another barracks. We were reunited and I couldn't have been happier! We had to keep marching because no talking was aloud. Al and I would catch up about our situations later on.

This first hike played havoc with my feet, and I knew after I arrived back at the base, I'd have a lot of blisters. The lieutenant colonel took the lead, with long strides, never seeming to tire out. He was a rebel from South Carolina and looked like a bronze statue with a dark complexion and a waxed mustache he was very proud of. Every now and then he would look back at us and holler out, "Come on girls, let's go! You're lagging behind! When I get through with you, you'll have blisters on your blisters!" He was smiling when his eyes faced forward again, enjoying the lead. The lieutenant colonel had been in the Corps at least fifteen years now and had served in different corners of the world. He was an "old salt" by Marine Corps standards. All through our stay at New River and during the war, we didn't care for him.

I never camped out in the woods as a boy, so this would be my first experience at the M1 training area. There was much commotion as we prepared for the mock attack with the hidden enemy. We would simulate with live ammo, which made all of us very nervous. Sides were picked by colors, and I was picked for the blue outfit, which would be fighting the green outfit. Wasn't I lucky? I had to get with the son of a bitch Sgt. Breeding—the rebel!

"Okay, Yankee girls," came Breeding's loud, crude voice, "fall in!" We wore blue arm bands, and our first objective was to cross this grassy field in the direction of the green outfit. At the other end of the field, rusting away, stood an old Model T Ford to simulate an Army tank. Our 105 howitzers opened fire, getting a direct hit on the old T. As we crossed the field, we opened up with our Springfield rifles and, as the tracer bullets left our rifles, there were many red streaks in the air like a display on the Fourth of July.

All of a sudden, machine gunfire opened up from behind us, and the bullets were flying over our heads. Every Marine hit the deck for safety from the bullets. We began crawling on our bellies as we advanced forward toward the enemy. Suddenly a brush fire broke out at the other end of the field. The officers ordered a ceasefire long enough to douse it. Once it was out, the maneuvers continued. It was a day well spent, learning to take cover when the bullets were flying and learning the discipline of battle.

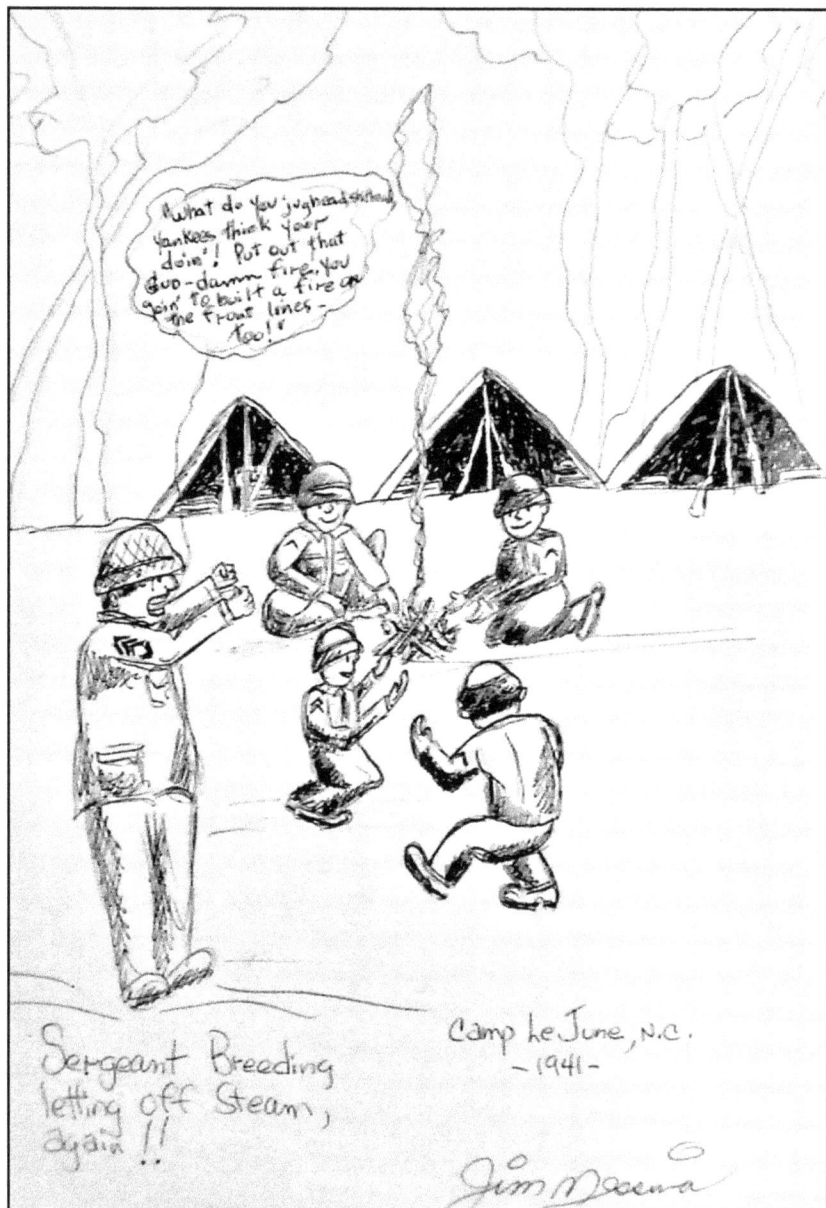

Around 1630 hours everything came to a halt. The field kitchen had been set up behind us, and we were ready to chow down. As we walked towards the area, we began digging out our mess kits. We moved closer to the field kitchen and the strong aroma of hot chow filled our nostrils. Boy, were we hungry! We had two slices of white bread, hot coffee, and beef stew. The coffee hit the spot because it was a very cold day in February.

It got dark early, and we were cold and shivering. Three of my buddies and I gathered some pieces of wood to make a nice warm little fire. We made the fire in front of our pup tents sitting cross legged and comfortable as we all lit up our cigarettes. We were so busy bullshitting we didn't notice Sgt. Breeding until he began kicking our little fire all over the place with sparks flying in our faces.

He steamed, "What the fugg do you jughead Yankees think you're doing? Put out that gud-damn fire! There will be no fires now or ever! You hear me, you fuggin' Yankees? Are you gonna build one every time your little Yankee asses get cold?" He looked at our squad leader, Corporal Albert Steve Podracky, and said, "Hey Pod, don't you know the rules? You're supposed to be a non-commissioned officer. Why didn't you stop them?" Podracky put his head down and didn't answer. Breeding walked away with the satisfaction of kicking hot embers on us.

Cpl. Podracky was a quiet man from Cleveland, Ohio.[16] He never seemed to get excited over serious matters. I remember once, even in real battle, when we were pinned down by enemy machine gunfire, he remained calm. God liked the corporal and protected him. When Breeding walked away, Podracky cracked a grin and said, "He was upset, wasn't he?" We all were snickering under our breath.

That night, as two men shared each pup tent, we had to cup every puff of our cigarettes so the glare wouldn't stand out in the pitch black of the night—another lesson we learned in battle. Boy, was it cold—around fifteen degrees!

This Marine I shared the pup tent with was a tall guy, and his feet stuck out of the tent. Each Marine carries two green wool blankets, so we had four all together. We put our ponchos on the ground first to keep from getting wet; one wool blanket to lay on and used the other three to cover us. Even with three blankets we shivered all through the bitterly cold night.

The next morning, the bugle blew at 0500 hours. We were up in a flash and hungry as bears. I was always hungry and never seemed to have enough food in my stomach. I could eat a big meal now and be starving an hour later. Breakfast this morning was a traditional meal of the armed forces: "Shit on a Shingle" and hot coffee. When you're hungry, anything can taste good in your mind. After breakfast, we got organized for the long ten miles back to Camp Lejeune. We followed the old railroad tracks back with two columns of men on each side of the track.

The trek back was very tiring with the heavy marching order on our backs and rifle strung over our shoulders. My feet were sore with blisters from the last hike. That rebel colonel of ours never seemed to get tired, and he was at least fifty years old. We all swore him up and down for walking at such a fast pace. The Marine Corps makes sure you are conditioned for battle and can take anything they dish out—to make a man out of you. There is no room in the Corps for pantywaists. Either they make you or they break you. It's up to the individual if he wants to become part of the fighting machine. So be it!

I came out of the Corps with a clean record because I did everything that was asked of me: I worked hard, followed orders, never was insubordinate, respected my officers, and never received a court martial of any kind. I really loved the Marine Corps and planned on staying in for thirty years.

The sound of the colonel's voice broke my train of thought as I heard him bellow his command: "Halt, ten-minute break!"

As Al and I sat down to rest, I lit up a cigarette. Al didn't smoke. "Boy," I said to him, "it sure feels good to get off my feet, and this cigarette sure tastes good!" We weren't allowed to smoke in ranks or while on the march.

I lay back, looking up at the clear blue sky, and thought about home. How's Mom and Pop feel about my being in the military? How worried were they about me? I wonder what Dom is doing. How was it at the roller rink in Monaca?

Pop sometimes talked about his younger days being a cook in the Italian Army, stationed in Venice, Italy. That's where he learned to make his tasty homemade bread and other specialties. On Halloween, he'd tell us spooky stories about the werewolves in Sicily. He said, in the old country, when a child was conceived during a new moon, it was believed they would grow up to be a werewolf. I remember a big oval picture of him hanging in the living room. He looked very handsome with his black, curled-up mustache.

My father was very strong and a hard worker. He had that get-up-and-go air about him. It seemed like he never wanted to take it easy wasting time sitting around doing nothing. I loved my father and what he stood for. He was a true Sicilian man who was devoted to his family. We were never without food on our table, whether it was macaroni and beans or bread and coffee.

"Okay, up off your asses, girls—time to march again!" These piercing words filled the air as the colonel commanded once again. My feet were hurting from the blisters, but I never complained to anyone. It was rough walking over the gravel along the old railroad tracks. There were many hikes to the M1 area, and with each hike my feet got worse with the blisters.

About a quarter mile ahead of us we could see Camp Lejeune. It was a welcome sight because we knew we would be able to sack-down before chow. It was very cold when we entered our barracks. One of the guys quickly lit the kerosene burners as we gathered around close holding our hands above the burner. The fatigue had taken over my body, so I stretched out on my bunk, covering myself with my two green wool blankets. It felt like I was in paradise. Now all nice and warm, I quickly dozed off.

Only forty-five minutes went by, and I suddenly awoke to the sound of the bugle blowing chow call. I jumped up, tired as I was, and headed for the mess hall. We were all starving, but there was only a little shoving and pushing in the chow line.

We had pork chops, biscuits, apple sauce, and red beets for chow, and then I had a peanut butter and jelly sandwich with my coffee. Even though it wasn't good, the hot coffee warmed my whole body. Most of our food was very bland. We always had to season it ourselves with whatever was on the table: ketchup, salt, pepper, mayonnaise, or Worcestershire dressing.

Our everyday routine of close-order drill, working parties, and twenty-mile hikes shaped us into elite fighting men. We were proud to claim our title and be a part of this tradition—The United States Marine Corps.

The month of February dragged on. It was a long, cold winter with howling winds and freezing temperatures. The winds kept knocking down the big circus tent. We barely were able to enjoy the movies they showed. Working details were rough in the bitter cold, and it was a challenge to keep warm. When the day was over, we welcomed our kerosene burners. North Carolina was almost as cold as Pennsylvania during the winter months. Winter reminded me of West Aliquippa. At that moment I pictured myself at home, sitting at the kitchen table, eating Pop's freshly baked bread with Mom's spaghetti and meatballs.

U.S. Naval History and Heritage Command Photograph

Soldiers and sailors crowd the decks of USS Wakefield, *c.1942-45.*

If there is a difference between Army and Marine Corps training, it is the degree of discipline imposed on its recruits by the Marine Corps. This, while an Army man may remember the size, the grand scale of his maneuvers, the length of his hike, the duration of his bivouac, the Marine is much more likely to recall the speed, the immediate obedience called for, during what might seem to be an otherwise no more demanding physical program. To the Marine, it's not what he does, as is the way he has to do it.[1]

14. LONE WOLF

Right after the attack on Pearl Harbor thousands of men flocked to the recruiting stations volunteering their service, and it sure helped our division. By the time we were ready to leave Camp Lejeune, our division strength quickly doubled in size as the Corps enlisted many courageous young men eager to defend their country. To our impaired Navy, the well-trained

Marine was to be a powerful fighting force. The 1st Marine Division went down in history as one of the first to strike back at the Japanese after Pearl Harbor. Our men sure were proud of this historic moment.

There had been a secret plan made to head overseas called Operation LONE WOLF, and we would soon be heading for Wellington, New Zealand, to train for combat.[2] But this destination wouldn't be revealed to us until our voyage was almost over. I didn't know where we were going but, I thought, I'm going to see a little of our world!

An advance party of two officers were assigned to pick our campsite. The encampment they selected—Camp McKay—was quickly erected by the New Zealanders to accommodate the American forces. The camp was located on the North Island near Paekākāriki , a town in the Kapiti Coast District about twenty-five miles north of Wellington. Situated between the coastline and Tararua Mountains, it had many rocks, gorges, and ravines.

One day we had to learn a little about ship's functions from the officer in charge (OIC). "Troop ships can carry thousands of men," he began. "On the port and starboard sides, you'll see landing boats secured to the ship. There are two types of landing boats. One is the Landing Craft Personnel, or LCP(L), and the other is the Higgins boat (LCVP). The LCP(L) requires the landing troops to jump off from her starboard and port sides and into the water when it lands on the beach. It's much easier to debark from the Higgins boat. Upon reaching the beach, the front ramp is lowered, and the men can rush right out with no difficulty. Is everyone following me?"

We answered with a resounding, "YES, SIR!"

He continued. "Once aboard a ship, there will be no smoking on deck; this refers only to nighttime. The glare of a cigarette can be seen for miles by enemy subs. You will only be allowed to smoke when you hear over the loudspeaker the words, 'the smoking lamp is lit.' On every deck each exit will be covered by a large black curtain so that no light will be seen out on the deck and give away our position.

"You'll be working with the sailors who run the ship, and you will pitch right in with them on working details. You will keep a tight ship. You are guests of the Navy, and their ship is their home. You will not pick fights with the sailors. Traditionally, the Navy and Marines don't like each other. If there are any fights that need broken up, it will lead to a deck court-martial. I don't care if the Marine is right or wrong. Same goes for smoking when the smoking lamp is out. I hope you remember all of these orders."

Then came a surprise when he said, "You'll be allowed to gamble on your way overseas. By the looks on your faces, you must be thinking, this officer has his wires crossed. I know the rules of the military are no gambling at any time, but we're making an exception. The only reason we're lifting this restriction is because you'll be heading into war, and some of you won't make it back, sad to say.

"There is a condition in regard to gambling aboard ship: you will not block any passageways. If you gamble near the passageways, it will have to be in the recesses of the doors. Also, there will be no gambling in the mess hall. There are plans for the 1st Marine Division to be moving out soon. The target date will be sometime in May. This is the end of my talk."

And with that we headed back towards our company barracks. My thoughts about going overseas were a little disturbing. Will I make it back alive? Where exactly are we headed? Will we have an escort overseas? Most of our Navy was knocked out at Pearl Harbor—how many aircraft carriers are left? Are we equipped with enough weapons, bombs, and shells? It would be a long, hard battle, as we would come to learn.

15. Maneuvers on the Chesapeake Bay

One morning after chow we were ordered out near the drill field. Capt. Hawkins told us we'd have a group picture of our whole company taken to send home to our families. I liked his idea, and so did the rest of the men. The group picture cost each of us a dollar seventy-five. My parents were very pleased with the photo; they framed it for me and hung it in our living room. It completed the setting for their one Blue Star service banner in the window of our front door. This made me feel proud to be serving our country as a Marine.

At Camp Lejeune, we had a nice-size PX, and articles were very reasonable—cigarettes and candy were a must with all Marines. Only one

Official U

Company B, First Battalion, F
New River, N
PFC James J. Messina, (sec

percent of Marines didn't smoke, but I don't think there was any Marine who didn't like pogey bait. Large bars of pogey bait were five cents, and cigarettes sold for a dime a pack. In those days, the only king-size cigarettes were Pall Malls and Wings; there were no such things as filters.

In February 1941, the 1st Marine Division had just been activated aboard USS *Texas* (BB 35) in Cuba.[3] On December 7, 1941, our division was small—518 officers and 6,871 enlisted men.[4] Ultimately, our division would reach a strength of almost 20,000 Marines. It consisted of four regiments: the 1st, 5th, 7th infantry regiments, and 11th artillery regiment.[5] The division's units were loosely dispersed throughout the Pacific. The 1st Division's 7th Marines were deployed to Samoa and thought they would be the first ones to see action after Pearl Harbor. They left the United States on April 10.[6] The month before, our regiment, the 5th, would be conducting fleet landing exercises at Solomons Island, Maryland.[7]

Towards the end of March, we departed Camp Lejeune for Norfolk, Virginia. On arrival, we boarded USS *Harry Lee* (APA 10), a small troop ship docked on the southern edge of the Chesapeake Bay. As we began to board, I noticed the ships rusting hull and the way she was listing to one side. I found out the ship had a leak on the starboard side. This had to be one of the worst small troop ships the Navy owned. After everyone was onboard,

;raph
nes, 1st Marine Division, F.M.F.
1942
from the top, sixth from the left)

Sgt. Breeding asked for KP volunteers. My hand went up first. I didn't mind working hard, but my main reason for volunteering was you got extra chow.

We settled down in the hold of the ship with its many bunks piled six high. I heard Breeding call my name. He ordered me to report to the bakery for KP duty. As I walked along the passageway on B deck, I could smell the fresh bread the Navy cooks were baking. There were Dutch doors into the bakery and the bread-slicing room. The top halves were open, and the bottoms were closed. I approached one of the Navy cooks and told him my name. He checked the KP list, "OK, Messina, follow me, and I'll assign you to your job." We walked from the bakery across into the bread-slicing room. "Now," the sailor began, "I'll show you how to operate the hand bread slicer. There's nothing to it. You place the bread on the board and pull down the handle of evenly lined wires—thus cutting clean slices of bread."

The cook was heavyset, sweating, and he had strong body odor. I held my breath when standing close to him but didn't say anything. This guy had a kind voice and talked slowly with a New York accent. When he left, I was on my own, and the fresh bread was being brought in to me. As I sliced the loaves, I placed them on sheets and lined them up on the shelves. It was an easy job, and I liked it. The fresh bread was making me hungry, so I slipped out a slice from the middle of a loaf and ate it. This bread was delicious! I did this a second and third time from the other loaves. When my hunger was satisfied, I finished my work and then looked at all the beautiful bread lined up on the shelves. The Navy served better chow aboard ship than the Marines did on our base.

We ate chow at 1700 hours, and afterwards someone said the men would be getting ready for landing exercises that night, going ashore for maneuvers. I was told to take the uneaten bread left over from chow back to the slicing room and place it on a different rack because the cooks would use it for bread pudding. As I was busy in the slicing room, the men began filing by along the passageway past my slicing room, all in full pack marching order with two blankets. I'd look up once in a while and thought nothing of it, until a voice rang out, "You bastard! You know when to volunteer for KP, don't you?" I was startled, and I looked up to see Negri was saying this.

I replied, "Bullshit, Negri! You had your chance to volunteer, didn't you?"

"I hate KP!"

"Well, don't be jealous of me then! Okay?" He just mumbled under his breath and continued down the passageway.

Negri was my best buddy—well, one of my best. We were like brothers, and he would stick up for me whenever I had a problem with anybody or anything. Aside from Negri, I had three more close buddies—Al, Larry Cokley, and S. A. Messina. Negri was much stronger than me and came from a tough neighborhood where there were many other Italians. He was proud of his first cousin Frankie from New Jersey, but I didn't know they were cousins until later—after Frank Sinatra became popular. That's when Negri told me!

I closed the Dutch doors of the slicing room and took a break to go up on the top deck to see the men off. When I walked out onto the open deck, there was an icy blast of winter wind sending chills through my bones. I thought to myself, Boy, am I glad I volunteered for KP. As the men started going over the side and down the cargo net, I noticed my buddy Negri glaring back at me. I knew he was swearing because I could

U.S. Naval History and Heritage Command Photograph

*USS Harry Lee (APA 10) off the coast of Puerto Rico during
fleet landing exercises, Feb. 3, 1941.*

read his lips. I didn't stay long on top deck because I wasn't wearing my Marine overcoat. It would be a cold, rough landing on the beach that night. I could tell because the strong winds were stirring up waves. I finished my work and went back to the hold, then lay down on my bunk.

The only other men in the hold were the five other guys who volunteered for KP. The troops were gone all night and the next day until nightfall. Mostly all of the sailors were still aboard the ship, and I brought trays of fresh bread to the mess hall for evening chow. Afterwards, I returned to the slicing room to finish my work. Just about then I heard muffled voices in the passageway. The Marines were returning from maneuvers.

Suddenly, a head popped in through the top part of the Dutch doors demanding a warm loaf of fresh bread. Would you believe it was my buddy Negri? I almost bust out laughing but kept a serious face. There were tiny icicles hanging from Negri's runny nose, and he was ready to kill if I didn't slip him a loaf of bread. I still kept a serious posture as I handed the bread to the wolf-in-waiting. He snatched it from my hand, quickly slipping it under his combat jacket. He just grunted with an icy satisfaction as though I had tossed a bone to a dog. Well, it wasn't the end of this episode, because I had to hand out a few more loaves of bread to some other hungry wolves, then rearrange the shelves to make it look like it wasn't too empty.

16. THE ART OF COMBAT

A week later we headed back to Norfolk and boarded our trucks to Camp Lejeune. About two days later, we were getting briefed about troop movements in battle. We sat on the ground at the edge of the woods listening to the lieutenant speak about the subject, but most of us really didn't pay attention. We whispered about different things and worried about going into battle.

Reveille blew at 0500. I was up and out of my bunk and went to the head to wash up and brush my teeth. After breakfast Sgt. Breeding ordered us out to the obstacle course for training in bayonet fighting and to learn how to lob grenades at the enemy. "All right, you Yankees, you will learn the art of close combat with the enemy! I'll show you, one time, how to use a bayonet if the occasion arises. Clear?"

"CLEAR!" was our loud response!

"Now, fix bayonets!" he ordered. "Remember now, the Japanese have a hook on their bayonets. In close combat, when they get a hook on your rifle, they yank it loose in a split second, and you're a dead Marine! When they get a hook on you, you're going to have to beat them to the punch and yank first. Clear?"

"CLEAR!"

"Now, you'll have to parry to left or right in close combat, whichever position suits you. Those Japs are tricky! The Chinese already know this. The Japs and Chinese have been goin' at it for the past two-hundred years, and the Chinese could tell you a lot about the fuggin' little bastards."

We learned about the art of bayonet fighting pretty well. Afterward came the lobbing of grenades through windows at different heights. The windows were rigged with two-by-fours, and there were three of them. "When you pull the pin," Breeding began, "you say to yourself, one one-thousand, two one-thousand, three one thousand...then throw the grenade. Whatever you do, do not—I repeat—do not throw it like a baseball! Keep your arm at your side and arc it in a wide swing over your head so it has time to reach its target before exploding! The grenade takes a full seven seconds before it shatters. Clear?"

Again, we responded with a resounding, "CLEAR!"

I did okay with the lobbing through the make-believe windows. Next came the remainder of the obstacle course. We had to clamber over a high wooden wall and then crawl under barbed wire, with live ammunition flying above our heads. After that we had to high jump over a stream of deep water, and we were forced to crawl along in deep mud. It was a long, endless course, and we were all dog-tired, but the best was yet to come.

Sgt. Breeding chose sides: 1st Platoon against the 2d Platoon in rough-and-tumble wrestling. Breeding lined us up on opposite sides of the field, and then he picked out a guy twenty-five pounds heavier than me to wrestle. Like I said, Breeding really didn't like us Yankees, especially the Italians. Salvatore Messina and a couple of other Italians got the same treatment from this platoon sergeant. When the big guy came at me, he got the first hold and put me down. But while I was down, I locked my arm around his neck in a vice-like grip. I didn't know where my strength was coming from. I guess it was all the good military living I'd been doing. In those days, at the age of twenty, I was very agile and moved fast like a monkey in the trees. Each time he tried to get up, I squeezed tighter, and by now I had his face in the dirt. I held on until Breeding's police whistle made the exercise come to a halt.

When I let him up, he came at me with every swear word in the book, saying, "There ain't no little dago gonna put me down!"

At this point Breeding stepped in and grabbed him. "Gud-damn-it! I said the exercise is over! Clear?" No answer from the Marine. Breeding barked again, "Clear?"

The Marine just nodded, then spoke up. "Messina," he said, "your ass is mine!" He was fuming and wasn't going to let any little shit-ass Marine like me shame him in front of the other guys.

Breeding spoke up again. "If I hear you and Messina get into it again, there will be a deck court-martial waiting for you, and you will lose your one stripe, boot! Am I clear, you jug-headed Marine?"

He finally said, "Clear," and walked back to his platoon. I didn't have any problems with him later, but I didn't let my guard down.

17. STEVIE

The next day at mail call I received my first letter from Stevie, and about five photos of her. Stevie was a pretty, nice looking, black-haired Croatian girl from Pittsburgh. She was the niece of my buddy John Loncar (Tarzan) back home.

One Sunday afternoon, before I enlisted in the service, I walked over to Tarzan's house to see his brother Tony. Whenever I bought a new record, I'd want Tony to hear it. We used to play 78 rpm records of big band music on his back porch. In those days, the stores let you play the record before you bought it. Record in hand, I approached his front porch and saw a pretty looking girl sitting there. I didn't know who she was, and I thought maybe Tarzan met her at the Monaca Roller Rink, not knowing he was her uncle.

I stepped up onto the porch, and she asked me if I was a friend of the Loncar family. She had a pretty face with milky skin. Her long black hair fell down over her shoulders. Stevie was also well built, wearing shorts that showed off her shapely legs. She caught me staring at her, and with a little grin, she said, "You looking for my Uncle John?"

"I'm looking for Tony," I answered.

"Just a minute, I'll go in and tell him you're here." She had a nice walk and swung her hips gracefully, and she knew I was taking it all in. Most women can sense this about a man.

Tony walked out about two minutes later. "What do you have there, Jinks, a new record?"

"Yeah," I answered. "Jimmy Dorsey's 'Green Eyes'."

"Let's go on the back porch, and I'll bring out the portable record player. Oh, and Jinks, this is my niece Stevie from Pittsburgh."

"Uncle Tony, did you say Jinks?"

"Yeah, Stevie. We call him Jinks the Storyteller."

"What's his real name?" she asked.

Tony laughed and said, "Okay, he's Jim Messina, and he lives over on the next street."

I guess girls don't go for nicknames. She put out her hand, "I'm glad to meet you, Jim. I like Jim better than Jinks."

Her hand was very warm and soft, and there was a gleam in her eyes. I could feel a sexual urge go through my body as I held the handshake. I was only eighteen years old then, and I never had a steady girl. "Stevie," I said, "would you like to hear Jimmy Dorsey on the back porch?"

"Sure," she replied. "Why not? I love his band." Then she followed Tony down the sidewalk to the rear of the house. I trailed along last and examined her body and swinging hips. Just like she had eyes in the back of her head, she turned and smiled at me again. I was getting the feeling she wanted a romance to start between us. We listened to records for about an hour, then Tony's mother sent him on an errand.

Stevie and I wound up on the front porch talking about her life and mine. She liked hearing about my stay in New Mexico when I was in the CCC camps a year before. She asked me if I had a good job in the mill. I told her I was a wire drawer, but I didn't make too much money. I averaged about six dollars a day while the other operators averaged nine and ten dollars for eight hours' work. She didn't comment, but she put her eyes down. I thought she thought I didn't make enough money.

But then she moved a little closer to me on the front porch swing, and I began feeling uneasy. We had only known each other for a matter of two hours. She questioned me about other girls in my life. When I told her I wasn't going steady, Stevie flashed a big smile, and I knew she was up to something.

"Would you send me a few postal cards when I'm back home in Pittsburgh?" she asked.

"Yeah," I replied. "I guess I can do that." But I never did because I realized she wanted to go steady.

Up until I joined the Marine Corps, I completely forgot about Stevie; my mind was set on leaving the wire mill and enlisting. I didn't enlist until the following year when I was nineteen years old. Well, when I read Stevie's letter, I still wasn't interested in going steady.

"Boy, did I have a heck of a time tracking you down," she wrote. "You know, first I called the Old Post Office Building and asked the recruiter about you. He told me you had left for Parris Island. Then I wrote them a letter. They told me you went to Camp Lejeune for advanced training. I contacted Camp Lejeune, and that's when I received the address of your company. I thought I would never be able to write to you before you went overseas. Please let me know. And write to me, because I fell in love with you the first hour I knew you!"

She threw me for a loop when I first read the letter. I never expected to hear from her or see her again. She completely was out of my mind when I enlisted. Well, not to be a jerk, I wrote to her telling her I was all right. But I never mentioned love, and I had to watch what I wrote. I ended my letter with "Jim" and not "Love, Jim."

After that I began getting many letters from Stevie, and more photographs, too. I felt bad because I didn't love her. It was just a casual acquaintance one Sunday afternoon. That's all it was. The only way I could break it was not to answer her letters again. When I left for overseas, I never heard from her again.

There was one other thing. Tarzan had a large photo of me, and Stevie asked her uncle for it. And until this day, she still has it. The reason I know this is Tarzan told me she still asks about me and still has the picture. He told me this upon my discharge from the Marine Corps. But my life with Stevie wasn't meant to be.

18. Two New Duties

We were ordered on another hike out to the M1 area to pull maneuvers again. Once we reached our designated area, we gathered together and split the company into the red and blue outfits to seek out and destroy each other. Our 1st Platoon had the blue armband, and Sgt. Breeding called out to Hennigan and me, "Front and center—Messina and Heidema! Move it, move it, move it!"

We both hurried over and stood in front of the rebel. He spoke again, "Messina, you will be head scout. Heidema, you are Messina's assistant scout. Clear?"

"CLEAR!" we yelled, trying to break his eardrums at such close range.

"Okay, now Messina, take the left flank and move slowly in front of the troops. Heidema, you will move to Messina's right, at about 150 feet. Clear?"

"Yes, Sir!" Hennigan replied sarcastically and walked away.

Hennigan was a good guy but was ever so slow in his movements. He never was in a hurry, and that was bad. I guess he hated the platoon sergeant so much, he always defied him. As we moved along, I'd motion to Hennigan to keep up with me. In return, he would hold his thumb up to his nose and flick it away with the "F--- you!" gesture. When he'd look back and see Breeding fuming, he'd have a smile on his face. He had that I-don't-give-a-shit attitude and showed it!

During the rest of the day, we did the same thing as we always did at the M1 area: we crawled with live ammunition over our heads and fired at an imaginary enemy and an old Model T Ford out in the field that represented an Army tank. But something always happened when the tracer bullets hit the Model T. The tracers missing the target would start a brush fire, so the whole company would work feverishly to extinguish it. With so many men there, it didn't take long to put the fire out.

When the chow call blew, with mess kits in hand we headed for the field kitchen. Our chow was hot beef stew, mashed potatoes, hot coffee, and white bread and butter. The beef stew wasn't so great, but we were hungry. I think the Marine Corps had the worst cooks of all the branches of the service.

That same night after we returned from maneuvers, I was dog tired from the ordeal and, on top of everything, I found my name on the duty roster to pull guard duty, from 0300 to 0700 hours, at the warehouses on the base. It was like adding insult to injury, and I wished I was on furlough at that very moment.

At about 0245 hours, I was awakened by the guard, who told me it was time to go on duty. As I got up from my bunk, I heard Glenn Miller's "String of Pearls" on the radio. It was the very first time I heard this song, and it was beautiful. To most people, Glenn Miller had the top big band of the era. His music was so soothing it would brighten up your whole day.

When I finished dressing, I checked my rifle, walked out of my barracks, and headed for the long warehouses made of wood. There was a chain-link fence surrounding the perimeter of the camp with barbed wire running across the top of it. I walked alone, and at the other end of the area another Marine walked to guard the other warehouses. I had guard duty once a week, for four hours, and really hated it. Our orders were to shoot if we were challenged by an intruder. If the intruder didn't know the password, our job was to hold him at bay and then take him to headquarters. As many times as I had four-hour guard duty, I never saw any intruder enter the base. I really didn't know if I would shoot an intruder; the occasion never arose.

19. Voyage to Aotearoa

It was now the beginning of May, and the first echelon would be departing soon. We began to break camp, taking our metal bunks back to the quartermaster. We kept the mattresses and slept on the wooden floor until the day came to leave. It was the day before we had to leave for port, and, would you believe, I sprained my ankle on a working detail. I didn't say anything to Sgt. Breeding for fear of getting left behind with the second echelon. I wanted to leave with the main body and not have someone say I was goldbricking. So, I tried to stay out of sight of the platoon sergeant and didn't report to sickbay. I told no one, not even Al or Negri. When they asked about my limp, I told them I had a blister.

The next morning, we headed for the trains to take the troops to Norfolk, Virginia, to board our ship. By this particular day, we had a new commander of the 1st Marine Division. His name was General Alexander A. Vandegrift, and he was the last to go aboard USS *Wakefield* (AP 21). She was formerly SS *Manhattan*, a huge luxury ocean liner that had sailed many transatlantic voyages. Shortly after her launch in 1931, she became known as "the fastest cabin ship in the world." After the Navy acquired her June 15, 1941, in New York, she was converted to a troop transport, with all her expensive furnishings removed and her exterior painted in Navy camouflage colors.[8] When I walked down the wooden deck and looked up at this big liner, it was like looking up at a ten-story building. This was the very first time in my life I was close to any ship of this size.

Left: *The Old Breed*; Right: Official USMC Photograph

Top: Marines boarding the train at Camp Lejeune, North Carolina, bound for Norfolk, Virginia, May 1942; Right: Major General Alexander A. Vandegrift, USMC.

As I looked in awe, the ship stood there like a giant waiting to be coaxed into action. Towards the water line of the ship, a gangplank was secured for us to come aboard. We climbed up and, before stepping onto the deck, it was a military rule to salute the flag at the stern of the ship. Before anybody could step onto the deck, they would first have to ask the officer of the deck (OOD), "Permission to come aboard?" The answer would then be, "Permission granted."

When Breeding saw me limping up the gangplank, he called me to one side and asked me what my problem was. I told him I had a blister on my foot. He didn't question me any further, and I was happy about it. I had to endure my sore ankle for a few more days before we shipped out. We spent that time in Norfolk loading the ship and getting prepared for our departure. I waited for the ship to weigh anchor, then quickly reported to sickbay. The corpsman wrapped an Ace bandage tightly around my ankle and told me to try to stay off it as much as possible. It felt much better afterwards.

Sgt. Breeding called for our platoon, and as we gathered around, he said, "This platoon is assigned to B deck, and there will be nine men sharing each stateroom." On three of the bulkheads, there were three bunks piled high. I took the top bunk, Al had the middle, and Negri took the bottom bunk. This deck was the second-class deck, and it was a very clean luxury liner. On May 20, we set sail for the Panama Canal with 4,725 Marines and 309 Navy and Army passengers.[9]

The word was out that there were German U-boats waiting for us beyond the three-mile limit, and it sent chills down my spine. How the hell can they get so close to U. S. soil and be undetected by the Navy ships we have left? Our escort was a light cruiser, USS *Philadelphia* (CL 41), and four tin cans (destroyers): USS *Aaron Ward* (DD 483), USS *Eberle* (DD 430), USS *Ericsson* (DD 440), and USS *Woolsey* (DD 437). There was also, another small passenger steamship, SS *Yarmouth Castle*, carrying several hundred nurses to Panama.[10] We figured we'd have these warships to protect us for the whole journey. Boy, we were wrong! Later on, we found out our warships' destination was only to Panama; after that they had other orders. From then on, we were on our own.

The first day out to sea, the gamblers didn't waste any time for the games to begin. In every recess of every deck there were mostly card games and a few crap games. Aboard ship, I preferred dice to cards because I was always lucky at this game. My luck continued throughout my entire time overseas.

The first couple of days at sea I didn't gamble. Al, Larry, and I went to explore the huge ship. We went up and down the steps of the different decks, from bow to stern, and it was tiring because the ship was a long one. I really enjoyed ocean travel, and I never got seasick like some of the other guys. As we strolled the decks, a lot of the Marines were lying down reading paperback novels, writing letters, conversing, or standing at the railings and looking out at the sea. We also liked watching the other ships of our convoy cutting through the ocean waves.

All of sudden, we heard some cheering, and saw a small group of Marines were pointing out to sea on our port side. There were many flying fish coming up out of the water, skimming the surface and then dropping back into the drink. They repeated this scenario for miles, and we kept watching until we got bored. It was a beautiful sight to behold. You know the old saying, "If you stay at home, you never see anything." I knew the war was on, but I was going to enjoy every minute I traveled. If I was lucky, and God allowed it, I'd live to tell about it after the war was over.

Two days after we sailed, one of the tin cans' sonar picked up a signal from a U-boat and steamed ahead of us to battle the Germans. We were all afraid of having USS *Wakefield* go down. Suddenly, as all the Marines lined the decks from bow to stern, there were explosions and water gushes the depth charges were creating, as the barrel-like charges tried to find their targets beneath the sea. After many explosions, we could see the debris and oil slick on the surface of the water. Word was out a tin can got one of the subs, while the others left the scene.[11] It was a hairy experience, and we all were relieved a torpedo didn't hit our ship.

It would take a total of twenty-six days to get to New Zealand. We'd have to run a zigzag course to avoid the submarine-infested waters of the Atlantic Ocean. The submarines lying in wait off Norfolk were our first experience of the war, and it was scary. You had to worry about being blown out of the water or getting eaten by sharks. Either way our minds were always thinking about survival and combat. Our convoy proceeded down the East Coast of the United States heading for Cristóbal, in the Colón Province of Panama. Along the way, we were lucky we had no more encounters with the German U-boats.

The second day was a Thursday, and the Navy served us beans for breakfast. At sea, the Navy always serves beans on Thursdays. I ate every last bit of mine, plus peanut butter-and-jelly sandwiches and two cups of coffee.

After chow, I was picked to swab the decks, while other Marines wiped down the railings, swept up, polished brass, and performed numerous other jobs that had to be done to keep everything shipshape. Breeding constantly checked on all working details so no one would be caught goofing off. Everything ran smoothly, and when our chores were done, the gambling would start all over the ship. Everyone had been paid before boarding at Norfolk, and the NCOs were loaded. They had the biggest games, and the greenbacks were flowing hand to hand in all the poker games.

Al and I stopped at one of the big games, only to watch because we couldn't afford to get in it. We only played the nickel-and-dime poker games or dice games. Before Pearl Harbor, a private only earned thirty-one dollars a month. After the attack, our pay was raised to fifty dollars a month. Since I made PFC before leaving the United States, my pay would be sixty dollars. The third day, I got into some of the smaller games, and I won a couple of bucks. I never lost the whole time I gambled in the Marine Corps.

There was this tall NCO from Texas, and boy was he raking it in. He was so lucky in this particular game that, when the voyage was over, he'd won 4,500 dollars. After we arrived in New Zealand, he radioed 4,000 dollars home, and kept 500. I remember chow being announced over the loudspeaker, and he asked one of the Marines to bring him back something to eat, and then paid the man five dollars for doing this. The Texan was so wrapped up in luck that if he left the game for chow, to him it would've been a bad omen and might have broken his winning streak.

Each day brought working details, talks on troop movements, exercises, field stripping our '03 rifles blindfolded, Japanese treachery coaching, booby traps, and many other things we needed to know before going into battle. I really enjoyed the ocean voyage, but there were only two meals a day on this large ship because there were too many men and not enough food for three meals a day.

Freshwater showering was turned on for ten minutes, once a day, but you had to be lucky to be there when it was on. Sure, we could shower anytime with saltwater and saltwater soap, but I only tried it once. My skin was so itchy from it I didn't bother with saltwater showers anymore.

On the fourth day, I was picked to pull KP with four other Marines on potato-peeling detail. I never saw so many potatoes in my life. It was a boring chore, and we made a lot of waste. I'm glad I only had KP once on this voyage, although I always liked volunteering for the Kitchen Police. It's different when you don't have to work for so many troops.

Each day would bring the repeated way of life aboard this ship, but our spare time in recreation gave us a breather, and we relaxed comfortably on the different decks.

We entered the Panama Canal on May 25, stayed overnight, and the

U.S. Naval History and Heritage Command Photo   Courtesy of the San Diego Air & Space Museum

Left: King Neptune (left) and his Royal Party on board the USS Wisconsin (BB 9) during Equator crossing ceremonies, 1908; Right: Pollywogs undergoing initiation aboard the USS Saratoga (CV 3).

whole next day. On May 27 it took about eight hours to pass through the canal. Thursday, May 28, we cleared the canal and began our long voyage to New Zealand.[12] USS *Borie* (DD 215), another tin can, escorted us out for two days.[13] After that, we were a lone troop transport all the way across the South Pacific Ocean. As the voyage continued, we were lucky there weren't any more submarine attacks. On the stern of our ship, we had one five-inch gun. Not much protection if we came under attack.

20. POLLYWOG TO SHELLBACK

Two days after leaving the Panama Canal, we approached the Equator, and it would be initiation time, done by the sailors to the Marines. One sailor told us, "If you have never crossed the Equator, you're called a 'pollywog.' Once you're initiated into the Domain of Neptunus Rex, you'll then be called a 'shellback'—meaning a veteran of the crossing." We were the victims of this naval tradition, and it sure was something to see and participate in.

First there were two long lines of sailors on top deck. At the other end of the line sat a large bruiser of a sailor dressed as King Neptune. Boy, did he look ugly in his getup, and when we approached him, we were in for a surprise! Each sailor in the line held a wide paddle full of holes. When the first Marine was pushed forward to go between the lines, a sailor would follow with a two-inch water hose aimed it at the Marine's backside. This helped you along for more punishment.

As you continued through the line, every paddle was whacking you on your wet ass, and boy, did it sting. The pollywogs were getting initiated. When you stood in front of King Neptune, he handed you a tablespoon of foul-tasting liquid to drink, and it made some of the guys vomit. The stuff we had to drink was the final part of becoming a shellback. Afterward we all received certificates officially welcoming us into the "Domain of Neptunus Rex."

There used to be another part of the initiation years before where they'd tie a rope around the pollywog's waist, throw him overboard into the drink for a couple of minutes, and then pull him back out. But they ended up getting rid of this part of the ritual after a tragedy happened to one of the men. Apparently, when they pulled him out, he had one leg missing—bitten off by a shark! So that part of the initiation was eliminated.

Halfway through our voyage the sky turned dark, and the sea began to heave huge swells. As soon as the ship started to sway, everyone quickly went below. We were being tossed around like a peanut and I was never so scared in my life! Someone said there were waves thirty to forty feet high crashing over the bow of our vessel. Negri tried not show his fear, but his face was white as ghost. We were all hanging on for dear life. If anyone was out on the deck of ship, they would easily get washed into the drink. This went on for four days and three nights and then gradually faded.[14] I think just about every man onboard got seasick during that harrowing experience except me, but it's one storm I'll never forget. Afterwards, everyone went up on the top deck. The sun was shining brightly, and the water was calm as if nothing ever happened. We all looked at one another and breathed a big sigh of relief it was finally over.

As our journey continued, each day was the same old routine. We all took turns carrying out the different working details the Navy handed us. This one day a voice cracked over the loudspeaker: "Now hear this! The smoking lamp is out. We are now crossing the International Date Line. Before we crossed the line, it was Thursday; now it's Friday. We moved up one day!" Later, we were handed another certificate, "Domain of the Golden Dragon," for crossing the International Date Line. We gained a day, and a ship going in the opposite direction would lose a day.

After we left Norfolk, I heard it would be a very long journey, but time had gone by quickly with all the work details, gambling, and preparations for combat. Negri and I would always be wrasslin' before it was time to retire. Boy, he was a powerful dago! We didn't hurt each other, though. We were like brothers who would do anything for one another.

In the early hours of June 14, our voyage was finally coming to an end when we saw the shoreline of Wellington, New Zealand, on the horizon.[15] It was a crisp, clear day as the sun was rising with a salty breeze blowing across my face. Loud cheers of joy rang out. I'll tell you, seeing land once again was the happiest moment for all of the Marines. As the ship steamed closer and closer, we noticed all of the houses had different colored roofs. What a beautiful sight! We were told, by one of the sailors that the native people, the Māori, called it Aotearoa, which means "land of the long white cloud."

We dropped anchor at Aotea Quay, and some New Zealanders were there to greet us. They even had the Royal New Zealand Air Force band playing the "Marines' Hymn" and "The Stars and Stripes Forever!"[16] All the Marines and sailors couldn't wait to get off the ship. Breeding came by and told us Vandegrift ordered the troops to stay on-board; only the NCOs were permitted to go on liberty. Everyone was surprised to hear this, hoping to get off the ship after such a long voyage.

Next, we were ordered to unload the supplies from our huge ship. There was much commotion as we busied ourselves on the dock. The supplies were unloaded from the ship and stacked high on the quay. For the next four days the troops were broken up into working parties and had to unload and reload the equipment for combat of the other American transports, USS *Bellatrix* (AK 20), USS *Electra* (AK 21), and SS *Delbrasil,* which were all docked nearby.[17] They arrived from New Orleans a few days before us.[18] They were loaded with bulldozers, landing craft, trucks, guns, ammunition, fuel, and other supplies. Word was the New Zealand dockworkers union refused to unload the American ships in the winter rains.[19] It was back-breaking work in the cold, winter rain, but we knew we had a job to do. It just felt good to be off the ship, and we all needed the exercise after being out at sea for our 10,000-mile journey.

Finally, after four days of unloading ships, we were given a four-hour liberty.[20] Negri and I went ashore together, but Al wanted to stay aboard ship and finish reading a novel. When Al told us this, we just looked at one another, shrugged our shoulders, and went on our way.

As we hurried along Negri said, "I can't believe Al wants to stay on the ship after all this time."

"Maybe reading keeps his mind off of thoughts of combat," I replied. Negri just shook his head as we shuffled down the gangplank.

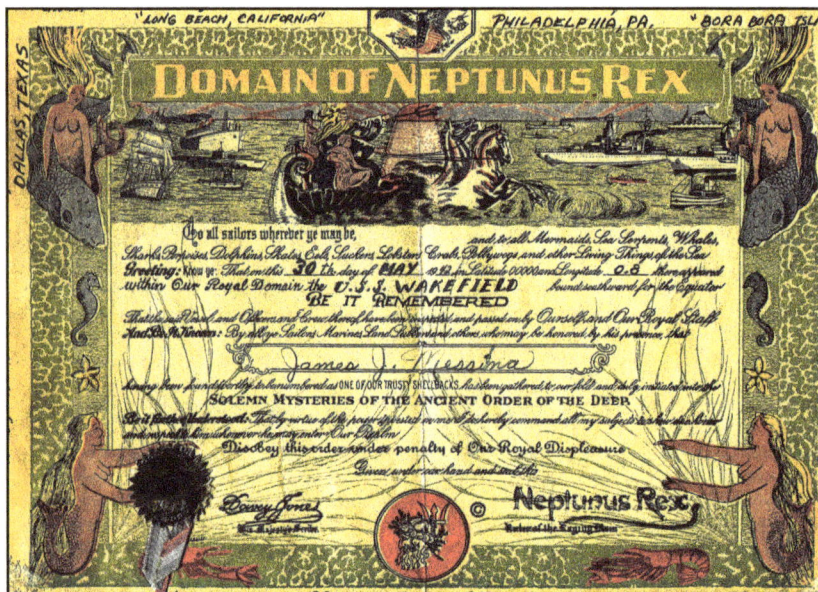

Shellback certificate awarded to James J. Messina, aboard USS Wakefield, *commemorating his first crossing of the Equator, May 30, 1942.*

CHAPTER 6: WELLINGTON

Archives New Zealand, Postcard, c.1942
Oriental Bay, Wellington, New Zealand, 1942.

21. FORBIDDEN FRUIT

We were so happy to be on liberty, even if it was only four hours. We looked like two little kids heading for a candy store. Negri and I didn't really know where we were going but just kept walking, saying hello to some pretty girls as we window shopped. We were also hungry and ducked into a fish and chips place and bought a bagful. Neither of us had New Zealand money, so we paid the man with American dollars, and he gave us change back in pounds and shillings. Now, we weren't sure if the guy cheated us, but it didn't take us long to learn their currency.

One thing we learned quickly in Wellington: stay away from the Māori native girls! The Māori were the indigenous Polynesian people of New Zealand, and they didn't like us fooling around with their women. Some Marines ignored their warning, however, and came back beat-up by four or five Māori adults. There were enough girls to go around, so we stayed clear of the forbidden fruit.

We stopped at a dance hall and were surprised to hear a New Zealand orchestra playing big band music. They sounded good but not as good as the regular American bands. The first couple of girls we met didn't understand our lingo. They were too strait-laced and weren't used to all the kidding taunts the American GI dished out. So, we asked the next two girls to dance.

Negri, with his New Jersey-style jitterbugging, was the kingpin on the dance floor, and his partner didn't know how to follow his lead. He danced all around her without noticing her predicament. When the dance was over, she told Negri he had a crazy way of dancing. Negri said she'd have to loosen up before she'd be able to dance New Jersey style.

We had to be back at the ship by 2200 hours, and it was now 2100 hours, so we left the dance hall and headed for the docks. Along the way, we walked past a bakery and noticed many different colored pastries. "Shall we?" asked Negri.

"Why not?" I replied. "I love sweets."

We walked in, studied the trays, and began saying, "One of these, two of those…" and so forth, until we wound up with a boxful. It cost us about a dollar and a quarter American.

Once we were aboard, we settled into our state room to eat our sweets. When the other seven men from our room walked in, they asked if it was okay to take some. "Help yourself," Negri and I answered. It wasn't long before all nine men emptied the boxful of goodies. Bellies full, we lay back and dozed off until reveille.

It was 0530 hours, Friday, June 19. "Now hear this!" a voice broke out over the ship's loudspeaker. "Chow will be at 0600 hours, then you will begin to disembark the ship."[1]

I jumped up and went to the head to wash up. For breakfast, we had shit on shingles, but I still ate it. It was really impressive seeing almost 5,000 men with full pack marching orders coming off this huge ocean liner. Once off the ship, we were ordered to board a train that would take us further north to where our temporary camp was located.

It was a very long train, and we all crowded aboard. Our seabags were hauled out on trucks. All of us men were very young, between the ages of seventeen and twenty years old. Some were married, but not too many.

Their worries were greater than the single men's. Since the attack on Pearl Harbor, almost forty percent of all servicemen and women enlisted to fight for their country.[2]

22. Paekākāriki

As our trainload of troops headed north, approaching this one station I noticed a peculiar name of the town. Its name was Paekākāriki, and we all laughed at the sign. I guess a lot of the names of towns and different things referred to the Māori people's heritage. We stopped laughing when we found out this was where our camp would be.

We finally arrived at Camp Mackay. Boy, what a sight it was! Muddy streets, wooded areas, mountains in the background, and a camp made of green lumber. It was so muddy they rigged the barracks up on wooden stilts about a foot off the ground. There were wide spaces between the floorboards, and an icy draft came up through them.

The small kerosene stove didn't heat the barracks very well, and we had to put up with the cold, rainy weather. The biting wind made our eyes water and freeze on our faces. We began stuffing rags, paper, or anything we could find to plug up the spaces between the floorboards. It was a losing battle. We still were chilled to the bone.

The next morning after chow we were ordered to carry rocks from the foothills to our camp. We made walkways to each building to avoid the heavy buildup of mud on our boots. It was miserably cold to go out on hikes into the mountains and do our work around camp. As the days went by, the routine here was very boring. We couldn't wait to leave New Zealand.

The third day here at camp was a nice day. We were asked if we'd like liberty in Wellington and jumped at the chance. Jonsey and I were buddies on this trip into town by train. The fare was very cheap, around thirty cents American. He was the likable type of guy, plus, being a rebel, he never brought up the subject of the Civil War, unlike some of those other rebels. Jonsey was also bashful around girls.

The train didn't take too long to go the twenty-five miles to Wellington, and we disembarked to seek out girls. We always made a pact in the Marine

Corps. When two Marine buddies meet a single girl, whoever starts talking to her first, the other guy departs. Two girls at one time, no problem. I liked this pact, and no one ever got mad when there was only one girl.

Jonsey and I walked into this restaurant and seated ourselves. About three tables away, I noticed these two girls, by themselves, sipping tea. One of them was looking my way, so I gave her a smile. She smiled too, put her head down, and then whispered to the other girl. They both looked our way. Just then Jonsey noticed, too, and we both smiled back. I said to Jonsey, "Let's walk over and talk to them."

He was getting red in the face when he answered, "Well, I don't know. They might be some guys' girlfriends, and we might have trouble."

"Come on," I urged, "only one way to find out."

Jonsey got up slowly and followed behind me. Both girls were good looking. I started to talk to the one who styled her hair in an upsweep. She was the older of the two, and they were sisters. "Hi," I said. "Are you two waiting for your boyfriends?"

They both giggled, and the older one said, "No, we don't have boyfriends!"

"Good," I replied. "Mind if we sit down?"

"No, it's okay with my sister and me," she replied. Jonsey was fumbling with the chair as he sat down next to the other girl. The older one said, "My name is Ann, and this is my sister, Esther."

I grinned. "I'm Jim, and my friend here is Jonsey."

The girl next to him said, "I like that name—Jonsey!" And again, his face reddened. Jonsey was a man of few words; he didn't think he was a lady's man.

"Ann," I asked, "do you live right here in Wellington?"

"No, I live in Brooklyn."

I didn't believe her. "Are you pulling my leg, Ann?"

"No," she said. "I'm not even touching you!"

I laughed and said, "No, that's slang for kidding someone."

"No, I'm not kidding," she insisted. "We live in Brooklyn!"

"Where's it located?" I asked.

"It's a suburb of Wellington, and by tram it's three miles up into the hills." Ann said a lot of the suburbs had American names, and "trams" are what Americans call "streetcars."

We bought them lunch and talked awhile as Jonsey squirmed. Ann said, "Esther, we best be getting back home. You know how father feels when we are in town."

They both rose from their seats, and I asked, "Can we see you home?"

"I guess it's okay," Ann replied. "Maybe my parents would like to meet you Americans." So, all four of us hopped onto the tram destined for Brooklyn. It was a slow-moving tram, but I enjoyed the ride.

Ann's parents had a nice little home with many antiques. Her parents asked about America and the way we lived. I gave Ann's father, a small man in his mid-forties, a pack of Lucky Strikes, and he was grateful for American cigarettes. Her mom, a short and stout woman with a high-pitched voice, began to brew a pot of tea as we conversed in the living room.

We all sat on the floor while Ann played a 78-rpm record on her phonograph. It was "longhair," aka classical, music and very soothing to the ear. I scooted close to Ann and held her hand as we talked about music. Jonsey sat next to Esther but not too close. He didn't have too much to say. Ann's father went to his study, and her mom was busy in the kitchen.

The next thing I did was slip my arm around Ann's waist and drew her close for a kiss. This took her by surprise because New Zealand men never kissed on the first date. Jonsey looked embarrassed, and Esther just giggled at our scenario. Now, these were two good girls, and I knew, sexually, it wasn't to be, so I just enjoyed her company and being in someone's home.

Soon her mom came out with a tray of cookies and a pot of tea. It was real nice being with them, and before we left, I thanked them for this day. I took down Ann's phone number, but we never saw them again. We returned to Camp Mackay satisfied with having this liberty.

One night, another Marine and I had to pull guard duty on the beach. It was around 1700 hours when we went to the beach for a four-hour watch. Suddenly, at 2200 hours, something happened that scared the wits out of us—EARTHQUAKE! It started with the trees swaying to and fro and the branches just about touching the ground. Then the sand began to wave like water in the sea. We tried to stand up, bracing ourselves with the butts of our rifles, but to no avail. We just kept getting knocked down on the sandy beach. The quake registered 6.1 on the Richter Scale.

Thoughts raced through my mind of all the movies I'd seen about earthquakes and the ground opening up to swallow you. It was another harrowing experience! It was my very first earthquake under my feet, and it didn't feel good at all. The ground didn't open up, but it lasted a full thirty seconds before simmering down to light tremors. I know now how all earthquake victims feel living in these regions. I don't know if there was any damage in Wellington; we were too busy getting ready for battle. The next day I forgot all about it. The officer of the day (OD) checked on us to see if we were okay. We told him we were shook up but fine.

Towards the end on June USS *Fomalhaut* (AK 22) and SS *Lipscomb Lykes* arrived carrying more cargo and equipment.[3] Around this time, we heard Gen. Vandegrift had gone to Auckland to have a meeting with Vice Admiral Robert Lee Ghormley, Commander of the South Pacific Area (COMSOPAC).[4] They were to discuss a dispatch the Joint Chiefs of Staff had sent concerning our combat assignment. The enlisted men knew nothing of the plans until the time was ripe. The orders at this meeting were to occupy and defend Tulagi and other Solomon Islands including Guadalcanal, Florida, and the Santa Cruz Islands. When our general asked, "Who will defend these islands?" The answer from the Joint Chiefs of Staff was, "The 1st Marine Division."[5]

The deadline was fast approaching for preparing our convoy to face the unknown. On June 30, all overnight liberty was cancelled.[6] July 2, we broke camp and headed back to the docks where we stayed until our departure. I was assigned to Combat Group A on the attack transport USS *American Legion* (AP 35).[7] Ships from the States kept coming in, but they weren't properly loaded for combat. Each ship's cargo had to be emptied and then sorted. There were teams of 300 men assigned to each ship, feverishly working around the clock.[8]

The cold winter rains drenched us, and our teeth never stopped

National Archives
Alexander Turnbull Library

Left: Marine Corps LVT(1) amphibian tractors crammed on the dock waiting to be loaded aboard ships of the Guadalcanal-Tulagi invasion force. USS McCawley *(AP 10) is in the background, 20 July 1942; Right: American supplies on the docks of Aotea Quay, Wellington, New Zealand, 1942.*

chattering until the job was done. The supplies were hurriedly dumped onto the docks and then had to be reloaded for our pending combat mission. They came in paper cartons, and the cartons, being rain-soaked, came apart, with the contents spilling out on the docks. You could see soggy cigarettes, mushy dry cereals, and a whole slew of C-ration cans rolling in all directions. Also, many cartons of pogey bait went to waste. The New Zealanders, when they witnessed this scenario, probably thought the Americans were crazy. This is one washout every Marine in our regiment would never forget.

As more ship's cargo arrived, it added to the disaster. The second echelon, consisting of the 1st Marines and supporting units, dropped anchor on July 11. They sailed from San Francisco aboard USS *Barnett* (AP 11), USS *George F. Elliot* (AP 13), and *John Ericsson,* another converted luxury liner.[9] Other supply ships arriving this day were USS *Alchiba* (AK 23), USS *Alcyone* (AK 24), USS *Libra* (AK 53), USS *Mizar* (AF 12), and USS *Jupiter* (AK 43).[10] We heard there weren't enough ships allotted to meet the combat-loading requirements for the entire 1st Division. Crucial supplies had to be left in Wellington to increase capacity for the troops. Rations and fuel were reduced from ninety to sixty days. Even our ammo had to be reduced for all the weapons![11]

National Archives

Photo taken from the USS Chicago (CA 29) of ships leaving Wellington, New Zealand, en route to Koro Island, Fiji, where they will rendezvous with the other components of the Task Force for the invasion at Guadalcanal -Tulagi, July 22, 1942.

The New Zealand Army loaned us their lorries, but our men had difficulty maneuvering the trucks through the disaster on the docks. It was one big soggy mess going down in Marine history. Despite this whole debacle, we met the deadline for the convoy to leave on July 22 for our destination.[12]

Finally, the troop transports and supporting vessels were all combat loaded and ready to sail. Around 0900 hours the ships began to leave Wellington Harbor in single file. All the Marines were worried because we noticed only the transports loaded with troops and a few destroyers. Oh no! I thought. Is this our only protection? We found out differently, though. Four days later, we rendezvoused with the other half of our armada out at sea and then proceeded to Koro Island to rehearse for our imminent attack against the Japanese in the Solomon Islands.[13]

National Archives

USS President Adams *(AP 38) crowded with Marines bound for the invasion of Guadalcanal, USS* Quincy *(CA 39) in the background.*

23. KORO ISLAND

Once out to sea, we discovered this first offensive against the Japanese in the southern Solomon Islands would be code-named Operation WATCHTOWER.[1] The convoy we were in, Task Force 62 (TF 62), was the landing force, and it had two transport groups.[2] Transport Group Yoke would carry the assault troops to Tulagi. My ship, USS *American Legion*, was part of Transport Group X-ray, in sub-group TransDiv A, landing at Guadalcanal.[3]

I think *American Legion* was even worse than *Harry Lee*. The bulkheads were thick with grease, and the railings were rusting. Its wooden deck was well-worn, and to boot, we were stuck down in the hold. All the bunks

U.S. Naval History and Heritage Command Photograph

USS American Legion *(APA 35), c.1944.*

were piled up seven-high, and as you slept there was a strong smell of stinking feet. I only slept one night in the hold. After that, I followed some other Marines and slept out on the deck.

As we sailed along, I prayed intently we didn't meet another storm like the one we experienced on USS *Wakefield*, coming across the South Pacific Ocean from the Panama Canal to New Zealand. That storm lasted four days as the ship rocked violently up and down and side to side. Later, on our voyage, we found out three men were lost while working guard duty out on deck, when the high waves swept them from the bow. *Wakefield* couldn't stop to rescue them, for fear of submarines, and the chance of losing all the men, as well as the ship.

On July 26 we noticed the other half of our convoy,[4] and we all rang out cheering for the United States Navy! Task Force 61(TF 61), our carrier force, had three aircraft carriers—USS *Enterprise* (CV 6), USS *Saratoga* (CV 3), and USS *Wasp* (CV 7), and one battleship, USS *North Carolina* (BB 55). There was a total of twenty-three troop and cargo transports, fourteen cruisers, thirty-one destroyers, five fleet oilers, and five minesweepers in our huge armada.[5] The Marine's strength would total 956 officers, and 18,146 enlisted men.[6] This Allied offensive would be the largest amphibious operations by the United States up to that time.

Our large transports were converted commercial vessels with limited cargo space, and our 155mm howitzers were left behind in Wellington.[7]

We figured the big artillery wouldn't be needed, knowing General Douglas MacArthur's Army would come in and defend the island once we established a beachhead. The plan was to capture one island at a time, like steppingstones to Japan, until we reached Tokyo. The sea battles that ensued prevented MacArthur from bringing in his troops. The Marines would have to defend Guadalcanal for four long months.

Early in July, Lieutenant Colonel Frank B. Goettge, our intelligence officer, shoved off to Australia to gather information. He scouted out men who had previously run the plantations in the Solomons, and others who operated trading vessels familiar with the waters around the islands. In Melbourne, he picked up the Japanese order of battle for the Solomons from the Army, and acquired the daily coastwatcher reports.[8] Meanwhile, a controlled photographic mosaic of Guadalcanal's beaches had been assembled, but never reached our Division.[9] At this point, we had very little information about where the Jap positions were, and exactly what we were up against.

Speaking of the Japanese and the Pacific Islands brings to mind what happened to Amelia Earhart and Fred Noonan ten years earlier on their around-the-world flight. They were supposed to land at Howland Island but never did. It was all over the news their plane had gone down somewhere in the Pacific Ocean. At the time, no one guessed the Japanese had been fortifying these islands starting in the 1930s.[10] There were a lot of theories, but I think they were shot down and taken hostage to prevent them from reporting what the Japanese were up too.

From Wellington we learned we'd be making pre-invasion landings at Koro Island, in the island nation of Fiji. We arrived July 28 and were there for three days of maneuvers.[11] Whoever had selected Koro Island had made a big mistake. Coral conditions on this island made it very difficult to land with the razor-sharp rocks on the beach.

On the first day, because of the poor conditions, our exercises abruptly came to a halt.[12] We pitched our pup tents, then sat and relaxed. I felt like trying a coconut, so I climbed up one of the trees and brought a couple of them down. When I removed the fiber husk and opened the coconut, it

Official USMC Photograph

*Task Force 62 (TF 62) conducts landing
rehearsals off the coast of Koro Island, Fiji, August 1942.*

was green and tasted very bad. I later learned when the husk turns brown, the coconut was ripe. It was better to wait until one would fall from the tree then we knew for sure it was ripe.

As we lay near our tents, smoking and bullshitting, a Marine from our platoon came up with a half-dozen huge, green, thick-skinned oranges. We each got a taste of the orange, and it was sweet as sugar. My squad leader, Cpl. Podracky, asked, "Where did you find those oranges?"

"About 1,000 yards in that direction," the Marine said pointing. When Podracky asked if we wanted to go after more oranges, our whole squad agreed. The corporal from the other squad told Podracky he wasn't supposed to leave the perimeter.

Podracky said, "Fuck it, let's go," as he motioned to his nine men.

When we came upon the oranges, the trees were loaded. They were as big as grapefruits. We stuffed as many as we could in our shirts, then headed back to our bivouac area. As we marched back in, we noticed Sgt. Breeding standing there with his hands on his hips, red faced, neck veins bulging, and crying out, "Where the fugg did you guys go? You knew the order, Podracky! You're supposed to be a non-com and control your men! No, you stoop down to a private's level and take off! You are going on report to Capt. Hawkins!

"Now Corporal," he continued, "what if the orders were to embark on the landing boats, back to the ship, and you weren't here? What would you have done? Cry mama like all of you Yankees do? If this wasn't wartime, I sure would see all ten of you would get a summary court-martial!"

Breeding was fuming when he walked away. He really hated us Yankees. It's not as if we loved the rebels. The Yankees won the Civil War, and as long as Breeding lives, he will never let us live it down. Cpl. Podracky did have to report to Capt. Hawkins, but what punishment could be given? After all, we were going into battle. The incident was forgotten. Sgt. Breeding was a son of a bitch, but also a good leader in the jungle.

On July 31 we embarked once again on *American Legion,* and at sunset departed Koro Island.[13] The first day out to sea, a gruff voice came over the ship's loudspeaker, "Now hear this, by orders of the United States Navy and the Joint Chiefs of Staff, this convoy is heading for Tulagi and Guadalcanal, of the British Solomon Islands. The Japanese have been fortifying these islands and our job is to stop them. The island of Tulagi is small, but of great importance, as they have established a small naval base there. Guadalcanal is much larger. It measures about ninety miles long, and thirty miles wide, and this is where they are building a large airfield. The troops on this transport will storm the beach at Guadalcanal. We will invade the island, hold there, and establish a beachhead for thirty-six hours. Gen. MacArthur's troops will then come in to hold and defend the captured islands. You Marines will receive further orders from your command."

When the Naval officer signed off, the question from one Marine to another, was, "Where the hell is Guadalcanal? Never heard of it in my history books." Then Breeding told us the 1st and 3d battalions of our regiment would be in the first wave, and 1st Marines (reinforced) would come in behind us.[14] My outfit was B (aka Baker) Company, 1st Battalion, 5th Regiment (1/5), with 186 men.[15] As our huge convoy churned through the waters, we were blessed with a low, overcast sky. It was our protection from the Japanese scout planes, and there were no signs of enemy subs.

The next morning out at sea, roll call found one man was missing. Later on, we got word he stayed behind with the Fiji Natives, purposely, because he was afraid to go into battle. Two weeks later he was brought to Guadalcanal by a PBY Catalina bomber. He received a general court-martial and was sent back to the states to serve a life imprisonment term at Portsmouth, New Hampshire. Before they took him away, he told a buddy he really enjoyed living on Koro Island and would have stayed there for the rest of his life.

It was now August 6, one day away from the invasion, and we were getting pretty nervous as we closed in on the Solomon Islands. As they hung suspended from their supports, sailors were busy testing the engines of the landing boats. They oiled up the cables so there would be no trouble lowering the boats into the drink. Along the deck, we could see coils of barbed wire and boxes of spare gun parts.

All of the Marines checked their packs, and some made camouflage nets for their helmets. A bunch of us went down to the machine shop and had our bayonets sharpened. That night was very quiet, and hardly anyone spoke. Tension was building. Thoughts raced through our minds. I thought, Will I get to the beach? Will I be lucky and make it inland? I prayed to God to watch over me and protect me from my enemy, so I could continue to live the life He gave me. My prayers were said the whole time I spent on Guadalcanal, and He answered them.

In 1948, Colonel Clifton B. Cates, commander of the 1st Marine Regiment and, at that time, commander of the Marine Corps, had this message for his men:

> *We are fighting for a just cause, there is no doubt about that. It is for right and freedom. We have enjoyed the many advantages given to us under our form of government, and, with the help of God, we will guarantee that same liberty and freedom for our loved ones, and to the people of America for generations to come.*[6]

The scuttlebutt spreading throughout the ship was the Japs were using explosive bullets. Well, there was an old salt among us, and he said if we made dumdums out of our bullets, it would tear a large hole in the enemy when they hit. We were all for it. Our question to him was, "How the hell do we do that?"

"Let's go down to the machine shop below and borrow cutters from the Navy," he said.

Following his instructions, we cut the tips of our .30-caliber bullets off, making them dumdums. We only cut the bullets in the clips of our cartridge belts, which were full of ammunition. Each cartridge belt carried eight to ten clips of five bullets. Plus, we carried two bandoliers of bullets crisscrossing our chests, which made us look like Mexican soldiers. With the combined weight of our heavy packs and the bandoliers, it was a little too much to swallow, but we couldn't complain.

Well, some bastard reported this to our platoon sergeant. He came storming in, yelling, "You sons-a-bitches, turn in your cartridge belts with those dumdums now! Don't you assholes know about the Geneva Convention?"

"The Japs have explosive bullets!" one Marine replied.

Breeding barked, "I don't give a damn what they have! Turn in the fuggin' ammo now and get a new issue! Am I clear assholes?" We had to hurry and get the reissue to be up on deck for the landing.

24. RED BEACH

At daybreak, the morning of D-Day, August 7, 1942, the big guns of the battleships and cruisers were pounding the beach as the planes from our carriers were swooping down on the island, strafing and bombing.[17] There was so much noise and so many explosions it was deafening. What a big show it was, and it scared the hell out of me! One of the shells from the battleship *North Carolina,* found a target of piled up drums of airplane fuel, and the ball of fire rising from it climbed to a height of about 150 feet.[18]

At 0910, Zero hour, we began to embark the landing craft and would be the first to hit Red Beach,[19] a 1,600-yard strip of sand situated four miles east of Lunga Point on the northern coast of the island.[20] Our squad moved up to the rails, and we could see all the landing craft taxiing around the ship, waiting for the troops. As we lined up on deck in four ranks, the men started going over the side and down the cargo nets into the boats.

I was so damn scared of being in the first assault wave, I thought for sure I'd get hit on the beach. As I lifted my legs over the railing, I got a good grip on the heavy cargo net and steadily lowered myself down. Many of us got banged on our helmets by shoes and rifle-butts as we tried to guide ourselves into the landing craft. The water was a little choppy, and we had to be careful to keep our legs clear of the boats bumping against the ship. It was a slow process boarding the landing craft because the Marines were heavily loaded with all their gear.

Once aboard I noticed it was an LCP(L). This meant we would have to jump off the port and starboard sides when it hit the beach. Our boats were a light-gray color, with each one carrying the American flag at its stern. I had a proud feeling when I noticed the flags fluttering in the wind. Each boat carried a whole platoon of men. A hush of silence hung over our heads, and there were blank stares among the men. I wished at that moment I could read everyone's mind. There was a Marine munching on an apple from breakfast just as though he was going on a picnic and had raided the picnic basket ahead of time. All the men around him gave him a funny stare. I think he was trying to put the fear of battle out of his mind.

Suddenly, all of the engines of the first wave were roaring and ready for full speed ahead. Before I knew it, we were all abreast—the first wave of the 1st and 3d Battalions of the 5th Marine Regiment was underway! As our boats sped within 1,300 yards of the beach, our warship's big guns ceased firing. The invasion had begun.[21]

As we began jumping over the side, we landed in at least two feet of water. The last Marine getting off the boat had help from the Navy coxswain, who was the operator. When this Marine came out of the water, he accidentally swung his rifle around towards the coxswain, but he'd already ducked down out of sight, steering the boat in reverse at full speed. The coxswain didn't want to stay near the beach any longer than he'd have

Clockwise from top left: U.S. Naval History and Heritage Command Photograph; National Archives; Critical Past (4)

Clockwise from top left: USS North Carolina *(BB 55) firing her forward 16/45 guns during her military trials, August 1941; Marines clambering down a net ladder on the side of a transport dropping into assault boats as the invasion of Guadalcanal is underway, August 7, 1942.*

Clockwise from top right: National Archives, U.S. Naval History and Heritage Command Photograph (2); Critical Past (4)

Clockwise from top right: SBD and TBDs prepare to take off from USS Enterprise (CV 6); Grumman F4F fighters in tactical formation; Smoke rises from Tulagi after bombing by US carrier aircraft; Marines conveyed in landing craft from transports storm ashore across Red Beach, Guadalcanal, August 7,1942.

THE
GUADALCANAL
LANDING
—0800 HOURS—
AUGUST 7, 1942

MY
OUTFIT

FIRST WAVE
—BY—
"B" COMPANY
1st. Battalion
Fifth Regiment
1st. MARINE DIVISION

to. One surprising thing about this invasion is there was no resistance at the time, except for a few Jap bombers that appeared briefly, damaging one of our destroyers.[22] We began hitting the beach. As we moved inland, my legs felt like lead from being so scared. As my 1st battalion charged to the right the 3d battalion went left.[23] There weren't any words spoken as the troops moved cautiously seeking out the enemy.

Sgt. Breeding shouted, "Scouts out!" There was no movement among men. "I said, Scouts ooout!" Still, no one moved out. In a low, growling roar, he ordered, "MESSINA—HEIDEMA, GUD-DAMIT! I SAID SCOUTS OUT!"

I turned to the platoon sergeant and said, "Since when are we scouts?"

He snarled, "Since maneuvers at the M1 area, asshole! Okay?" There was no argument I could give the rebel.

I started to move out through the tall, razor-sharp grass and into the jungle, ahead of the main body. I motioned to Hennigan, who was on my right flank, to move out also. But he thumbed his nose at me like, who the hell are you to be giving me orders? When Breeding saw this, he aimed his .45 weapon in Hennigan's direction, and it was only then that he stepped out.

We moved ahead in complete silence, knowing we were encountering a treacherous enemy. We had heard many stories about the Japanese booby traps and the way they were camouflaged. Just then my eye caught something in the wind, or so I thought. On my right flank, past Hennigan's direction, I noticed a clump of leaves at the top of a tree. I put my hand up for our company to halt. With a hand motion, I summoned Breeding in my direction.

Sgt. Breeding came to my side gesturing, "What's the problem?" I pointed to the tree. He had some doubt, and motioned Negri to our side. Negri carried a Browning Automatic Rifle (BAR), each clip contained twenty rounds of .30-caliber ammo. Breeding signaled Negri to open up on the clump of leaves. Negri fired half-a-clip into the tree, and then a Jap sniper fell loose, hanging by a rope. They always tied themselves to the tree for better firepower. Breeding said, as he looked my way, "Well, chalk one up for the Yankee scout who was on the ball!"

Official USMC Photograph

A Marine patrol wading across a jungle river on Guadalcanal, c.1942.

The sniper could have shot three or four of us before we knew what happened. I was just happy he didn't get any of our men. In our ranks, we also had Thompson sub-machine guns like the Mafia used in Al Capone's days. This gun used a round drum magazine carrying ninety rounds of ammo.

All of a sudden, there was enemy machine-gun fire ahead of us in a thick part of the jungle. Word got back that some other Marines came upon a machine-gun nest, but they quickly took care of it.

As we advanced further, we had to wade across the Tenaru River.[24] The streams they classified as rivers, were no wider, or deeper than some of the creeks back home, in Pennsylvania, where I went fishing. On the other side, we came upon the first Japanese camp with about twelve pyramid tents. Two fires were burning with huge cast iron pots, filled with water, hanging above them, probably to boil rice. We cautiously moved into the camp, with fixed bayonets, but the Japs all took off when our ships and planes bombarded the island.

Slowly, we entered the tents, looking for souvenirs, careful of booby traps. There were Japanese naval insignias on the wooden lockers and seabags. Whenever any of us tugged at anything, we made sure there were no hidden strings to set off a trap. I can tell you one thing; every Japanese soldier's wooden locker held a jar of opium. The opium was in large-brown-pill form, and they were round like a marble. I'll bet one of those pint jars was worth a lot of money in the United States. There were also these long-stemmed pipes made out of bamboo with a very small bowl that could hold one ball.

Curiosity got the best of me because I knew very little about dope. In fact, I never thought about it. I had to try one. I placed a ball on the tiny bowl and lit it. When I puffed, the ball just glowed to a reddish color, and immediately, I didn't like it. Well, all I can say is you know how garbage smells? Well, that's how this dope tasted. I flung the jar against a coconut tree, and the glass and opium shattered all over the ground. Then, I broke the pipe in half. None of the other Marines liked it either when they too had to satisfy their curiosity.

There wasn't much to find in the Jap's belongings—mostly clothes, no valuables or Japanese money. There was one fellow who came down the road with sixteen Japanese wristwatches up his arm. I couldn't believe it! "Where the hell did you find all of those watches?" I asked him.

"About an eighth-of-a-mile in that direction," he said, pointing to another Jap camp," he replied. "You want to buy one?"

"HELL NO!" everyone answered in unison.

My battalion continued to advance westward through the jungle parallel to the beach.[25] What we found on the first day of our invasion were many of the Japanese civilians who built the camps and helped with the construction of runway at the airfield they were building a short distance from Lunga Point. Most of the Japanese construction battalions had fled to western part of the island after our invasion, but there were a few hundred Jap soldiers spread throughout the vast jungle.

Our intelligence misjudged the enemy's presence on Guadalcanal. They thought the Japanese garrison totaled 8,400. As it turned out, the actual count was around 2,500.[26] We had many skirmishes with the Jap soldiers who were already there. They never expected the Americans to attack in August 1942. We drove them deeper and deeper into the jungle. In the coming months, the Imperial Japanese military would send thousands of soldiers to fight the Americans.

The natives on Guadalcanal were known as the Melanesian people. They knew we were there to fight the Japs and were very friendly with us.

Most had reddish-blond, wooly hair, were big in size, and very cunning jungle fighters. One Marine said, "I'd rather the Japs be our enemy, than those natives." Later on, we gave some of the natives our M1 carbine rifles with folding wire stocks to defend themselves because none of us Marines liked this weapon. We depended on, "Old Faithful," the Springfield '03 rifle. Most Japanese soldiers carried a .25-caliber bolt action, clip-fed long rifle, with a hooked bayonet.[27]

At midday we got word there was an air raid of Jap bombers attacking our convoy. A coastwatcher, Paul Mason, 350 miles north at Bougainville, transmitted by radio: "From S.T.O. twenty-four Jap torpedo bombers headed yours."[28] Thanks to his warning, eighteen Wildcat fighters from our aircraft carriers greeted them.[29] The bombers damaged one of our destroyers, USS *Mugford* (DD 389), but no ships were sunk.[30] These coastwatchers proved to be the most valuable source of intelligence for the Americans. Captain Martin Clemens was the most famous coastwatcher on Guadalcanal. He had served as a district officer on the island, and also played a big part in the resistance to Japanese occupation. The story we heard is Capt. Clemens and his native scouts took off into the mountains when the Japanese began construction of the airfield. The Jap patrols used radio detectors to zero in on their positions, forcing them to constantly relocate. They eventually ran out of supplies, and the rumor was Clemens' shoes had completely disintegrated and he had to walk barefoot in the jungle.[31] It was a dangerous and lonely life for the coastwatchers, who were always on the move.

Our landing craft were busy working from ship to shore, bringing in rations, ammunition, and supplies from the cargo transports, and dumping everything on the beach. While five battalions of Marines pushed the Japs further into the dense forest, the rest of the division was busy working, carrying the supplies to each outfit's bivouac. As the officers were all shouting commands, crews were unloading the landing boats, while other crews were loading the trucks. Everyone was cursing on the beach because we landed on this godforsaken island none of us had ever heard of.

After trudging two miles through the hot, putrid jungle from Red

Official USMC Photograph   Official USMC Photograph

*Left: Coastwatcher Captain Martin Clemens and his native policemen;
Right: Marines hauling supplies and reinforcements on Guadalcanal,
August 1942.*

Beach, the 1st Battalion set up a perimeter defense near the mouth of Alligator Creek.[32] We immediately began digging foxholes but couldn't go any deeper than five feet without hitting water. That night, Cpl. Podracky and I shared a cramped pup tent. We were worried B Company's position was too close to the beach and thought we should be at least a little farther back into the jungle. The supplies had been hauled over to our bivouac area from the transports, and the beach was too crowded to move about. It reminded us of the docks in New Zealand. The only difference here was we didn't have the rain. It was August though, and the wet season on Guadalcanal would soon be upon us. In the months to come we'd get more than our share. And boy, was the rain cold!

Across the channel, about twenty miles, was the island of Tulagi. On this first day of the invasion, the landing force there included the 1st Raider Battalion; 1st Battalion, 2d Marines; 1st Parachute Battalion; and 2d Battalion, 5th Marines (2/5).[33] These units would suffer many more casualties than we did at Guadalcanal on their initial landing.

The sneaky Japs were holed up in many pockets of caves. They were notorious for this method of fortification. Marines would toss grenades into the caves, and they would throw them right back out. It got to the point where one of the sergeants suggested dynamite. The Marines who did this job had to climb up and around the caves, then dangle down on heavy ropes suspended above the opening. They would light the fuse, wait until it would burn down to an inch or two, and then fling it into the cave. The flamethrower soldiers also moved in close and would shoot a steady stream of hot liquid fire into the mouth of the cave. Some of the Japs would come running out engulfed in flames, and the Marines would mow them down with machine-gun fire. The smell of burning flesh nauseated the Marines, but they had a job to do.

Our paratroopers got a dirty deal. After going through intense training, jumping from airplanes, they ended up in the landing boats along with the infantry. Half of the paratroopers only got a little way up on the beach before they were caught in the Japanese crossfire.

25. THE BLACK STILL OF NIGHT

The first night we were all afraid of the many shadows that popped up around us. In everyone's mind the thought of the Japs infiltrating through the night kept us awake and alert.

Suddenly, a voice in the night rang out. "Messina and Heidema, front and center!" It was that bastard rebel Sgt. Breeding. "You both go on guard duty now! You will stay near the beach, under the coconut trees, close to the mouth of the river. Keep your eyes out for any movements among the trees and for rubber boats trying to land on the beach. Clear?"

"Yeah," we said in disgust, and went on our way. We both locked and loaded our '03 Springfields. It was almost midnight now, and we'd be on duty until 0300.

It was a pitch-black night, and we were supposed to walk guard in different directions, but we didn't. Hennigan and I put our rifle butts down against a coconut tree. He faced the ocean, and I faced the jungle. Then we laid our rifles on our laps. We whispered in low tones, because your voice could carry in the black still of the night. It was very spooky, and we were both afraid, this being our very first night in the jungle.

In Richard B. Frank's *Guadalcanal,* Private Robert Leckie writes:

It was darkness without time. It was an impenetrable darkness.
To the right and left of men rose up those terrible formless things of

my imagination, which I could not see, but I dared not close my eyes least the darkness crawl beneath my eyelids and suffocate me.[34]

We had to be on constant alert fearing this treacherous enemy we were learning to fight. The Japanese soldier was a cunning son of a bitch who learned his trade in Burma and other places where they fought against the Chinese. The Japanese persecuted the Chinese for the past 300 years, and they were experts in jungle warfare. You could walk right past a Jap in camouflage lying on the ground, and you would never know he was there. A lot of our Marines would cut down palm fronds and tie them to their helmets for concealment, but I never did it.

It was around 0200 hours when both Hennigan and I heard a movement among the trees, about forty feet in front of us. We both got up and moved slowly towards the sound. I spoke out, "Halt! Who goes there?" No answer. I unlocked my rifle, fired one-round, and then a second. We heard a thump. Someone was hit and fell to the ground. Our first Jap, I thought!

I started to move forward, rifle at the ready, when Hennigan grabbed my arm and whispered, "No, he might not be dead. Wait about five minutes, then check him out. He might be booby-trapped with a grenade. We'll both die, Messina!"

"We have to check it out," I whispered back. "He might just be wounded, and we can take him prisoner." Hennigan didn't like it but followed me anyway. We stepped lightly ahead, hearts pounding, sweat rolling down our faces, both fearful of walking into a trap. I told Hennigan to hit the deck, and we crawled slowly on our bellies because we'd be able to make out the body easier being silhouetted against the sky. About fifteen feet in front of us was a huge form on the ground, and it wasn't moving. We kept inching closer to the form. I was in for a big surprise when we figured out what it was. Instead of a dead Jap, we saw a dead cow!

We both busted out laughing, but at the same time, I knew I was in for a razzing. Hennigan, through his heavy laughing, blurted out, "Messina shot a cow! Messina shot a cow! Wait until Baker Company hears about this!"

"Hennigan, you son of a bitch, you better not say anything about this!"

"Fuck you," he snorted. "I can't wait to tell them." He couldn't stop laughing.

Then I said, "Hey, Henny, remember, there's two bullets in that cow! One of them is yours, and one is mine!"

"Bullshit, you shot both of them!"

"Oh no," I countered, "that's not what I'll tell our buddies. Who are they going to believe, you or me? They know what kind of guy you are. You've lied before, and they know it." Hennigan stopped laughing. He knew I was right. It was his word against mine. The incident never came out in the open, and it was killing Hennigan.

We went back to our guard positions and noticed it was about ten minutes before relief time, so we both walked our posts to make it look good. Two men approached, and we gave them the "Halt, who goes there!" They identified themselves as the guards who were relieving us.

26. Battle of Savo Island

At daybreak, August 8, the day after D-Day, the whole beach was a mess. Our platoon was put on a working detail loading food and supplies. There were many Japanese stake body trucks on the island, and the motor transport battalion made good use of them. They resembled the American Chevy trucks and could carry three tons. We also took over two huge bamboo warehouses loaded with Japanese goods. Half of one warehouse had stacks of 100-pound bags of rice. There were also many cases of quart bottles of Japanese beer, and many bottles of sake along with dried, whole smoked fish in wooden buckets with tight lids. The rest were all canned goods: grasshoppers, tangerines, crab meat, octopus, crackers, noodles, and many other varieties. The only way the Marines could learn what was in each can was to open one of every size. Whenever you wanted a certain food, you'd know it by the size of its can. There were also two types of cigarettes. One came in a pack of twenty, with cone shaped tips, so the paper wouldn't stick to your lips. About five drags and the cigarette was gone. It was very lousy tobacco. The other one I liked better. They came in small boxes of ten cigarettes. They were called the Rising Sun, and they were a lot thicker than the American cigarettes.

At 1215 hours there was an air raid of Japanese bombers on our convoy, and we all scrambled for cover.[35] Dogfights broke out between our Grumman Wildcat fighters and the Japanese Zeros, sometimes with sickening outcomes. One of our Wildcats was hit, the pilot bailed out, and as his parachute drifted down to the ocean, a Jap Zero machine-gunned him to death. Voices rang out among us, "You dirty little bastard!" This kind of thing would happen many more times throughout the Pacific war. The Zeros outmaneuvered our Wildcats, but many Japanese planes were brought down by our pilots.

The Jap torpedo planes were flying low, skimming the surface of the water, dropping deadly torpedoes aimed at the American vessels. As they flew by, we could see the shit-eatin' grins on their faces in triumph after a direct hit to USS *Jarvis* (DD 393), one our destroyers. Another Jap Betty did a death dive crashing into our transport, USS *George F. Elliott*, setting her on fire.[36] We cursed them over and over for declaring war on the United States.

After the raid we were busy again moving supplies off the beach. At dusk we received a radio message from an allied search plane that a Japanese surface force was on its way. A little after 2300, four Japanese float planes flew over the island and dropped flares illuminating the area.[37] They would be sending back a report of our positions on the island, and also where the allied ships were in the channel between Guadalcanal and Tulagi. The planes disappeared as fast as they appeared. We figured we would be in for one hell of a fight.

That night around midnight the Japanese warships arrived in the channel. At first there was silence, but around 0145 all hell broke loose.[38] The battle for Guadalcanal had begun! The bursting shells were deafening. This naval battle would later be known as the Battle of Savo Island.

We had ringside seats on the beach as we watched the bright flashes from the big guns, the direct hits, the explosions, the noise, the confusion, and deaths of both Japanese and American sailors. One of their ships sent

Top: National Archives; Bottom: U.S. Naval History and Heritage Command Photograph

Top: Japanese twin-engine G4M torpedo bombers (later named "Betty") flying low through anti-aircraft gunfire between Guadalcanal and Tulagi; Bottom: USS George F. Elliott (AP 13) is set ablaze in left center after a Japanese plane crashed into her. The other plumes of smoke are downed aircraft, August 8, 1942.

up a star shell, and when it exploded in the sky, the channel lit up like it was a bright, sunny day. What a scene it was, right in front of our eyes! It was actually breathtaking to see the many ships spread out, spilling the fires of death.

The American cruisers, USS *Astoria* (CA 34), USS *Quincy* (CA 39), and USS *Vincennes* (CA 44), were all sunk, and the destroyer USS *Talbot* (DD 114), and the cruiser USS *Chicago* (CA 29) were severely damaged. The Australian heavy cruiser, HMAS *Canberra* (D33), burned all night, and had to be sunk with American torpedoes the next morning.[39] She split in half, the bow going down in one direction and the stern in the other. She sank, in a matter of seconds, as though a giant vacuum pulled her down.

We also witnessed the transport ship *George F. Elliot* go down, which was still ablaze from the earlier air raid after the Japanese G4M bomber struck her starboard side. As the sailors were abandoning their ship, the Jap machine guns opened up on them, and the screams of many men could be heard in the night.

The naval battle went on for over an hour. Star shells kept the sky lit up for about three minutes each, and the sea battle wasn't a pleasant sight to see. Our ships had gotten the worst of it. Later on, some of the sailors were discussing this sea battle, and I learned about a trick our ships would use. In the dark of the night, one of our destroyers would steam between two Japanese warships and then fire simultaneously from port and starboard sides at both ships. It would accelerate at full speed ahead into safety. Both Jap ships would then open fire on each other, thinking each was the enemy. They claimed it was one of the tactics used by our Navy in future sea battles.

In this assault the Japanese heavy cruiser, *Chōkai*, was damaged, and all of a sudden left the area without sinking any of our other transports anchored near Tulagi.[40] The Japanese fleet quickly pulled out, heading away from the American ships. We got word later one of our hits knocked out *Chōkai's* operation room, so there were no charts to help it lead the Japanese force in the dark of night.[41]

The morning of August 9th the Allied losses were 1,077 dead and 700 wounded.[42] The Japs only lost 129 men, with 85 wounded.[43] This surprise attack by the Japanese Imperial Navy was a devastating blow to the United States-Australian force and was documented as one of the worst defeats in American naval history.

27. STARVATION ISLAND

After the Japanese task force departed from the scene, our transports returned that morning to continue unloading supplies. But by sunset they all had left the area and set sail for Noumea.[44] None of us knew about the Navy's plan to withdraw their ships. We found out later that, before the naval battle had ensued, Vice Admiral Frank Jack Fletcher, commander of Task Force 61, had requested permission from V. Adm. Ghormley to withdraw his aircraft carriers. He feared losing his remaining aircraft carriers, as he had already lost two at the Battle of the Coral Sea and Midway.[45] The transports and cargo vessels were forced to withdraw after Fletcher's carriers left, because they had no air support to protect them, and the offloading of supplies was never completed.[46] Gen. Vandegrift strongly objected to this withdrawal, but it didn't stop the departure.

All the Marines called this the "great Navy bug-out." Much of our medical supplies, rations, and ammunition had not been unloaded. Along with the supplies, some 1,800 men, elements of the 2d Marines, went away with the transports. They left us with 10,819 men to defend Guadalcanal, while 6,075 men remained in the Tulagi and Gavutu-Tanambogo area.[47] We were totally unprotected from the Jap air raids and nightly shelling by the Imperial Japanese Navy's ships. The Japanese had naval and air bases in Rabaul, at the northern tip of New Britain Island. They would come through the "Slot" (New Georgia Sound), cutting right through the center of the Solomon Islands.

As word spread that the Navy left, we all felt like we'd never get off the island alive. There was a feeling of abandonment among us, and it intensified our fear. Our nerves were getting the best of us, not knowing what to expect from the enemy. We were immediately put on short rations, and our chow was reduced to two meals a day. Most of our rations were the captured Japanese food, which was mostly fish and rice. We lost a lot of weight during that time.

> *The feeling of expendability is difficult to define. It is the loneliness, it is a feeling of being abandoned, and it is something more, too: it is as if events over which you have no control have put a ridiculously low price-tag on your life.*[48]

In the early days of the invasion, after our Navy departed from Guadalcanal, we were without naval and air support. Knowing our situation, the Japanese surface craft and submarines prowled the waters between Guadalcanal and Tulagi constantly disrupting our shore operations. Their seaplanes were watching our every move and would conduct low-level attacks, day and night, on whatever targets they could find. They were in command for the time being, but that would soon change.

There was a beautiful coconut plantation nearby, but much of it was left in ruins from the many explosions. The island's banana groves didn't see any damage at all. They were located towards the middle of the island in the southern direction. There were also many pineapple patches and pecan trees throughout the island. The British shipped all of these agricultural commodities and copra (dried coconut kernels) to different parts of the globe.

Heavy rains gradually increased and soaked us to the skin. Half the time on the island we were sopping wet, and the ice-cold rain made you shiver to the bone. Add to that the extreme heat and humidity, lack of clean clothing, and no permanent living quarters. We also had annoying land crabs, giant bush rats, snakes, wild dogs, and crocodiles. The worst were the multitudes of insects, including scorpions and deadly, venomous spiders. Our flooded camps were also infested with swarms of huge mosquitoes. The Marines were stricken with various types of diseases and infections that were hard to treat in the hot, moist conditions. Sleep was nearly impossible with the constant bombing and shelling. At first sight the island looked like paradise, but it soon became sheer hell!

28. AIR RAID

By the third day, the 1st Battalion established a 9,600-yard-long beach defense between the east branch of the Lunga River to 1,000 yards west of Kukum Creek.[49] The same thing happened here when we started digging our foxholes, just like near the river. If you dug deeper than five feet, you'd hit water. The Japs had built an ice plant and bakery out of green timber. The ice plant was run with a gasoline-driven generator. To have ice in this ninety-degree heat was a godsend. We didn't get too much bread made in the bakery, on account of the constant raids from the air and sea.

Quart bottles of beer and sake were plentiful. The beer only lasted two weeks, and the sake was destroyed by order of Gen. Vandegrift. Too many Marines were acting crazy from drinking the rice wine. I'd see the MPs gather the bottles of sake, place them in a big pile, then smash them. A lot of the Marines buried bottles of sake anyway. The beer was distributed and carried to every outfit on the captured Japanese trucks. It was plenty good beer, but I never was much of a beer drinker. I was happy just with plain drinking water.

It was now 1200, and a high-pitched voice rang out, "Condition Yellow!" We knew what it meant: the Japanese bombers were heading for Guadalcanal. Five minutes later, again the voice rang out, "Condition Red!" This meant the bombers could be seen with the naked eye. The air-raid siren whirled, and we looked up to see a formation of Japanese bombers flying at high altitude.

I had an eerie feeling come over me. The bombers were not camouflaged. The silver fuselages gave off a transparent effect and looked like ghosts in the glare of the hot sun. I began praying to God to spare me from the dropping bombs.

I remembered the orders given to us in training: In a raid of any kind—bombs or shells—lay flat on the ground, lift your stomach, and keep your mouth open to prevent concussion. This was my first bombing, and these words were branded in my brain. But I was still scared and very confused thinking about dying. Everyone was running around looking for a place to hide from the bombs. No matter where I stopped to take cover, it felt like the wrong spot.

Before we knew it, the planes disappeared. My heart was still pounding as I stood up and brushed myself off. I looked at my other comrades as we all breathed a sigh of relief. We were expecting to be pummeled with bombs, but they never came. One of the NCOs told us afterwards that the Japs were most likely doing reconnaissance to relay information back to their base. This time we were lucky. But from August until December, the Jap planes thundered over us daily at noon like clockwork, dropping bombs on the airfield and surrounding installations.

At night throughout the campaign, the Japanese warships would come in around 0300 to shell the island. When their ships would appear, first-off they would scan the beach with their powerful searchlights to see if they could spot any movement. When the lights went out, they would lob the shells in, hoping to destroy men and installations. I don't think any of the Marines got more than three hours sleep at night the whole time we were there. We'd all try to catch catnaps during the day.

The Japanese started this fight, and we, sure as hell, were going to finish it. The Marines went into the battle of Guadalcanal with revenge on their minds for the losses of Pearl Harbor. Our Navy was pretty good at figuring out the next move of the Japanese high command. The enemy was determined to get Guadalcanal back, but it never happened. The Marines held strong!

Our Navy was lacking until the folks back home began producing ships, planes, bombs, ammunition, and whatever else the American fighting machine needed. Most of the men were very young like me and didn't know the meaning of battle, but we learned quickly in a costly way.

All men are afraid to die, and thank God, the noncommissioned officers were good leaders, even though we didn't like some of them. Some of the other officers were excellent leaders, but others couldn't find their way out of serious situations. A lot of them were "ninety-day wonders" out of Officer's Candidate School, who were as green as the young, enlisted men. Our best leaders were the NCOs, who had anywhere from four to twenty years' experience in the Corps.

There would be many medals for Marines for acts of bravery throughout the campaign, and also many Purple Hearts. One of our heroes, Al Schmid from Philadelphia, was awarded the Navy Cross.[50] He was part of a machine-gun squad of the 1st Marines and was credited for killing 200 Japanese soldiers at the Battle of the Tenaru.[51]

When night fell everyone became trigger-happy again. We began firing at anything that moved, even a weed in the wind. We were very nervous and inexperienced.

"Knock off the fuggin' shootin,' you assholes!" came a voice in the night. It was Sgt. Breeding. No one paid any attention to his command. The shots rang out the whole night until dawn. In the jungle the nights turned very cold, and we used our wool blankets to try and keep warm. Just like we learned back at camp, we'd spread our ponchos out on the ground, with a blanket on top, and then use the other to cover-up with. The thin blanket wasn't enough to keep us warm, but we had to make do. At the first sight of dawn, the jungle would begin to steam as the sun penetrated through the trees.

29. Patrol

Guadalcanal had many horses and a large herd of cattle owned by the British. These animals scattered out in all directions to survive the pounding destruction of the planes and warships on our initial landing. An incident I never forgot was one time when the Japs dropped a bomb, causing the cattle to stampede, and they plowed straight through the 1st Marine's command post (CP) destroying everything in their path.[52]

The morning of the fourth day our platoon was picked to go out on patrol into the jungle. Breeding led us southwest from our camp near Kukum to see if we could stake out the Jap positions. Each man carried a full canteen of water, can of C-rations, two bandoliers of .30-caliber ammunition, and a cartridge belt with two hand grenades clipped on the back. We trekked a good distance through the dense jungle. There were large trees that shot up over 100 feet high, with huge roots flaring out like fans that extended into a thick ground layer of ferns, vines, and sharp

Critical Past

Marines on patrol advancing through the jungle, c. 1942.

thorn bushes. The process was very slow as we hacked our way through the tangled mess with machetes.

As we advanced into the jungle, our eyes constantly scanned the trees for snipers or any movements in front of us. In the upper canopy of the trees, exotic jungle birds were clamoring in song, adding to the tense feeling of fear as we slowly trudged along. We came upon a freshly killed wild boar tied to a long carrying pole. I guess the Japs must have heard us coming and fled for their lives. We figured whoever it was must have been a couple of stragglers and not someone from the main body of the Jap garrison.

We proceeded to push forward cautiously, hearts pounding, eyes searching, tripping over vines through the impenetrable jungle, expecting at any moment a camouflaged Jap sniper would open fire upon us. No one spoke as we advanced. We searched the trees, looking intently into the thick vegetation for any signs of the enemy, but nothing happened.

After we had walked another quarter of a mile, suddenly Sgt. Breeding yelled, "Halt!" The two men who advanced in front of Breeding were called to his side. He said, "Do you notice anything where my .45 is pointing?" The sergeant had his weapon pointing to the ground, just to the right of the path.

"No, Sarge," the two men said in puzzlement.

"Gud-damn it, there's a Jap lying right there!" Pointing his weapon at the same time, he kicked the little bastard. The Japanese soldier jumped up from his concealment with his hands over his head in surrender. He was a short, stocky little Jap wearing horned-rim glasses, and he had a fat, round face. He had fresh blood on his uniform and was one of the Japs who had killed the wild boar. He was caught by surprise when our patrol approached. The two Marines now learned the Japanese fighter was very good at camouflage, and they wondered how Breeding had spotted him. He told all of us we would have to keep in our minds that the enemy is always there, and to concentrate on that and not think about anything else.

Sgt. Breeding also told us to look out for booby traps, especially the ones made with bamboo stakes stuck into the ground at a forty-five-degree angle with sharpened ends pointed outward. The Jap prisoner's hands were tied behind his back, and he quietly walked along with us, wondering when he would get a bullet in his back. His eyes searched all of the Marines with fear written on his face. He would later be interrogated by our commanding officer when we got back to our bivouac area.

The long hike through the jungle was coming to an end. We had advanced about eight miles through the mosquito-infested jungle, and we didn't find any Japanese positions. If we had located any, we wouldn't have fought them. The objective of any patrol was to locate, move quietly away, and report back to headquarters. Then an offensive operation would be organized.

Sgt. Breeding ordered an about-face, single file, to move out back to where we came from. We headed back towards the Lunga River where our bivouac area was located. Back at camp our prisoner was turned over to Division Headquarters where an interpreter would question him for information about the island of Guadalcanal. After the interrogation they found out he was part of a unit of soldiers in command of the civilian Japanese construction crews working on various projects, including the airstrip.

He was easily persuaded to give information and wasn't like the traditional "die for your country" Japanese soldier he was supposed to be. He told our command there were at least 2,000 Japanese soldiers dispersed throughout the jungle, west of the Matanikau River towards the northern tip of the island. There were also more supplies and ammunition in this vicinity. He said the high command in Japan were determined to get the island back and would be sending reinforcements. With this information, we began preparing for the upcoming battles.

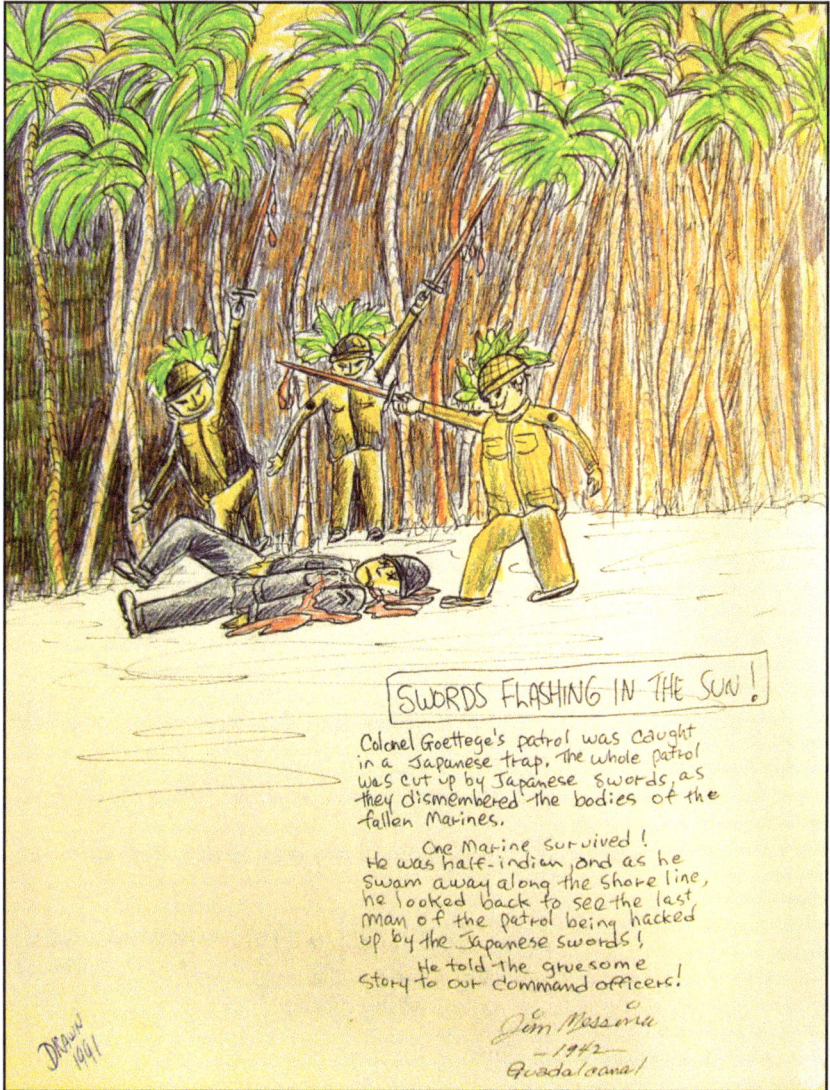

SWORDS FLASHING IN THE SUN!

Colonel Goettege's patrol was caught in a Japanese trap. The whole patrol was cut up by Japanese swords, as they dismembered the bodies of the fallen Marines.

One Marine survived! He was half-indian, and as he swam away along the shore line, he looked back to see the last man of the patrol being hacked up by the Japanese swords!

He told the gruesome story to our command officers!

Jim Messina
— 1942
Guadalcanal

Drawn 1941

30. Japanese Trickery

One of our other patrols captured a hostile and scraggly looking Japanese warrant officer. After he was offered generous amounts of liquor, he suggested to our command that some of his buddies were without food, around the mouth of the Matanikau River, near a tiny peninsula called Point Cruz. He said, if given the chance, they wanted to surrender.[1]

The Jap officer claimed his men were starving and didn't want to fight anymore. There was also a rumor one of our Marines had seen a white flag flying in the Jap bivouac area.[2] After listening to the prisoner and considering the information he related, Lt. Col. Goettge felt we would gain vital information by capturing the Japs, and it would also be the humane thing to do. Our command was hesitant, but obliged, and found out later it was a mistake. He organized twenty-five of our best men to seek-out a Japanese surrender. His patrol consisted of infantry men, scouts, a language officer, intelligence specialists, and the assistant division surgeon.[3]

The colonel's patrol shoved-off on August 12 from Kukum Beach in a Higgins boat after sunset. They headed west towards the Matanikau area, not knowing what was in store for them. The sad part of this scenario was only three Marines returned. According to Marine records, there were never any traces of the missing Marines, including Goettge.[4] The Japs had done their sneaky trick well, and it would be a reminder for the future to never believe the stories of captured Nips.

The author of *The Old Breed*, George McMillan, interviewed Sergeant Charles C. (Monk) Arndt, one of three survivors. The following short account of the events of that fateful expedition and of his experience consists of extracts from McMillan's interview:

> *...there was a Japanese party in the Matanikau area that was willing to surrender. Our idea was that this was a reconnaissance patrol and that no fighting would take place...we got into lighters and went down to the area at night. There were 25 men in one boat, 4 officers and 21 enlisted men, plus the Navy cox'n... (the boat) hit this sandbar and we waded ashore...It was real dark, no moon or stars, it was a little cloudy that night. I couldn't see much...Colonel Goettge was in the lead. He got hit... Then a couple of other men were hit...Right after that, the Japanese machine guns opened up...a corporal went out to the water's edge and started firing tracers, trying to get an SOS back. We*

didn't have a radio. The fighting went on until about 1 o'clock....the captain said someone had to go back for reinforcements...and I told him that if anybody could get through the line, I thought I could... There was no chance to leave by land and I was a pretty good swimmer. I went into the water just like a snake, on stomach, hands, and knees, and I went like this just as far as I could without swimming at all. Out for about thirty yards....As I waded out I did take my clothes off. I had all my clothes off except my shoes and socks, the only things I couldn't get off. And my helmet. I still had that on...(swimming) was very easy with the breaststroke... I'd go into the beach once and awhile and there was a lot of coral that I had to hold on to and I have scars yet on my hands and legs where I was pushing around this coral...when I crossed that damned sandbar, I must have made some noise. Somebody fired at me. (My pistol was) under my helmet, (I had) hooked the butt under my chin strap... I had a good clip in the pistol and the other one was wet, but I kept it just the same. Then I saw a man, and shot him, and I heard no running away from where I shot...I saw a native boat beached. I crawled in it and...I pushed out ... There was an old plank in it. I paddled away until I got back down to the boat base and there everybody was challenging me. I didn't know the password so I kept yelling, "Million, million." That had a lot of "l's" in it. And when I hit the shore and guys started looking at me funny, I realized I was bleeding all over. I was cut all the way to the hips from the coral. They told me later that the bones were sticking out from my fingers. Then they wrapped a blanket around me, and I told them that I had to get word to Colonel Hunt, and they got him on the phone, and I told him that the patrol was all cut up and was being shot all to pieces.

Sergeant Arndt ended the harrowing story: Of the other men who got back, the last was a half Indian. He did not leave until nearly daybreak and as he splashed out into the water to start his swim to safety, he looked back to see (he told a correspondent) "Swords flashing in the sun," the Japs hacking up the last of our people.[5]

After this tragedy, Colonel Leroy Phillip Hunt, Commanding Officer, 5th Marines, immediately dispatched his reinforced L Company to land west of Point Cruz. This patrol swept back searching for information on the fate of the men only to find a few helmets and the surgeon's medical bag.[6]

31. Shell-Shocked

The next day was very hectic and exhausting. We worked round-the-clock, clearing a pathway through the jungle. There were many other tasks to be accomplished in order to defeat the sneaky little bastards who started this war. At midday, we took a ten-minute break to eat our C-rations, drink water, and smoke cigarettes. Afterwards, we laid down barbed wire until dusk. Working tirelessly, all day long, made us very hungry. The order was given to knock-off. We headed towards the field kitchen, where large cans were used for cooking. Most days rice was the main course.

Only two men had chow in their mess kits when, suddenly, we heard the whooshing of an artillery shell over our heads. It exploded very close to the chow line. As we scattered, shrapnel flew all around. Pandemonium was unleashed as shells from a Japanese submarine kept flying in. We ran in all directions looking for foxholes or any kind of protection from the exploding shells. Almost immediately my battalion's three-inch guns returned fire, along with the Weapons Company's half-tracks' 75mm guns.[7]

Jonsey hollered, "I'm hit!" Looking in his direction, I saw him rolling on the ground holding his leg just above the knee. I started towards him when he suddenly got up and staggered into one of the foxholes.

I continued to run, and as I jumped into a very large hole, I felt myself being lifted up and thrown back out of it. Talk about being scared! I couldn't believe what just happened. There were about twelve Marines in the hole, and I guess I made one more too many. The shells were coming in about every three minutes, and just the whooshing sound alone made the hair on my head prickle with fear.

The feeling of dying was very strong. I started to pray again as I ran around frantically searching for cover. I was afraid to die, along with all the other Marines. Finally, I crawled into a foxhole covered with sandbags and coconut logs. There was only one other man in there, my buddy Shuford. Boy, was I glad to see him.

Just as I entered, two shells exploded near the foxhole, one right after the other. The force of the blasts felt like they detonated ten feet away from us. The concussion jolted our bodies and slammed us against one end of the hole. After this, I don't know what happened. I was knocked out.

This bombardment lasted for fifteen minutes. Afterwards, my buddies told me I was in hysterics, and Shuford suffered the same fate. We must have been completely delirious clambering out of the hole. In WWI this was called "shell shock," and now it is called "combat fatigue," or post-traumatic stress disorder (PSTD). The concussion also did damage to my lower back, and as time went by, it would continue to be a problem. We were both taken to the Division Field Hospital.

Three days later, I recovered from the shock. I felt a sharp pain in my lower back but didn't say anything. My buddies might have thought I was goldbricking. We had a few goldbrickers—guys shooting off their toes to get out of combat. The men in our company let them know they didn't like it. I had no enemies in B Company, not even Sgt. Breeding. Yes, I disliked the sergeant, along with the other guys, but I didn't hate him. God's law is not to hate, but to love; not to judge, but to be judged by Him. There wasn't a single day that went by on that island I didn't pray to God for protection. Until this very day, I never stop thanking Him for the gift of life He gave me.

32. BLOODY RIVER

Gen. Vandegrift cooked up a plan to avenge Lt. Col. Goettge and his patrol. Three of the 5th Regiment's companies—B, I, and L—were assigned to find the bodies of our comrades and snuff out the Japs who slaughtered our Marines. Command figured, from the massacre, that the Japanese garrison was concentrated west of the Matanikau River area.[8]

On August 18 at 0800, L Company hacked their way through the thick vegetation inland, advancing southwest through jungle, crossing the river upstream, then circled back on the western bank, where they camped until daybreak.[9]

At 0930, artillery fire from our guns rained down on the village of Kokumbona, near the mouth of the river. That afternoon, Capt. Hawkins ordered B Company to move out parallel to the beach and advance northwest towards the river's bank.[10] As we pushed forward, progress was slowed by the dense undergrowth and sharp coral mounds. Before reaching the east bank of the river, we held back behind a low ridge. We remained undercover in our attack position for the following morning. My platoon stayed close together—Al and Negri on my left flank, with Larry on my right. The rest of my comrades were nearby. By this time, we were like brothers, always looking out for one another. That night we heard explosions back in the regimental area from enemy naval gunfire.[11] Each time a bomb exploded, the ground shook, and I feared the shells would reach us like before. We were all on edge. Plus, with all the rumbling, it was impossible to get any sleep that night.

This was my outfit's first encounter with the enemy, and most of the enlisted men weren't seasoned fighters. We all wanted revenge on the little Jap bastards who slaughtered the Goettge Patrol, but at the same time we were scared shitless. Everyone inspected their rifles and equipment for the upcoming battle. Sgt. Breeding was checking out each man in his platoon. He kept a close eye on everyone to make sure no one fired off any rounds. This night we learned the importance of absolute silence before combat, only using hand signals to communicate. It would be one of many lessons in our induction to becoming seasoned, jungle warriors.

The following morning before daybreak, I Company boarded landing boats and headed west past Point Cruz and got off at Kokumbona. Their mission was to land, then advance eastward parallel to the beach at the mouth of the Matanikau River, where all three companies would converge, surrounding the enemy. The Japs directed machine-gun fire at our landing boats, while enemy naval artillery shelled the beach, making it difficult for them to reach their objective.[12]

Our artillery bombed the village and surrounding area again at 0830.[13]

The shelling was ear-splitting, and some of the shells came in very close to where we were hunkered down. Shuford and I were still spooked from the blast we took a few days ago back at camp. We kept looking at each other each time a shell exploded, hoping we wouldn't find ourselves in the same predicament. The battle hadn't even begun, and the explosions were enough to make us all petrified. My heart was pounding out of my chest.

The order was given to attack across the sandbar, near the mouth of river. Negri yelled out, "Let's kill the Jap bastards!" As we moved out down the coral ridge, the Japs sprayed us with machine-gun fire. A rapid stream of bullets flew over my head, and I immediately dove to the ground.

Sgt. Breeding shouted, "Retreat!" We all scrambled back up the ridge as the bullets kept coming in from every direction. I heard a loud ping, and when I looked over, I saw Al's canteen spouting water all over him as he clambered back up the steep slope. Once we got back behind the ridge, Al and I ended up huddled together. I could tell he was shook-up because his face was white as ghost. I sure was glad the bullet hit his canteen and not him, and so was he. Later on, after the battle, we razzed him that he was so scared he pissed his pants!

Shortly after we took cover, Lieutenant Colonel William E. Maxwell, commander of our 1st Battalion, approached our company commander with these orders:

"Hawkins, I want you to take B Company and charge the enemy across the river."

Capt. Hawkins looked the colonel straight in the eye and said, "Very bad decision, sir."

"Are you refusing the order, captain?"

Hawkins replied, "Yes, sir!"

The colonel was fuming. "Who the hell are you to refuse my order?"

"Well, sir, it would be suicide to take my men across."

"Pray, tell me captain, why?"

"The Jap machine-gun positions would make mincemeat out of us in no time at all, sir."

"What are you saying, Hawkins?"

"Again, colonel, I refuse your suicidal order."

The colonel's face turned red as a beet. "You know what this means, don't you?"

"Yes, I know what it means colonel, and I stand pat. I'm protecting my men from the enemy." The colonel, with fire in his eyes, turned around and stormed away to report the incident to higher command. He'd make sure Capt. Hawkins would have to answer to a court-martial.

No sooner had the colonel walked away, we heard the loud cry of a Japanese officer. At the top of his lungs, he hollered the Japanese war cry to attack. "Banzai, Banzai!" Swinging a golden sword over his head, the Jap officer led his men into the river towards us. We opened up with gunfire, at the same time lobbing grenades and trench mortars. It was a sorry sight. The jungle river quickly turned red as Japanese blood spilled into water. This could have happened to us, had our captain followed the colonel's orders. Capt. Hawkins had saved our lives.

B Company gave the Nips everything we had, firing continuously, keeping their attention on us. My ears were ringing loudly from the deafening noise. The order had been given to L Company to advance through the jungle towards the beach. They ambushed the enemy from behind, attacking with rifles and bayonets, killing many Jap soldiers.[14] There were more Japs hiding behind a coral ridge on the western bank that opened fire. Once again, we heard them shout, "Banzai," as the enemy charged with fixed bayonets. The Marines spun around and mowed them down at close range.[15] There were many screams of pain and death coming from the enemy as bullets tore through their flesh. I Company fought their way down the beach through enemy machine-gun fire, taking the village of Kokumbona. The remaining Japs managed to high tail it up into the hills.[16]

The battle persisted for almost six hours. In the end, sixty-five Japs were dead. We only lost four Marines, but that was four too many.[17] Some of the dead Jap bodies drifted slowly downstream with the current to where the river met the ocean. The blood in the river began clearing up, and the river soon turned back to its original muddy color. Orders were given to wade across the river to the other side to mop-up.

Once across, the scenario in front of us was a sickening sight to behold. Bodies were scattered all over the blood-soaked ground. I got sick to my stomach when I saw the Jap soldiers torn apart by our trench mortars. There were Japs with no heads and others with gaping holes in their torsos. Arms and legs were missing and strewn about. But the worst was a man with his brains leaking out of his head. He looked like a deflated football with no air in it. The trench mortars had done their job well.

This was my first-time witnessing death in battle, up-close, and the image was branded on my brain. It was a hellish scene I'll always remember for the rest of my life—the horrors of war. It was a shameful waste of human life. For three days, I couldn't eat. All I did was drink water. Just the smell of food made me nauseous.

It would be another hard lesson in becoming a jungle warrior. It's either kill or be killed. Something we all learned very quickly. This first action on the Matanikau River would become known as the "Battle of Little Tokyo" among the men of B Company's 1st Platoon.

Our fallen comrades were carried back to the regimental area for proper burial, and it was a sad moment for us. I wasn't picked for burial detail and was glad. The Jap's bodies would be gathered and thrown into a mass grave.

Capt. Hawkins was relieved of his command and punished for disobeying Maxwell's order back at the Matanikau River. On September 9, B Company's executive officer, First Lieutenant Walter S. McIlhenny, would be promoted to captain, replacing Hawkins.[18] The scuttlebutt was they transferred him to the French island territory of New Caledonia, located about 850 miles directly south of the Solomons. There, in Nouméa, they ran a medical facility, Mobile Hospital No. 5, and his new job would be with supplies.[19] We were sad to lose Capt. Hawkins and talked about how much we would miss him. He would forever live in everyone's memory for saving the lives of B Company.

33. Condition Red!

The next day we were back at the bivouac area. A few moments after we woke up, the air-raid siren went off. Someone was yelling, "Condition

Red, Condition Red!" Everyone dove for their foxholes! The Japanese were constantly coming in, day and night, bombing, strafing, and shelling us at will.

We'd been without air support since the initial landing on August 7 and were sitting ducks. There wasn't a whole lot we could do to fight back from the heavy bombardments. Not too far above the trees, a squadron of planes roared over us. We all started to scatter. As they got closer, someone yelled, "They're ours! They're ours!" Our planes had finally arrived, and now we could show the Japs a thing or two. One by one, a head popped up from a foxhole looking up in awe. What a beautiful sight this was for all the Marines! It was a squadron of twelve Douglas SBD Dauntless dive-bombers, led by Lieutenant Colonel Dick Mangrum. Later, Captain John Smith would lead another large squadron of nineteen Grumman Wildcat fighter planes onto the airfield.[20] Both Navy and Marine pilots flew these planes. Whenever the captured Japanese siren mounted on a bamboo tower would sound off, our planes were instantly in the air, intercepting the Japanese Zeros. The Jap pilots didn't expect to be hit so hard by the Wildcat fighter planes' surprise attacks. Their Zero fighters outmaneuvered our heavy planes, but we brought down more of theirs, than they did ours.

The Douglas dive-bombers started to hit the Japanese shipping lanes. Our coastwatchers would always radio in ahead with information of both Japanese ships and planes heading towards the island.[22] The newly arrived American aircraft were creating havoc on the Japanese. They couldn't figure out how strong our air support was on Guadalcanal.

The news got back to Japanese Prime Minister Hideki Tojo in Tokyo. He was raving mad and didn't know how much the island of Guadalcanal was going to cost him in lives and equipment. He now realized it was a mistake—a big mistake. He started to send reinforcements continually and was determined to win back the island.

Although the Japanese destroyed many ships at Pearl Harbor, Tojo still didn't know how strong our Navy was. The Japanese fleet commander who directed the bombing of Pearl Harbor didn't see any aircraft carriers in the bay, or anywhere near Pearl Harbor. This worried him. Where were they?

U.S. Naval History and Heritage Command Photograph

The F4F-4 Wildcat in formation. It was a single-seat mid-wing plane with a top speed of 320 m.p.h. and had six fifty caliber machine guns mounted in the wings, c.1938.[21]

Now, with our newly arrived air support, the sinking of the Japanese ships, and downing many of their planes, the Japanese high command thought twice before they made their next move. I heard later that the count of planes brought down was five Japanese for every American fighter.

Back home, civilians were working twenty-four hours a day to produce the equipment we so badly needed. Steel production was stepped-up. Many of the men's wives and girlfriends went to work in factories and mills to help the war effort. They made planes, tanks, bombs, bullets, and many other essential supplies. Every American did what they could do to help. The will to win was all we needed to push forward until we arrived at Tokyo's front door!

34. ANTAGONISTS

In the beginning, the Japs knew we didn't have any aircraft, and they used many tactics to harass the Marines on the island. One of these pests was the little Jap bastard we called "Washing Machine Charlie." This pilot flew around in a twin engine night bomber keeping us awake.[23] The drone of his

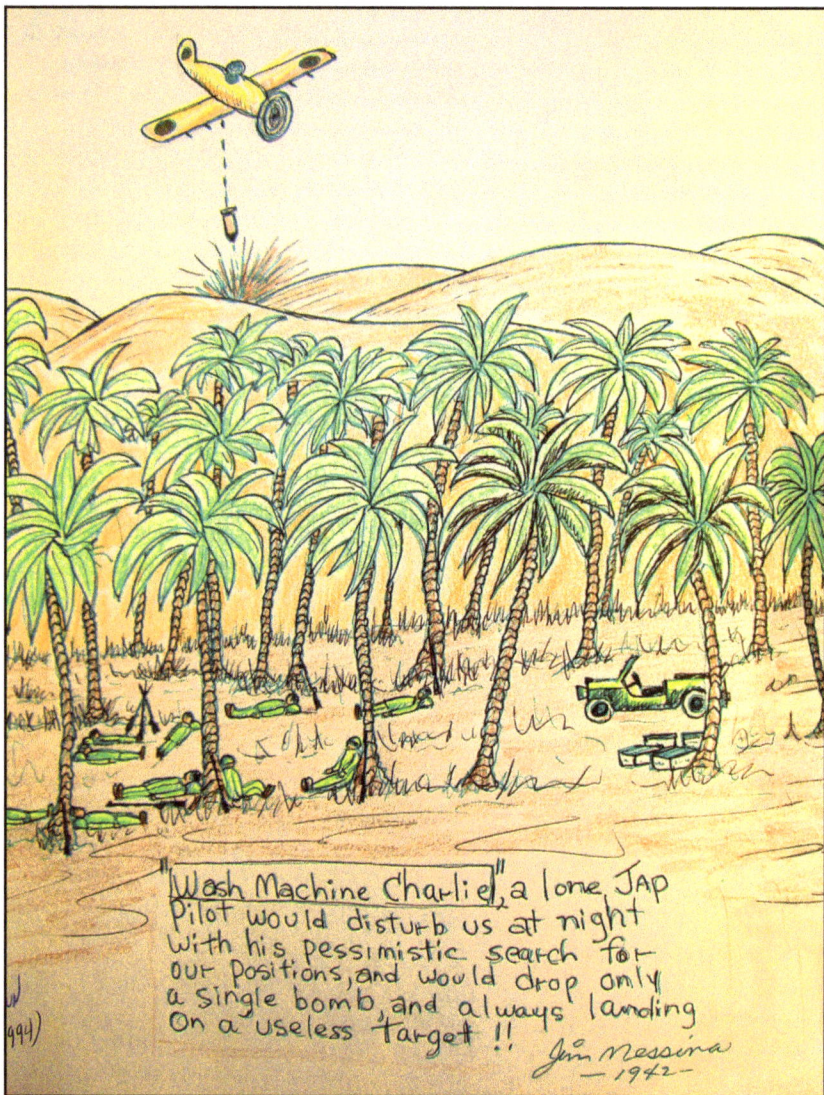

"Wash Machine Charlie", a lone JAP pilot would disturb us at night with his pessimistic search for our positions, and would drop only a single bomb, and always landing on a useless target !!

Jim Messina
—1942—

engines was very annoying. You could hear the engines at different intervals, as though he was turning them on and off. He would cruise around at night covering a wide area. Our planes couldn't take off in the dark because it would disclose our positions if we used lights for the runway. But Charlie flew at his own will. He would keep us on our toes for at least two hours every night. In the end, his bomb was always dropped where it didn't do much damage. The target was supposed to be the airfield, but he rarely ever found it. It was scary though, so we always took the precaution to sleep in our foxholes and never walked around in the open.

We had another disturbance around 0300 that was a lot scarier. First, a cruiser floatplane dubbed "Louie the Louse" would fly over the perimeter dropping flares.[24] Then a Japanese cruiser or destroyer would come into the channel. First, the ship would turn on its powerful searchlight. Next, it would scan the beach from one end to the other looking for any movements. It was like clockwork. Once the searchlight went out, shells were fired at random, hoping for a direct hit on something.

This one night the worst shelling was from a Japanese battleship. This was the first time in naval history that combat troops were shelled by a battleship. Jonsey and I were on guard duty this night, and as soon as the searchlight went out, we took cover behind some coconut trees. We thought it was a routine destroyer appearance, but we soon found out different. The island rocked as though it were hit by an earthquake. Jonsey and I were stunned when we realized fourteen-inch shells were flying in. These shells were as big as a small automobile!

A salvo of six shells came in, one after the other, searching for a target. With each explosion, the ground trembled as shrapnel and debris rained down all around us. The whole perimeter was in a panic. Marines were running in every direction, seeking cover from this attack, which, according to the Geneva Convention, was illegal. But Tojo was determined to get his island back at any cost. Jonsey and I got up and ran deeper into the jungle looking for safer shelter. The best we could do was put our heads up against the base of a tree and pray real hard.

The salvos kept coming in, and the shells were now exploding closer

to the airfield. It was a terrifying experience. We cursed the enemy over and over as we ran for cover. One shell exploded fifty yards in front of us. A large chunk of metal flew above our heads and slammed into the ground about thirty feet behind us. Later on, we searched for it, but only found a large, scorched area. The huge projectile must have been buried at least six to ten feet deep.

In my whole life, I will never forget this battleship shelling our troops on the island. We talked about it for many days, but it wouldn't be the last time the Imperial Japanese Navy launched two-ton bombs at us. This evil act added more fuel to the fire. Our pilots were skilled airmen, already seeking revenge for Pearl Harbor. They were determined to defeat the Jap bastards!

We also had the "Noon Special," which happened almost every day. A small group of Japanese bombers always appeared at 40,000 feet.[25] Many of the bombs found their target among the infantry positions, and lot of Marines lost their lives. If you got wounded, the worst place to be hospitalized was the Division Field Hospital, located northeast of the airstrip.[26] It was the Nip's prime target. After Jonsey got hit by shrapnel, he had to spend a week there. He told me it was worse than being back at camp, because bombs constantly exploded all around them.

NEGRI AND MYSELF
CARRYING OUR WOUNDED LIETENANT GIERE
BACK BEHIND THE LINES FOR FIRST AID
HE TOOK SHRAPNEL ONE INCH FROM HIS HEART   1942

35. Jacob Vouza

It was now exactly two weeks after the invasion of Guadalcanal. Back at camp, following our first encounter with the enemy, there was some bad news about a native chieftain they called Vouza.

All the natives on the island were in top, physical condition. Even the twelve-year-old boys had the strength of an adult. They could carry twice their weight and would lug around bunches of bananas, handing them out to the Marines. Vouza, likewise, was a very strong native with red, bushy hair. He and his men served as scouts and would travel with the coastwatchers and Marines whenever patrols were sent out. Vouza loved the Americans. A Marine befriended him and gave him a small American flag, which he carried everywhere he went.

One day, Vouza and his natives went out on a patrol by themselves, when he realized having the flag on his person probably wasn't safe. Leaving the patrol, he turned off alone to hide the flag in a nearby bamboo village. But it was too late, and Vouza walked right into the path of an enemy platoon on patrol. The flag was all of the evidence the Jap platoon leader needed to see; Vouza couldn't deny he was on the American's side.[1] The Japs tied him to a tree and tortured him and left him to die. Vouza chewed through the rope, however, and escaped. By the time he dragged himself, crawling, into the Marine lines west of the Ilu River, he'd lost a lot of blood.[2] Despite his gaping throat wound, he wouldn't accept any medical attention until he was able to communicate what he knew. The information was extremely helpful to the 1st Marine Regiment on the Japanese numbers and weapons.

At the time, we didn't know the full story about Vouza. We thought it was only scuttlebutt. Later on, I read about the true story of what had happened in *The Old Breed*:

> *Lieutenant Colonel Al Pollock did not get to the wounded man, to the scene of the firing. A runner caught him mid-way to tell him that a native, badly wounded, bayoneted in many places, gurgling news of many Japs on the other side of the stream, had come in through our lines, was back at the command post.*
>
> *Pollock hustled back to his CP, not many yards behind the lines along the riverbank. The native was there. He tried to talk, blood streaming out of his wounds. What the native (he was Sergeant Major Vouza) said must have been something like the letter he wrote to an*

English friend after the war describing the episode:

"Well, I was caughted by the Japs," Vouza wrote, "and one of the Japanese Naval Officer questioned me but I was refuse to answer and I was bayoneted by a long sword twice on my chest, through my throat, and cutted by side of my tongue and I was got up from the enemies and walked through the American front line..."

Pollock listened intently through this recital, and then pressed Vouza for Japanese strength. "Maybe 250, maybe 300," was Vouza's reply. Round figures were enough for Pollock: "By this time I knew something was up." He called the Division to come for Vouza, and while he was on the phone, he could hear firing down by the banks of the river.[3]

Official USMC Photograph

Sir Jacob Charles Vouza

Fortunately, Jacob Vouza survived the ordeal, thanks to the help of the American doctors, many pints of blood, and two weeks of rest. He would live on and lead many more patrols against the Japanese.[4] He received several decorations of valor from the United States, including the Silver Star and the Legion of Merit medal, presented to him personally by Gen. Alexander A. Vandergrift. He was also made an honorary Sergeant Major of the United States Marine Corps. The British awarded him the George Medal and the Police Long Service and Good Conduct Medal. In 1957, he was made a Member of the British Empire, and in 1979 he was knighted by Queen Elizabeth II. He passed away on March 15, 1984, as a hero to the Americans, British, and his native people.[5]

36. ALLIGATOR CREEK

In the early hours of August 21, shortly after the bloodied and half-dead native scout Vouza appeared choking out his warning, fierce combat was about to erupt. Anticipating the enemy, the 1st Marines had dug in along the west branch of the Ilu River.[6] A tidal lagoon infested with crocodiles, it was dubbed "Alligator Creek."[7]

Two days earlier on August 19, the Imperial Japanese Army dispatched Colonel Kiyonao Ichiki and over 900 men to land about twenty-two miles east at Taivu Point.[8] Their mission was to retake the airfield. From there, they marched down the beach and through jungle.

At 0200 on August 21, green flares were shot into the night sky casting a bizarre glow over the lagoon as the Japs stormed over the sandbar near the mouth of the river. They were immediately met with small-arms, machine-gun, and mortar fire by the 2d Battalion, 1st Regiment.[9]

Sgt. Breeding routed us out of our so-called sleep. "Everybody gear up," he hollered. "Let's go! The 1st Marines are getting the shit kicked out of them, and they need our help!"

It was the fastest time I'd ever thrown all my gear together, and all the equipment, ammunition, and tools we had to lug was heavy and awkward. As we hurriedly marched down the beach through the coconut trees, we could hear the sound of the raging battle a short distance away. There was no talking among the troops. All the while I was thinking, will this be it? Will I survive again? As we trudged along my thoughts turned to God in silent prayer.

About a half-mile from the battle, we came to a halt as a runner approached our captain with a message. We were ordered to lay back in reserve until notified to help the 1st Marines.[10] We all sat down and waited for further orders. A short time later, another runner brought back a message the 1st Battalion, 1st Regiment had advanced south down the stream and came up behind enemy, surrounding them.[11] As it turned out, they had the situation well in hand.

From 0400 to daybreak, the battle continued on a smaller scale as the Marines dealt with a few Jap soldiers who'd snuck in behind the lines. Some of the enemy who got through ended up in the tall jungle grass, only to be met with a horrible death by our flame throwers. Later the same morning, our planes took to the air and began strafing the Japs, as the 1st

Marines closed in and obliterated them.[12] The remaining Japanese died from bayonets or hand-to-hand fighting.

There were many acts of bravery during this battle, but one that stands out is the heroic story of Al Schmid, who I mentioned earlier in my story. Al was part of a three-man machine-gun crew. One of the gunners, Private John Rivers, was shot in the face, but stubbornly kept firing rounds, even after he expired; his finger was frozen on the trigger. Corporal Lee Diamond stepped in and took over until his arm got shot up. Noticing his predicament, Al Schmid jumped in and continued mowing down the oncoming Japs. Suddenly, a hand grenade exploded right in front of him, and the hot metal shrapnel burned through both his eyes, blinding him. Word was he grabbed his pistol and continued firing at the advancing enemy.[13]

Other daring stories involved our light tanks. As the armored vehicles heaved across the sand pit into a coconut grove, they knocked down trees, chasing down Japs and running over them.[14] Someone commented later that the tank's track plates looked like raw hamburger. A lot of Marines who witnessed this scenario said it was something that haunted them for the rest of their lives. This was one of the many gruesome calamities that took place on that godforsaken island.

Official USMC Photograph   Critical Past

Left: They were known as the "Mop Up Unit." Two Marines stand guard beside their small tank used as part of the final blow against the Japanese in the Battle of the Tenaru; Right: In the aftermath of battle over 700 Japanese soldiers lie dead, scattered among the sand and surf, August 1942.

The Marines also learned more about Japanese deception from this battle. There were stories of our men searching to help the wounded among the many corpses strewn all over the sand pit.[15] Some of the wounded Japs would play dead and wait for our men to get close. Then, suddenly, they'd roll over and fire their rifles or toss hand grenades. After a few of these incidents our men opened fire on any Jap who made the slightest twitch, until they were sure all of them were dead.[16]

The final reward for us Marines was the suicide of Colonel Kiyonao Ichiki. After the annihilation of his detachment, Ichiki shot himself in the head.[17] I guess he felt completely humiliated after the Marines wiped out all of his troops.

Our company was still at standby when a runner approached with the good news. By dusk, what would later be called the "Battle of the Tenaru" was over. In the end, we lost forty-four Marines, with seventy-one wounded. Half-buried, scattered on the beach, and floating in the surf were 777 dead Jap soldiers.[18] This battle would be a turning point for the Marines against this sneaky and ruthless foe.

37. The Fog of War

The next day, our captain gave us permission to take a quick dip in the ocean. Guards were posted while a sergeant stood ready with a police whistle to warn us of any danger. We romped in the water, acting crazy and cooling off from the scorching sun. It was fun until a black torpedo—about twenty inches in diameter and twenty-four feet long—sped right past us and landed on the beach! We all sloshed onto the sand as an officer spotted a periscope receding into the water. He ordered a half-track 75mm gun to fire at it, but the shells couldn't reach the Jap submarine.

As Hennigan ran up and put his hands on the torpedo, Breeding rushed over and barked, "Get away from that thing, you jughead Yankee!"

Hennigan hated Breeding, slowly backing away with a look of defiance.

We all thought those dumb Japs must have been really desperate to be firing a torpedo at a bunch of naked men in the water. Later on,

"B" company was called to stand by to help the First regiment, if we were needed. We were standing by, fully equipped for battle, just a stone's throw from where the battle near the beach was going on against the Japanese Imperial Marines!

James J. Messina
— 1942 —

DRAWN (1994)

A runner came up to Captain Hawkins, and told him the order was to secure our company. The First regiment had the situation well-in-hand against the Japanese Imperial Marines. We gathered into two colums, and headed back to our bivouac area, ten miles down the beach...

— 1942

command informed us the Jap sub had intended to hit USS *Fomalhaut* but completely missed.[19]

After we wiped out the Ichiki detachment, the fighting switched to the sky for the next week or so. The Japs weren't happy about their defeat at the Tenaru, and a huge sea battle developed as the they continued to build up their naval presence. The "Battle of the Eastern Solomons" took place August 23 - 25. All the fighting was carried out by land and carrier-based aircraft from both the Japanese and Americans.[20]

We were getting intense bombing from Jap aircraft during the day and naval shelling in the dead of night. The bombers would always appear around noon and pound the perimeter surrounding the airfield. Between the shelling and air raids, we were constantly running for cover, never getting much sleep. Our Wildcats had a hard time keeping up with the superior Jap Zeros in the dogfights. But with the help of the coastwatchers warning them on the approach of enemy aircraft positions, our fighters had enough time to climb above the enemy and dive down, unseen, and then shoot them down.[21] It was reported our fighters shot down 21 enemy planes in one day![22]

Division command thought a significant part of the Japanese forces were still concentrated in the Matanikau area. On August 26, the 1st Battalion moved to an assembly position near Kukum beach to prepare for a daylight embarkation.[23] The following morning orders were given to board the Higgins boats and move out to that section of the island.

Three companies of Marines, including mine, fell under the command of Lt. Col. Maxwell.[24] Weighed down with our marching gear, tools, ammunition, canteen of water, and three cans of C-rations, we boarded the landing boats. There must have been twelve or fourteen boatloads of men. This would be our second battle, and I was right smack in the middle of it because I was the head scout. Hennigan was my assistant, and Negri was also in the same squad as me. The other guys from the 1st Platoon were Jonsey, Shuford, Yanno, Johnson, and Salvatore Messina.

Once all the Marines were aboard, the engines revved up. We moved out about fifty yards parallel to the beach and kept that same distance all the way to the Matanikau area. A silent hush hung over the boat as we stared

The Old Breed
Marines in landing craft heading towards the beach, c.1942.

blankly at one another. Some of us were going to die. We felt it in our bones. Some men had their heads bowed in prayer as they made the sign of the cross. Some men smoked, some whispered, some were jotting down a letter to whoever back home, and some checked their weapons for dirt.

Many thoughts were racing through my mind. Is God going to tire of me repeatedly asking him to spare my life in battle? I wanted to live, and I prayed for us to be the victors of the upcoming battle.

Cpl. Podracky addressed our squad. "Follow my orders, and you'll stay alive," he said to the ones nearest him. "Don't panic. Take cover, if possible. Don't bunch up together. Spread out at all times. Don't do anything on your own and get killed. Follow orders, and we may have a chance!"

Podracky made a lot of sense. We followed his orders, along with those from Breeding and 2nd Lt. Guyer.

About two hours went by before the Matanikau River came into view. The area where we'd come ashore was covered with coconut trees and coral mounds protruding out between them. The large coral rocks made a perfect cover for the enemy waiting to attack.

At 0700 the coxswain steered our landing boat onto the beach west of Kokumbona village.[25] As the front end of the Higgins boat dropped down, we rushed out to the protection of the trees, where we found rice still steaming in a large kettle with a fire burning underneath it.[26] The Japs must have heard the boat engines and took off in a hurry.

When all the troops were ashore, our company took up the lead. Sgt. Breeding summoned Hennigan and me to his side. "Okay, scouts, I want you to move out in the direction of the coral rock. Clear?"

"Yeah, sarge," I replied. "We know our job." Then we moved out. Hennigan cautiously followed on my left flank and, boy, was I scared to be about 500 feet in front of the main body. As we moved along and got closer to the coral, we caught a glimpse of a couple of Japs peering at us through the rocks, but they didn't open fire. I motioned to Hennigan to drop back to the rear. We had to report this to Sgt. Breeding.

After I told him about it, Breeding had our whole platoon move out in front of the main body. We were now a scout platoon, and we were about to walk right into a trap. As we proceeded to advance up the slope of a low ridge,[27] about 1,000 yards ahead of the rest of the troops, I felt an intense uneasiness. Hidden behind the huge coral rock, the Japs were setup with machine guns and trench mortars. They waited until our whole platoon was within their aim, and that's when the shit hit the fan.[28]

My position was on the right flank with Jonsey, Cpl. Podracky, Negri, Yanno, Shufford, and Johnson. Hennigan, Sgt. Breeding, and Robert Hilsky were on the left flank. The lieutenant summoned three runners to go back to the main body and report that our platoon was caught in a trap.[29] We needed help quick. At that moment we were outnumbered.

On my left flank, where the trench mortars were heavy, I heard many screams of pain. Men were getting killed or badly wounded. Our position was also under fire from small arms, machine guns, and grenades

As the bullets from the machine guns streamed over my head, I melted into the ground behind one of the coconut trees. I couldn't see the little camouflaged bastards, but I fired in the direction of the coral mound. I kept my head in the dirt as their bullets tore bark off the tree. To my surprise, my head was resting in a nest of red ants, and they were biting the shit out of my face. But it was better than a bullet in the head. I laid there on my belly, firing my rifle while the red ants had a feast on my face.

2nd Lt. Guyer, who carried a .45 automatic pistol, was hollering for us to retreat and reorganize. No one made a move. We were frozen with fear, too close to the Jap positions to retreat now. We wanted to continue fighting and clean them out. Guyer knew it would be suicide. He began waving his .45 at us, saying, "I will start shooting if you gyrenes don't retreat—NOW!" Slowly, one by one, we started to drop back.

The Japs kept lobbing trench mortars at us as we retreated. As a Marine lay in the prone position firing at the enemy, one exploded between his legs and blew him in half. His legs completely gone; he moaned in agonizing pain. Robert Hilsky was closest to him and quickly scooped him up and lifted him across his shoulders. Blood flowed down all over Hilsky as he strained to hold the man up. He began to sprint while dodging bullets and mortar shells.

Suddenly, a blast knocked them both to the ground.[30] Hilsky was dazed and disoriented; the wounded Marine was knocked out, blood still gushing from the stubs of his legs. Robert staggered to his feet. Once again, he heaved the man over his shoulders and pressed on. Just then a Jap popped up from the camouflage and was about to finish Hilsky off, when Negri spotted him and opened up with his BAR, spinning the Jap around like a top. Negri let him have all twenty rounds of his clip. As the bullets hit the Jap's body, blood spurted in every direction.

Right then, a bullet ripped through Guyer's chest, knocking him down.[31] As soon as Negri saw Guyer get hit, he motioned to me to help lift the lieutenant and carry him back to a corpsman. I sprang up, slung my rifle over my shoulder, and picked up Guyer by his feet while Negri held him under the arms. We started running in zigzag fashion, like we were taught back at Camp Lejeune.

Shortly after we started running, Negri got hit in the gut.[32] He froze for a split second, and at that instant our eyes locked. I was terrified as bullets flew past our heads, ripping through the vegetation and ricocheting off trees. The noise of the mortar blasts was deafening, and my ears started to ring. I mouthed to Negri, "Are you okay?" He had a blank stare on his face, and I thought it was the end for all three of us.

Suddenly, Negri yelled, "Go, go, go!" My adrenaline instantly kicked in and we continued zigzagging through a thick cloud of smoke, flying bullets, and debris raining down on us. All the while, loud cries of pain could be heard over the loud clamor of gunfire. It was hell on earth.

We were lucky to get the lieutenant back behind the lines without getting killed ourselves. Once we got Guyer to safety, a corpsman immediately took over, dressing his wound. He was hit one inch from his heart and was very fortunate he didn't meet his fate that day. Meanwhile, Negri completely ignored his own gunshot wound and started heading back to battle. As the corpsman busily worked on Guyer's wound, he glanced at Negri's bloodied shirt and ordered him to stay put. He was shot in the abdomen and acted as if a mosquito had bit him. Negri was a brave Marine and would always be like a brother to me.

Hilsky was panting heavily as he brought our critically wounded comrade back behind the lines. He had completely disregarded his own safety to save his close friend, and his clothes were now completely drenched in his friend's blood. As he gently lifted him off his shoulders and onto the ground, the corpsman ran over and checked the man's pulse. It was too late; the Marine had died in a matter of seconds. It was a big blow to Hilsky, and he cried like a baby. After this battle, he was nervous and shaky all the time. He became a quiet person who hardly ever spoke and never smiled.

Guyer, Hilsky, and Negri were all transferred to the Division Field Hospital.[33] Guyer's wound was critical, and therefore, four days later he was evacuated aboard USS *Zeilin* (APA 3) to Wellington, New Zealand.[34] From there, they would transfer him by train seventeen miles north to U.S.N. Mobile Hospital No. 6.[35] Hilsky spent one day at the Division Field Hospital and was treated for war neurosis before he was released back to active duty.[36] Negri was also evacuated off the island, but we didn't know where they took him.[37] In the fog of war I guess it was hard to keep track everyone. I was sorry my good friend got wounded, but grateful God had sparred his life. The battle would be an experience my whole platoon would never forget.

38. A New Order

Once my wounded comrades were in good hands, I headed back in the direction of the battle to rejoin our company but was halted by Captain William P. Kaempfer of A Company.[38]

"Son," he ordered, "I want you to help put the wounded on that Higgins boat anchored over there. Stay with them until you reach the area of the field hospital area and help unload the men."

"But sir," I responded, "my captain and sergeant won't know where I am, and they might think I'm a deserter."

"You do what I ordered," he replied. "I'll notify 1st Lt. McIlhenny of your duty and whereabouts. Now snap to it and unload the wounded!"

I meekly replied, "Aye, aye, sir." I kept thinking about Sgt. Breeding, the son-of-a-bitch rebel, who would not believe the word of a Yankee. But I had wounded men to attend to, so I brushed it out of my mind.

I approached the wounded lying on the ground. The first Marine I glanced down at had a gaping hole in the side of his face. The corpsman had poured powdered iodine over the hole to stop the bleeding. Large blowflies were buzzing around and trying to get to his wound. I immediately began shooing them away from his face. I tried to comfort him as he moaned in pain.

There were about twelve wounded men to be brought aboard the landing craft. Another PFC and I began carrying the wounded onto the boat. As we lowered the first man on the deck, I felt a sharp pain in my lower back but didn't utter a word. The Japs began launching trench mortars towards our position. Boy, was I scared when the first shell exploded on the starboard side! As it rained shrapnel all over the place, we tried to protect the wounded as best we could. Luckily, no one got hit. God was throwing a shield over our boat. I can't tell you how many times on Guadalcanal I gave thanks to Him for sparing my life.

We kept running back and forth for more wounded until we had the last man aboard. Meanwhile, mortars continued to explode around the landing boats, all of them near misses. The other PFC, the coxswain, and I were the only ones ordered to go back with the wounded. The coxswain revved the engine, and we were on our way back to the safety of the field hospital about fifteen miles down the beach.

As our Higgins boat sped away, shards of metal were pinging the boat, while gushes of water sprayed down on us. We were drenched. It took about an hour to get back to the camp area, and we were relieved to make it back alive. When we hit the beach, ten Marines were on hand to help unload the wounded. Apparently, they had radioed ahead of our arrival. We quickly began carrying the men to open-stake body trucks. Just then, a colonel put his hand on my shoulder and said, "You men did a fine job getting the wounded back here to safety."

"Sir," I began, "my company officers aren't aware I was caught up with this command to assist with the wounded. They may think I'm a deserter. I have to get back to the battle."

He said, "Okay son, don't worry about it. I'm heading in that direction with some of my men. You'll go with me. If anyone gives you any static, you let me know, and I'll come down on them real hard."

I didn't realize it at the time, but the colonel was Leroy P. Hunt, regimental commander of the 5th Marines.

39. RETURN TO BATTLE

There were some other officers and at least fifty Marines with full marching pack that accompanied Col. Hunt during the trek back. Some of these men were from the 11th Marines (artillery) and some from the mess hall. As we marched down to the Higgins boats, the bow ramps lowered and we all quickly scrambled aboard. No one spoke as the two landing craft headed back to the battle scene. By this time, I was thinking my comrades probably thought I had been shot.

Another hour passed before the boats slid to a stop up on the beach. The front ramps dropped down and we cautiously filed out, rifles in hand.

I went along with the wounded by order of another officer of a different Com
The Colonel questioned me about the situation of the battle —
"Tell me everything that happened back there at the Mataniku!"
I rode back with him and his men on a landing craft, and returned to "B" Company. —
— 1942
Jim Messina

DRAWN (1993)

We scanned the perimeter but saw no one. There were no trench mortars to greet us, and the place was quiet. Where was everyone? Why wasn't there the sound of gunfire? We would soon find out.

Col. Hunt took the lead and we followed. I kept glancing up at the trees for snipers. We headed into the coconut trees near the beach and were met by the Capt. Kaempfer.

"The scout platoon that got caught in the trap was ordered to fall back," I overheard the captain say to Hunt.

As they continued talking, I proceeded to look for the rest of my company. I found them a short distance down the beach. I went straight to 1st Lt. McIlhenny and told him my story. He was satisfied and didn't question Capt. Kaempfer about his order.

Sgt. Breeding, however, would be a different story. He hadn't seen me talking to McIlhenny. When he finally did see me, he blustered out, "Well, you fuggin' Yankee deserter! Where in the fuggin' hell ya been?"

"I already talked to McIlhenny, sarge. Go and see him if you want to know." Then I sat down next to Larry and lit up a cigarette. I was too tired and scared from the ordeal to have to answer to the platoon sergeant. Breeding stormed away madder than a hornet, heading straight for the captain. About a half hour later he came back and, to my surprise, made no comment. He glared at me with the genuine look of a die-hard rebel who hated Yankees with a passion. Oh, I knew I would soon get a shit detail from him—no two ways about it!

Col. Hunt looked angry as he conferred with some officers on the beach. Lt. Col. Maxwell was then summoned to the group and was relieved of duty for how poorly he handled our situation. Hunt personally took over command of the 1st Battalion.[39] The men of B Company felt this was payback time after Maxwell had put Capt. Hawkins on report for refusing his death order back at the Matanikau River. Maxwell boarded a Higgins boat and chugged away, and we were glad to see him go.

McIlhenny returned to our company and called for all the NCOs to inform them of a new plan. Afterwards, Breeding gave our platoon the straight dope, while the other platoon sergeants briefed their men. The plan

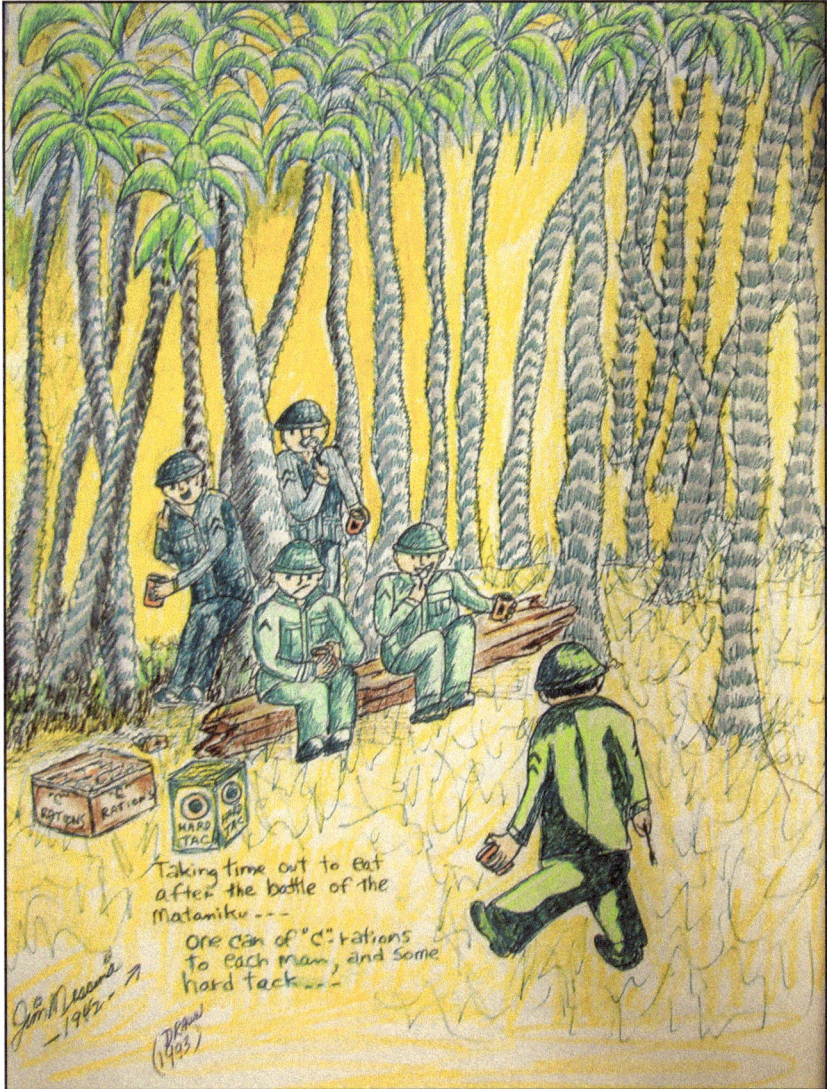

Taking time out to eat after the battle of the Mataniku---

One can of "C" rations to each man, and some hard tack---

was to regroup and surround the perimeter. It would be a surprise attack.

Sgt. Breeding cleared his throat. "Shitheads," he began, "as soon as it gets dark, we'll move out with our company, reconnoiter, and surround the Jap positions. At the very first crack of dawn, we'll attack the little bastards. I want every man to stay in his position and not be moving around in the dark. There will be no talking, no whispering, no smoking. I want complete silence as you get into your positions. Understood?" We all nodded yes as we got ready to move out.

It was dark now, and we had to feel our way through the vegetation using only hand signals to communicate. Our cover was the trees and underbrush. We had to be careful not to snap twigs or branches as we walked. Once our company and the other companies had the perimeter surrounded, we all sat down quietly and opened up a can of C-rations and some hard tack. The last time I had eaten a can of food was early that morning between exploding trench mortars. I was thirsty and starving. I took my canteen full of water and guzzled it. The best C-rations were beans. Unfortunately, I got stuck with corned-beef hash.

Not one Marine uttered a word as we ate our meager meal. We were all fearful the Japs might spot our movements as we surrounded the perimeter and attack us first. There was a deadly stillness that made chills run down my spine. Why did the Japs suddenly stop firing? What were they up to? We were fighting a sneaky, cunning enemy who had lots of experience with jungle fighting.

Throughout the night we caught a few catnaps. We were too afraid to go into a deep sleep, for fear the Japs might infiltrate and stab us in our sleep. It was a black, moonless night, and we were ready for any outbursts or silent movements from the enemy.

Before we knew it, dawn was breaking. The sun's heat penetrated through the trees without warning, and the whole jungle began to steam. Everyone was ready for the onslaught to begin. How many Japs were in the perimeter? Who would live and who would die? No one knew.

Orders came with hand signals to move out as an infantry unit. Our trench mortars opened up on their positions as hand grenades were

Official USMC Photograph

The hot morning sun permeates through the dense jungle growth as steam rises enveloping a Marine encampment, Guadalcanal, c.1942.

thrown. Meanwhile, our machine guns opened up, spraying the whole area. It seemed as though another fierce battle was about to begin again.

But the noise was all coming from our guns. The enemy didn't return any gunfire. They weren't there. During the night, they had retreated.[40] McIlhenny told us the Japs might have thought we were a larger force, outnumbering them, and decided to withdraw. They'd probably regroup with more men and come back soon to fight again.

Since the Japanese had fled, we geared up for our return back to the bivouac area. Command radioed back to Division Headquarters to send out landing boats to retrieve our men for a return trip. In a prior search for survivors, they found a total of twenty dead Japs scattered around the area. We lost five men and had eighteen wounded back there in the trap.[41]

About two hours later, we could hear the engines of the landing boats approaching the shore. We lined up in single-file and headed for the beach. We were tired, beat up, and hungry for a hot meal. When Red Beach came in sight, we were all happy to be back alive. The field cooks had a hot meal of beans, rice, coffee, and hardtack. The hot coffee provided a welcome aroma.

OUR COMPANY OPENED UP WITH TRENCH MORTARS,
HAND GRENADES, and MACHINE-GUN FIRE, and THE
JAPS TOOK OFF and HEADED FOR SAFER GROUNDS —

Official USMC Photograph

A detachment of Marines pauses in a jungle clearing for a brief rest on their way to the front on Guadalcanal, c.1942.

40. TASIMBOKO

The Japs were mad as hell, and the next two weeks brought increased daily attacks. Every day we were getting hit by air and sea. They pummeled the regimental perimeter and airfield with a constant barrage of bombs falling from the sky and shells flying in from Japanese naval vessels. The air-raid siren's wailing moan was nonstop, warning us of a never-ending commotion of explosions.

As the bombs fell through the air, they made a strange sound, like someone ripping a piece of canvas; not the high-pitched whistle I'd heard at the movies when I was a kid. We ran around like chickens without heads, diving into foxholes or whatever shelter we could find. Throughout all the mayhem, orders were continuously dealt out to fortify our positions and unload supplies from our boats.

During the day, the stagnant heat was stifling, and the giant, malaria-carrying mosquitoes would constantly attack us. There were also many other pests in the jungle to put up with, robbing us of our precious sleep. At night, the temperature would drop, making us shiver. Our thin, wool blankets didn't help much in keeping us warm. It was a whole new experience no one cared for. As far as I was concerned, the natives could have this wretched jungle.

Some days our meals consisted of only two tablespoons of rice. The Marines on the island lost a lot of weight and looked like walking skeletons. We had nowhere to bathe except in the muddy Lunga River. After many ships sunk and planes crashed, the water became polluted with oil. All this made for a miserable day-to-day existence. We were dirty, sweaty, hungry, and irritable, but we never lost our spunk in seeking revenge for the American lives lost at Pearl Harbor!

September 6 and 7 were relatively quiet and a welcome break.[1] We finally caught up on some much-needed sleep. But this break made us anxious, and we couldn't help but think the Japs were up to no good. I slept half-awake with my rifle loaded at arm's reach in case of an ambush. At night, I kept waking up thinking the Japs were infiltrating our perimeter. It turned out later I wasn't too far-off in my suspicions.

Under the cover of darkness, the sneaky Imperial Japanese Navy were landing significant reinforcements. They found out quickly their transport ships were too slow and vulnerable for the Allied air superiority during the daylight hours. The enemy decided to use smaller, faster warships (destroyers) to deliver troops, supplies, and equipment to counter the American offensive. This nightly conveyance became known as the "Tokyo Express."[2] Between August 29 and September 11, over 6,000 Jap troops were dispatched and split in two parts. The smaller group concentrated west near Kokumbona; the larger unit off to the east at Taivu Point.[3]

In the early hours of September 8, two of our destroyer transports, USS *McKean* (APD 5) and USS *Manley* (APD 1), accompanied by two patrol boats, USS *YP 346* and USS *YP 298,* former civilian tuna boats, or "yippies" as the Marines called them,[4] anchored near Taivu Point. Lieutenant Colonel Merrit A. Edson and his 1st Raider Battalion splashed onto the beach and advanced west along the coast. After discovering a Japanese supply base at the Tasimboko Village, he attacked. His attachment of the 1st Parachute Battalion, also known as Paramarines or Marine paratroopers, came ashore in a second wave later that morning. After this clash, the enemy took off retreating further into the jungle.[5] The Marines found large amounts of food, guns, ammo, and medical supplies. Edson also seized important documents revealing information the Japs were advancing southwest behind our perimeter.[6] The price paid for this cache was two Marines killed and six wounded. The Japanese lost twenty-seven men in the encounter.[7]

Although the skirmish that took place at Tasimboko was on a small scale, the information obtained from the documents proved vital to the entire campaign. The upcoming onslaught that ensued in the following days would go down in history as one of the most famous and bloody conflicts waged at Guadalcanal. Without the information Lt. Col. Edson had captured, the Allied Forces may have lost the crucial battle to the Japanese, and possibly the war.[8]

41. A Gruesome Discovery

The next morning at 0500 hours, we were abruptly woken out of our sleep to go out on patrol. We had to be ready to move out into the jungle by 0530. Our breakfast consisted of a can of C-rations and a cup of purified water. Living in the jungle denied us the breakfast we would get aboard a ship or in our military camps back home. It was always rice or cold food out of a can.

We were ordered to saddle-up our heavy marching gear, plus entrenching tools, and two cans of C-rations. Sgt. Breeding came out and gave the hand signal to move out and begin our trek, southwest through the jungle. Once in the jungle, there was complete silence in the ranks. Everyone used hand signals for the safety of the patrol.

As we approached the banks of the Lunga River, the order was given to cross. We held our rifles overhead to keep them dry. Progress was slow as we waded through the chest-deep water. Upon reaching the opposite shore, Sgt. Breeding summoned Hennigan and me to his side. In a low growl he ordered, "Scouts out!"

Hennigan and I were both nervous, having to enter the foreboding jungle ahead of our platoon. In many spots it seemed impenetrable. The twisted vines on the ground slowed us down, and it was easy to trip if you weren't careful. Our bayonets were used to hack through the thick mass of vegetation. We sweated profusely, our clothes sticking to our skin. To top it off, the half-inch long mosquitoes made us irritable. These pests were very annoying to fight off as we trudged along.

There were many sounds in the jungle, mostly from all different kinds of birds overhead. The loudest were the cockatoos, jungle crows, and myna birds. Their constant chatter went on all day long, from sunrise to sunset. One species made a low, groaning sound. Of all the birds chattering throughout the day, this one in particular gave me the creeps because it sounded as if someone was dying. I found out later this bird was the Buff-headed Coucal—a large black bird with a bright, yellow head.[9]

Eventually, we found a trail another squad cleared earlier. As the scouts, we walked about fifty feet in front of our platoon. Hennigan was on my left as we scanned the trees and underbrush, searching for the slightest movement. The fear of Japs lying in wait, ready to kill you, was always present. No one liked patrol duty, but every platoon had to take their turn. We were moving slowly on the alert every second, checking the trees for snipers and the dense vegetation for booby traps.

At one point, the jungle suddenly became quiet. It was a heart-stopper, not knowing what was happening. Maybe there were Japs up ahead, causing the birds to stop their calls. I raised my hand up, signaling the platoon to come to a halt. We scanned the perimeter and saw nothing. It was really scary. Were we gonna to die in a Nip trap?

The platoon froze at the ready, waiting to hear "Banzai!" For two whole minutes nothing happened. Suddenly, the birds began singing again and the jungle was back to normal. I signaled to move out again. To this

Official USMC Photograph

*A Marine patrol moves stealthily among the coconut trees
on a beach at Guadalcanal, c.1942.*

day, no one knows the mystery of what caused the entire jungle to pause. Not even the officers could figure it out.

We trekked through the jungle at least two miles and were sweaty, tired, and thirsty. By this time, we didn't encounter the enemy, but we were ordered to continue forward on the patrol. I thought, where are all the Jap positions? Then Hennigan and I noticed some movement about fifty feet ahead of us. We both dropped back to report to Sgt. Breeding. I whispered to him there might be something up ahead. He ordered us to take cover on both sides of the jungle trail. He also motioned not to open up with any gunfire if the Japs came into view and to stay concealed. The only time a patrol was supposed to fight was if the enemy spotted us first.

The platoon stayed perfectly still. It was a Japanese unit on patrol, doing the same thing we were. We stayed very still and hidden but also at the ready. The huge mosquitoes were biting us, but we didn't flinch, fearing exposing ourselves to the enemy. Once the Japs were out of sight, Breeding gave a hand signal to move out in the opposite direction of the Jap patrol. We hacked our way through the jungle for about another three miles.

There were no other signs of Jap positions camped anywhere in the perimeter. Sgt. Breeding signaled us to turn around towards the direction of our bivouac area. He didn't want to run into the Jap patrol, so he ordered a different route as a precaution to make it safely back to our camp. We moved silently among the coconut trees along the beach.

We continued to advance, with no talking in the ranks. About twenty minutes later, we encountered an ungodly sight. Hennigan signaled us to halt. He was in the lead and beckoned our sergeant to see what he discovered. Off to one side of the path, under a coconut tree, he found a shriveled-up female body that had turned completely black. She had been dead for a long time. There were many bayonet wounds on her body, and she had a large Rosary dangling around her neck. She was a nun, and her habit was bunched up next to her.

Later, we heard the story about how the nun ended up in the jungle. Before the Japanese came to the island, two priests and three nuns from the Society of Mary were stationed at the Ruavatu Catholic Mission between the perimeter and Aola.[10] They came to teach the natives the Word of God. All had gone well with teaching the bushy-haired natives. They loved the missionaries, and most wore a religious pendant, or scapular, as a symbol they were proud Catholics.

These religious martyrs met their fate at the hands of the Japanese, who tortured and killed them. The native Chief Vouza swore revenge for these unspeakable acts. The natives were very friendly with the Americans but hostile towards the Japanese. They were cunning and moved very quietly as they struck out at their enemy—the Japanese soldier.

Sgt. Breeding ordered us to dig a hole so we could give the nun a decent burial. Afterward, one of our NCOs said a prayer over her grave. All of the Catholics ended the ceremony with the sign of the cross. This horrific scene would haunt me for the rest of my life.

After the nun's burial, we continued advancing through the jungle and came upon a small stream of stagnant water. We all were parched and quickly filled our canteens. Breeding yelled out, "Don't drink that water, you knuckleheads!" Back at camp, before we went out on patrol, halazone tablets had been distributed to purify the river water.[11] Everyone was so thirsty, we completely forgot about this precaution. So, we plopped a few tablets into our canteens but had to wait a half hour for the water to become purified. It seemed like an eternity! Everyone guzzled the water, and not one of us became ill.

The Lunga River came into view after our long trek. Our strength had been completely drained as we waded slowly across the river, finally making it back to the bivouac area. In my pup tent, I lay down exhausted, and soon fell into a deep sleep. Not long afterward, I woke up suddenly after having a nightmare about the Japs attacking and raping the nun.

42. The Ridge

The main objective after capturing the airstrip was to finish construction the Japanese had begun. This small landing strip became the main focal point of the entire Guadalcanal campaign. The 1st Pioneer Battalion started the job using captured Japanese construction equipment,[12] consisting of steamrollers, tractors, cement mixers, automobiles, and a large fleet of trucks. There were also bicycles, drums of gasoline, bags of cement, tar paper, and many other supplies. We all gestured by bowing our heads, mockingly thanking the emperor of Japan for his kind gifts.

Marine command named the airfield Henderson Field after Major Lofton R. Henderson, a naval aviator hero of the Marine Corps who had been killed in action at the Battle of Midway. He was the first Marine aviator to die attacking the Japanese carrier forces.[13]

Once the Seabees' 6th Naval Construction Battalion (NCB) of 357 men arrived on September 1, they were put in charge of completing and maintaining the integrity of the airstrip.[14] They brought their own equipment and utilized the captured machinery to lay down a portable runway of perforated steel mats, or Marston mats, which interlocked together.[15] After completion, the runway was 3,778 feet long, running east to west.[16] On September 9, they completed a second runway of tamped-down sod running 4,600 feet long, a mile east of Henderson, naming it "Fighter One." The Marine fighter squadrons began using the airstrip, renaming it "Bomber Field No. 1."[17] The allied air force converging on Guadalcanal became known as the "Cactus Air Force."[18]

There were many ridges and ravines surrounding Henderson Field. About a mile south of the airfield stood a very high ridge where Gen. Vandegrift had decided to build his new CP. It quickly became a prime target of the high-flying Japanese bombers. This ridge was very steep. The Lunga River was near the base of its west slope, and the Tenaru River (Alligator Creek) was off to the east. It also had a few smaller spurs extending out from both sides of the main spine. From the air, it looked like a large insect with legs. The Japanese called it the "centipede."[19]

Edson suspected the enemy had more troops than he previously assumed and had planned to attack this high ridge based on the captured documents from the raid at Tasimboko. He and Colonel Gerald Thomas, Vandegrift's operations officer, presented their theory to the commander the day after the raid. Their suspicions were further verified by Capt. Clemens and his scouts when they reported columns of Jap soldiers moving in a southwesterly direction.[20] Vandegrift believed they were on to something and decided to move his CP under a smaller spur of the ridge.[21]

The next day, Edson moved his Raiders to the forward spur of the high ridge near the Lunga River, and the Parachutists were positioned on one of the smaller, forward spurs. Vandegrift positioned the 2d Battalion, 5th Marines, south of the airfield in reserve, and moved the 1st Battalion, 1st Marines behind them as a backup.[22] We knew there was going to be some action, but we never could have imagined the carnage about to unfold.

The Raiders were a special unit trained to fight the crafty Japs at their own game. Back in March 1942, the most experienced officers and men had been hand-picked from our 1st Battalion, 5th Regiment, by Edson himself to create the Raiders elite force.[23] They were considered the United States' first special operations forces created to engage in combat during WWII.[24]

At noon on September 11, fierce dogfights broke out between a dozen of our Wildcats and a squadron of twenty-seven Bettys and fifteen Zeros.[25]

Louie the Louse appeared at midnight, dropping his bright flares and casting an unearthly green glow over the area. Shortly afterwards, off in the distance, we heard loud booms from the large guns of Jap ships. For the next two hours, shells came flying in and exploding all around the perimeter. The next morning, we discovered an annex of the Division Field Hospital had been hit, and it was a bloody mess. Sadly, some of our wounded comrades had met their fate.[26]

Twenty-six Japanese bombers appeared once more at 40,000 feet the next day. The "Twelve O'clock Special" was back to bust up Henderson Field.[27] Al, Larry, Yanno, S. A. Messina, and myself were swimming in the Lunga River, not far from our bivouac area, when a loud voice rang out: "Condition Yellow!" We knew this meant Jap bombers were heading towards the island. Everyone grabbed their clothes and headed for the coconut trees.

Running frantically, we ran smack into a large air-raid shelter made of logs and sandbags, which also served as a communication center. As we cautiously entered, the radio men were surprised to see us. They told us to sit down anywhere and stay as long as we needed. There was plenty of room in the shelter. It was about thirty feet long, eight feet wide, and loaded with equipment. There were four Marines on duty. One of them was adjusting the knobs of a shortwave radio, and he tuned in "Fibber McGee and Molly," a radio comedy series from America. Listening to the comedians tell their jokes, we all bust out laughing. It reminded all of us of being back home.

Outside the shelter, we heard another voice ring out again: "CONDITION RED!" Now, the bombers were directly overhead. We could hear the low drone of the big bombers' engines above us, almost sounding like they were hesitating. The bombs began to fall, making the strange, ripping-canvas noise, as they cut through the atmosphere. This sound was implanted in my brain and it was very scary.

We were sitting directly in the target area. I began to silently pray, as I could see the fear on the faces of each man around me. The blasts of the bombs shook the ground under us. Each concussion loosened the logs more and more, and sand seeped down all over us. One of the explosions was about fifty yards from the air-raid shelter. There was a radio shack on this spot, and it received a direct hit.[28]

When the air raid was over and the smoke cleared, we emerged from the shelter. The scene before our eyes was very sad. Debris was scattered everywhere, and there was no trace of the two men who were in the radio shack, only tiny pieces of flesh splattered all over the area. Markers were placed on this spot to indicate two men had been killed.

It had been a close call for all of us. Fortunately, my prayers had been answered. For about ten minutes, we all stood in silence gazing at the destruction. We looked at each other with great sadness, thankful it wasn't us this time. Then we turned and walked away.

Back at our bivouac, we sat around discussing the radio shack getting blown up. Then the subject turned to home. How were the people of the United States taking the war? How was the war going in Europe? We knew lots of our WWI veterans were working as air-raid wardens. They'd help in directing people to shelters if the U. S. was attacked. Many women were working long hours in steel mills and factories to keep us supplied with the necessary armaments we needed. Citizens also invested in war bonds, lending our government the money needed for the war effort. The fighting men knew our people back home were doing their share to help win the war.

That night, like clockwork, Louie droned over us releasing his green blaze of light in the night sky. Shortly afterwards, naval shelling started pounding us again, then stopped abruptly. This time it was followed by a ferocious ground assault. The Japs were famous for nighttime infiltration when they were concealed by the cover of darkness. They were a cunning, well-camouflaged enemy, and the Marines would fight hard to win this battle.

One of our officers told us a large group of Jap soldiers was moving towards the Raiders up on the ridge.[29] Flares shot into the sky to illuminate the battle area. Then, all of a sudden, the sounds of battle erupted ahead of us. The enemy was surprised when the Marines on the ridge opened fire on them. The Japs charged up the ridge hollering "Banzai," only to be mowed down with our machine guns, BARs, trench mortars, and grenades.

The loud pops of gunfire and shells exploding, and the constant rat-a-tat-tat of machine guns was ear-splitting. Over the clamor of combat, you could hear screams in the night from both the American and Japanese men who'd been wounded by bullets or shrapnel. The confusion of battle was extremely exhausting, and I wondered if it would ever end.

One of the Raiders commented later on how frightening it was to see so many faces of the enemy advancing in a freakish glow of light. Streaks of orange light from the tracer bullets crisscrossed through the night, trying to find their mark, as grenades were thrown in the Jap's positions. There were also bright bursts of light from mortar explosions.

Our battalion was ordered to hold in a reserve position and await orders to move into battle. We all took cover, and I was lucky to find a foxhole among the trees. There were many holes throughout the perimeter that had been previously dug, and it was easy to find a hideout. The thick smoke from guns and mortars clung to the moist air, making it difficult to breathe. I was frightened as I peered out through the smog.

Earlier that day, a Marine from A Company showed me a trick he used in combat, where he placed a small white piece of paper in the sight of his rifle. In night fighting, he told me, when you could only make out the dark shapes, aim at the white paper in the direction of the enemy. I thought of this as I cocked and loaded my rifle, but I was still scared as hell. I began praying to God again to spare me and the rest of our division so we could return home in one piece and be back with our families. Images of Mom and Pop flashed in my mind. After the war, my sisters told me they were all worried for my life. Mom prayed the Rosary every day, and everyone was glued to the radio listening for the progress of the Marines on Guadalcanal.

As the battle raged on, we couldn't make out the orders Sgt. Breeding was trying to give us over the deafening noise. The only thing he could do was send out runners to each platoon. When a runner came crawling to our positions, we were ordered to drop back. We retreated, moving silently in single file, communicating only with hand-signals.

We fell back to the Lunga River and waded across, withdrawing into the jungle. A runner came up to Captain McIlhenny with an order for us to hold our present position. Our job was to protect the Marines on the ridge from any other Japanese forces attempting to come up behind the main line of resistance (MLR). I didn't feel right about this order. The boys on the ridge were getting their asses kicked, and I thought we should've been moved up to help them. I figured, in the fog of war, sometimes the commanding officers get confused when giving orders.

The battle lasted until the first hint of dawn, and it ended as quickly as it began. The enemy withdrew, disappearing into the canopy of the thick jungle, only to regroup and fight again the next night. Edson knew they'd be back. Later the same day, he fortified his defenses on the ridge. In addition, Gen. Vandegrift ordered the 2d Battalion, 5th Marines to move directly behind Edson's troops as reinforcements.[30]

At dusk on September 13, over 3,000 Japanese troops amassed, confronting 830 Marines. A short time later, heavy Japanese naval shelling pounded the ridge. Fierce combat continued throughout the night. By mid-afternoon on September 14, the Japs once again retreated back into the jungle.[31] This time, however, they did not return, and the battle finally ended.

It wasn't all Japanese losses, though. We also lost many men in this conflict, and bodies were strewn out on both sides of the ridge's spine. Of the combined American units engaged in this battle, 96 were killed or missing, with 222 wounded. The Japanese suffered 708 killed, and 506 wounded.[32] The big task of removing dead Marines from the steep slope for burial had begun. We moved silently among our slain comrades, and there were tears on the faces of many of the Marines as the dead soldiers were lifted onto the trucks.

Our fallen warriors were taken to an open area that had been cleared among the tall coconut trees. This would be their permanent resting place on Guadalcanal, lined with many wooden crosses. Bulldozers pushed most of the Japanese dead into mass graves; others were burned.[33] The stubborn, hard-fighting little bastards' graves would be the large shell holes their own ships or bombers made.

During our time on the island there were a number of clashes that took place on this ridge because it was strategic to the airfield. Following this bloodiest of battles between September 12 and 14, the ridge was given many names: "Edson's Ridge," "Bloody Knob," or "Bloody Ridge." We just called it "The Ridge."

43. BAD LUCK MARINE

The day after the ferocious battle on the ridge, eighteen enemy bombers struck again in the afternoon, but there was little damage to our bivouac. The 1st and 3d Battalions were sent out on patrol south and west of the perimeter.[34] As we trudged through the steamy jungle, machine-gun fire opened up on us. I was scrambling to find cover when someone yanked me from behind by the belt and into a muddy foxhole. Turns out it was my buddy S. A. Messina! He was always looking out for me. It must have been a small enemy unit, because they stopped firing the moment we hit back with mortars. We took a few prisoners, and they looked pretty beat up.[35] I got the feeling they were almost happy to be captured, knowing they would get something to eat. We thought we had it bad, but these Japs looked half-starved and completely battered. Word was they had run out of food on the ridge two days ago. We handed them over to command for interrogation after returning to camp.

The next day, we continued working on consolidating our positions. After running out of barbed wire, Breeding instructed us to erect large poles of bamboo in a crisscross fashion. We cut the ends of each pole at an angle to make them razor sharp, creating a lethal defense obstacle called a cheval de frise. He told us this type of defense measure dated all the way back to medieval times.[36] It took all day to complete this chore. Completely exhausted, we returned to our bivouac area and were surprised to hear about the orders given. We were told not to load our rifles that night until we got the order. I thought to myself, I'm not going to be caught with an empty rifle, if the Japs attack our position tonight.

At about 2100 I loaded my rifle and, damn it, as I closed the bolt, my little finger hit the trigger, firing off a round. Everyone jumped out of

Official USMC Photographs

Top: Marines firing a .50 caliber machine gun west of the Matanikau River;
Bottom: Marine patrol with Japanese prisoner, Guadalcanal, c.1942.

their pup tents and grabbed their weapons, thinking the Japs had begun to infiltrate. Fortunately, the round went into the ground, where my muzzle was pointing.

Sgt. Breeding came up in a hurry. "Who the fugg fired their rifle?"

I answered, "It was me, sarge."

He snarled. "What the fugg were your orders?"

"I wasn't going to wait to the last minute!" I replied.

"Gimme the fuggin' rifle and go see the captain!" He snatched my rifle and ordered me towards the CP. I didn't know the password, though, and had to ask Breeding what it was. "Just go see the captain," he growled. "I ain't tellin' you the password, and I hope his sentry guns you down!" Then he stormed off ranting and raving.

As I started for the CP, my corporal said, "Honolulu, Jim."

"Thanks, Podracky," I said, relieved. Passwords usually had Ls in them because the Japs couldn't pronounce this letter correctly. For example, the Japanese would say, "Honoruru." This was a tactic the Marines used at night to ensure the person was an American.

I slowly felt my way down the ravine and then climbed up to the CP on the opposite ridge, cautiously edging through the thick underbrush and straining my eyes to see in the black of night. Suddenly, I heard the click of a round going into the chamber of a rifle. "Halt! Who goes there?"

"Messina, Baker Company," I replied. "I need to see Capt. McIlhenny."

"What's the password?" the sentry barked.

"Honolulu."

"Advance and be recognized." After the sentry checked my ID, he let me pass.

Approaching the CP, I could see Capt. McIlhenny's silhouette framed against the night sky through the light in his tent. He was scanning the jungle for enemy infiltration. As I got nearer to him, my shoe snapped a twig, and he reached for his side arm. I spoke out: "It's Messina, sir!"

He said, "Okay, come forward son. What's your problem?"

"Sgt. Breeding sent me."

"Yes, I know about the round you let off. He told me about it over the field phone. What do you have to say for yourself, son?"

"Well, sir," I began, "I knew about the orders, but I was afraid of being caught by surprise with an unloaded rifle. I'm on edge with these jungle nights, and I'm afraid to fall asleep, always thinking about getting a bayonet in my back!"

"Enough reason," the captain replied. "I'm afraid too. I don't want to die, either." Then the captain talked about his personal life, his career as an officer, and much more. I was surprised to hear him going on and on about these things. I felt at ease, but at the same time wondered what my discipline would be.

He continued. "An officer has a lonely life on the battlefield, especially black nights like this. He wants his men to like him, but at the same time he has to rule with an iron fist. I was in the Virginia National Guard until I joined the Marine Corps.[37] As a field officer, life isn't easy. Many decisions need to be made to try to protect the men under you, and I value every one of my Marines the same as I value my own life. I'm not going to punish you. I know what you're feeling. Every man feels what you feel. Don't repeat this Messina but know my own .45 automatic is always loaded. Sometimes orders don't make sense, and this is one of those times." He gave me a nod as if to say, don't worry about what happened, go back to your pup tent.

"Captain," I asked, "what about my rifle? Sgt. Breeding said he wasn't going to give it back, and I would have to fight with only my bayonet!"

"Tell Breeding I said to return it to you. The incident is forgotten."

When I returned to bivouac, Breeding had a big, triumphant smile on his face. He thought I got some severe punishment.

As I approached him, I said, "Captain said to return my rifle, sarge."

"Like hell I will," he stammered, and then he stomped away.

I was preparing to enter my tent for another sleepless night when, all of a sudden, a rifle was thrown to the ground on my right side. "Here's your fuggin' rifle, Yankee! Lucky for you the captain likes Yankees!" Then, Breeding stormed off, cussing all Yankees.

As I crawled into my tent to lay down, I clutched my rifle for dear life. Cpl. Podracky and I shared this pup tent, and I thanked him again for telling me the password. He was one hell of a nice guy, and I liked him a lot. I was so scared, thinking I might get a knife or a bayonet in me, knowing the Japs liked to infiltrate under the cover of darkness. Finally, I fell asleep, completely exhausted.

About a half-hour later, I awoke with a stinging pain on my face and my right hand. I was moaning in agony.

Podracky cupped his flashlight and shined it on me. "What the hell?" were his first words as the light hit me. "Your face is all swelled up and look at your hand!" My face was disfigured from my lips to the side of my cheek, and my hand was a big as a boxing glove! "Something bit you," Podracky said. Then he aimed the flashlight to the ground next to my body and found a tiny blue-and-red spider with three stingers protruding from its head. It was smaller than a dime. He immediately crushed it with his flashlight, fearing it would bite him too.

Cpl. Podracky sprang up and made a beeline for Breeding's tent to report this incident. The-son of a bitch took his time coming over to check me out.

"Well, Yankee Messina," said Breeding, "I see the Japs got to you and injected some poison! Ha, ha!"

Podracky clenched his fists, wanting to tear into him, but he kept his cool. "Hey, sarge, you gonna get on the radio for help, or do I have to?"

"Yeah, yeah Pod, I'm going over to the radio man now," replied Breeding, busting out with laughter. At that moment, I was ready to put another round in my rifle and let him have it, once and for all. The sad part of it was, we needed Breeding to guide us in battle. He was very good with the logistics of deployment and troop movement. There were many men in our company who wanted to shoot him, but knew we needed him.

Breeding took his time calling regimental headquarters, who sent a jeep with a doctor. The long wait was unbearable, as my hand and face throbbed with pain. The jeep finally showed up two-and-a-half hours later. Upon their arrival, the driver told Breeding they had a flat tire, which had to be changed in the dark. Plus, they were halted a few times by the Marine sentries on guard. After Podracky explained what the spider looked like, the doctor checked me out and told me the bite wasn't fatal. He administered a shot of morphine, and the pain disappeared immediately.

The doctor gave our corpsman extra morphine and instructed him to give me a shot every six hours. I settled down and dozed off, not a worry about Japs in my mind. It seemed like I slept for two days, but it was only a matter of a few hours. When the shot wore off, I was in agonizing pain again, and it seemed like forever before the corpsman gave me the next shot of morphine. After three days, my hand and face returned to normal size.

44. Expanding the Perimeter

On September 18, Admiral Richmond Kelly Turner's five transports appeared on the horizon carrying the 7th Marine Regiment of our Division, reinforced with the 1st Battalion, 11th Marines from Samoa.[38] He kept his promise to Gen. Vandegrift that he would bring more reinforcements to Guadalcanal.[39] A separate convoy of three transports brought in more vehicles, fuel, ammo, and rations. We were so relieved to have over 4,000 additional Marines and much-needed supplies come ashore and join our forces.[40]

Ten of us went down to the beach to watch them land. They charged onto the beach with fixed bayonets, ready and eager to fight. As soon as they saw a group of us standing there to greet them, instead of the enemy, they felt silly. The first few days on the island, the 7th Marines would be doing the same routine our other units had been doing all along. They'd have to begin patrolling the jungle, lay barbed wire, dig foxholes, put up with snipers, follow orders, and perform many different duties. They seemed like a great, highly trained bunch of guys, and we were glad to have them here to help us win upcoming battles on Guadalcanal.

The ships delivering the 7th Marines also took many of our wounded soldiers back out to the Allied base in Espiritu Santo, part of the New Hebrides Islands.[41] Most of them were from the 1st Parachute Division,[42] and they hadn't been receiving proper care at the Division Field Hospital. Jonsey told me after getting hit with shrapnel, when he was laid up there, they didn't have enough medical supplies to keep up with all the incoming wounded.

Official USMC Photograph

A Marine is loaded on a landing barge to be taken to a hospital ship lying off shore after being wounded in the fighting on the island of Guadalcanal, c.1942.

A few days before they landed, Japanese submarines were prowling the waters in the path of Turner's convoy (Task Force 65), carrying the 7th Marines. In a surprise attack, torpedoes struck the covering force hitting the aircraft carrier USS *Wasp*, battleship USS *North Carolina*, and destroyer USS *O'Brien* (DD 415). The *Wasp* was so badly damaged she eventually had to be scuttled by our Navy. Of the seventy-one aircraft on this huge carrier, forty-five of them were lost. This left our Navy with only one aircraft carrier, USS *Hornet* (CV 8), to face six Japanese carriers in the South Pacific. The severely impaired *North Carolina* and *O'Brien* were forced to leave the area for repairs.[43]

As Japanese submarines attacked the American convoy on the night of September 15-16, seven of their destroyers delivered 1,000 more men while bombing our perimeter. Two nights later, they delivered 170 men and more equipment.[44]

In the early morning hours of September 19, our perimeter was hit again by shells from Japanese warships. By this time, the 5th Marines were no strangers to the endless shelling attacks in the middle of the night. But the 7th Marines, bivouacked in our area, had not experienced the Japs' dirty tactics. Sadly, in this bombardment they lost two of their men and had four wounded.[45]

Around this time Gen. Vandegrift made some changes in command throughout the Division. He decided to replace Col. Hunt, commander of the 5th Marines, with Lt. Col. Edson, commander of the 1st Raider Battalion.[46] The troops in my regiment seemed to like this change in command, on account of Edson's conquest at Bloody Ridge.

During the remainder of September, Gen. Vandegrift extended our lines and established an inner-ground defense ring around the perimeter of the airfield.[47] The ring was divided into ten sub-sectors from Alligator Creek stretching to ridges west of the Lunga River. My regiment was part of seven sectors that faced inland and were assigned two for each regiment.[48] The 5th Marines defended Sector's Three and Four, with a ridge on our left flank and reinforced support defense for the Pioneer Battalion at Sector Two.[49]

Within a few days, our lines were extended further west, and my battalion (1-5) was ordered to advance to a ridge beyond where we were positioned at the time.[50] The next day two companies from the 2d Battalion, 5th Marines (2-5), left to patrol the ridges southwest of my battalion's position and caught a glimpse of a small group of Japs but didn't confront them.[51]'

On September 24, an observation post (OP) was established near my battalion's position.[52] Gen. Vandegrift decided to expand the perimeter by utilizing the 1st Battalion, 7th Marines (1-7), commanded by Colonel Lewis "Chesty" Puller, ordering them to move inland then patrol north past the Mount Austen,[53] a grassy mound rising above the jungle about 1,200 feet.[54] Later that same day, Puller's battalion clashed with Japanese troops encamped on the Austen's slopes, and an intense firefight broke out, killing seven Marines and wounding twenty-five.[55]

For the next three days, another battle at the Matanikau River ensued. Our 2d Battalion (2-5), and 1st Raider Battalion joined the 7th Marines to beat back the Japs, but to no avail. By September 27, the 7th Marines were ambushed and trapped inland. One of our destroyers, USS *Ballard* (DD 660), shelled the area while a Marine SBD swooped down strafing with machine-gun fire. The 7th Marines fought their way to the beach where a force of landing craft moved in to rescue them. As the boats returned to our perimeter, the Raiders and 5th Marines retreated. In all, 60 Marines were lost and 100 left wounded.[56]

One morning, my battalion was ordered on patrol again, this time passing the OP to reconnoiter near Mount Austen.[57] On our way back through the forbidden jungle, we heard a loud scream in the ranks. A Marine from another platoon had gotten caught in a Jap booby trap. It was set up like a bear trap, made of sharp pointed bamboo sticks. As he stepped into the hidden trap, it snapped up, the sharp tips piercing his ankle. A corpsman rushed up, tied a tourniquet around his leg, and gave the Marine a shot of morphine. Then he removed the bamboo stakes. His comrades rigged a makeshift stretcher made of bamboo, twine, and palm leaves to carry him. It was slow progress getting this guy back to regimental sickbay. We finally arrived at bivouac, all dog-tired.

Our captain gave the motor transport officer an order to bring some captured Japanese beer to our company. The officers had kept a stash for themselves. He told us we'd earned it and that he had a hankering for a beer himself.

The beer was warm but still tasted good. It sure was better than the river water we were forced to drink. A lot of the Marines weren't satisfied with drinking only beer. The boozehounds also wanted sake, which some had hidden away in their foxholes. They fetched the rice alcohol, drank it, and got pie-eyed drunk. Two gung-ho Marines grabbed their rifles and headed into the jungle saying they were gonna kill some Japs. Cpl. Podracky informed Sgt. Breeding about the two drunk Marines, and the sergeant sent out six men to find them. They were brought back with no trouble and sent to their pup tents. They sang "God Bless America" as they flopped down into their tents and passed out.

Later on, we heard the engines of one Wildcat after another taking off from Henderson Field, and we wondered was going on. We found out later thirty-four of them rushed to intercept twenty-five Jap Bettys and forty Zeros headed for Guadalcanal. It turned out to be one of the largest air battles during our time on the island. Our pilots brought down seven Japanese aircraft and damaged many others. Meanwhile, all of the American Allied planes returned to the airfield with only minor damage.[58]

45. FIGHTING INTENSIFIES

The following week we hacked our way through the tangled vegetation, cutting trails to make getting through the hot jungle a little easier.[59] By then we were scrawny and weak, which made this arduous task more difficult.

On October 1, our comrade PFC Robert Joseph Hilsky was promoted to corporal by Sgt. Breeding.[60] Two days later Gen. Vandegrift presented him with the Navy Cross for "extraordinary heroism" in connection with military operations against the enemy at Kokumbona on August 27, 1942.[61] Vandegrift took a few moments to recite the actions Corporal Robert Joseph Hilsky had taken, jeopardizing his own life to save another. It was a proud moment for the men of Baker Company. Robert stood there stoically as the commander pinned the medal on his shirt. He didn't appreciate the great honor bestowed upon him. Robert always kept to himself and barely talked to anyone. We knew how much he missed his good friend and was sad he couldn't save his life. After receiving the award, Robert never mentioned the medal again and kept it locked up in his seabag.

The month passed with increased fighting on land, sea, and in the air. There was yet another major action at the Matanikau River between October 6-9 involving the 5th Marines (minus my 1st Battalion), a Scout-Sniper detachment, 3d Battalion, 2d Marines, and 7th Marines (minus the 3d Battalion).[62] As the rest of my regiment fought in this battle, my battalion continued to hold and defend Sector's Three and Four of the defense perimeter near the Matanikau.[63]

On October 7, five Japanese destroyers delivered 600 more men, along with ammo and provisions, to Tassafaronga Point, northwest of Point Cruz.[64] The next day, ice-cold rain was coming down so hard it halted the forward progress of our troops, but the fighting continued.[65] This time the Marine forces successfully crossed the river attacking the Japs, wreaking havoc on their troops and causing heavy casualties. The Japs lost over 690 men, forcing them to retreat further into the jungle. We lost sixty-five men, with 125 wounded.[66]

October 11-12 saw the Battle of Cape Esperance unfold. This event happened with a surprise attack as our Navy intercepted Japanese ships bringing troops and supplies to the island. As a result of this action, we threw a wrench into the nightly runs of Japanese reinforcements. In this major sea battle, we lost two cruisers and one destroyer, with 163 men killed and 125 wounded. The Japs had three destroyers and one heavy cruiser sunk and 454 killed. Plus, we took 111 prisoners.[67] Then, on October 12, four waves of Jap bombers and Zeros attacked the perimeter for two solid hours.[68]

The morning of October 13, Turner's transports, USS *Zeilin* and USS *McCawley* (APA 4), anchored off Lunga Point and delivered over 3,000 more men from the 164th Infantry of the Americal Division, 1st Marine Air Wing, and additional Marine replacements.[69] Along with these fresh troops, badly needed rations, supplies, fuel, and vehicles were brought ashore. As the soldiers were landing, Jap planes began dropping bombs and, at the same time, shells were fired from their 150mm Howitzers, causing considerable damage to the airfield.[70] With these additional reinforcements, a Division Operation order reorganized the perimeter into five regimental sectors, strengthening forces by one regiment west of Lunga Point.[71] The 5th Marines would defend Sector Five near a high ridge.[72]

That same day, during all the commotion, I needed a cigarette to calm me down, but I'd lost my matches. I ran around asking if anyone had one, but no luck. Then someone's arm extended from behind me with a lit match. Puffing on my Lucky Strike, I turned around to thank them and saw it was Negri! I couldn't believe my eyes! I grabbed him by the shoulders and said, "You son of bitch! Where the hell have you been?"

Grinning, he said, "They took me to a mobile hospital (Mobile Hospital No. 5) in Nouméa, New Caledonia."[73] He pulled his shirt up exposing a small scar. "Turned out the bullet just grazed my side. It was only a flesh wound, and I only needed a couple stitches. Man, you should see all the gorgeous nurses there! They were a sight for sore eyes!"

I laughed and said, "All this time, I thought I'd never see you again. I kept thinking, poor Negri, I hope he's okay. And here you are getting dates with pretty nurses!"

He chuckled. "I'm gonna try and get shot again, just so I can go back! Hey Jim, can I bum a cigarette?"

I smiled and handed him the pack. "Keep it." It was good to have my old friend back.

Our joyous reunion was short-lived, however, when twenty-four Jap bombers laid down a barrage of explosions on the airfield. Negri and I took off running in hurry and found a foxhole nearby. Back to our daily routine. We waited awhile before emerging from our shelter, when suddenly, another group of enemy bombers thundered in dropping more bombs. This time they hit our aviation gasoline tanks with a huge explosion, spilling flames all over the airfield.[74]

That night Louie the Louse once again lit-up the night sky with his flares. Afterwards, brilliant naval star shells exploded with streams of light dripping down from the heavens. We looked up in awe, as if we were watching a fireworks display. Then, fourteen-inch shells whooshed into the perimeter from two Japanese battleships, *Haruna* and *Kongo*. Five- and eight-inch shells were also flying in from Jap cruisers and destroyers, while their aircraft pounded the area for over an hour.[75] The Japs threw everything at us but the kitchen sink!

There was no safe place to hide, especially from the enormous naval shells. Large metal fragments ripped through air destroying everything in their path. The whole day and night we were running around like maniacs, scrambling for cover. A total of 973 enemy shells were fired into the perimeter that night.[76] This was the U.S. Army's induction to our miserable home.

The next day at Henderson Field, we discovered forty-two Cactus aircraft were damaged or destroyed in this bombardment. The airstrip was riddled with craters, rendered unusable, and forty-one men were killed.[77] Many were buried alive in their shelters. The concussions were so intense some men's ears bled and they couldn't hear for days. Almost everyone ended up with shellshock.

Later the same day, two separate Japanese convoys deposited about 4,500 Japanese troops around the area of Tassafaronga.[78] Our Douglas dive bombers (SBDs) of the 1st Marine Aircraft Wing attacked the Japs while they were unloading troops and supplies.[79] The American fighters managed to sink one transport and left two others burning on the beach,[80] but they were only able to prevent a small percentage of troops from coming ashore. This brought the Japanese strength on the island to about 15,000.[81] The estimate for the American fighting men, mostly Marines, stationed on Guadalcanal was 23,088.[82] The Japanese and Americans were building up their forces rapidly to see who would become the victors in this struggle. Guadalcanal had quickly turned into a strategic flashpoint.

You could feel the tension in the air as we anticipated more fierce fighting with the buildup of forces on both sides. We continued to occupy and defend our newly designated Sector Five, working tirelessly on installations around the revised Matanikau horseshoe defense perimeter.[83] Its line now extended from the mouth of the Matanikau River 2,000 yards inland to the Nippon bridge. The right flank curved along the beach, while the left flank was situated on high ground overlooking the first stream junction.[84] My platoon was slashing through vines, digging foxholes, and laying barbed wire to fortify the forward defensive line.[85]

Official USMC Photograph

Marines battling against a tropical hurricane on Guadalcanal to prevent their food supplies from getting soaked, c.1942.

46. A Buzz in the Air

Many of the men were coming down with malaria.[1] The first signs of the disease were feeling hot, breaking out in a cold sweat, chills, and then the fever. It would end up leaving you in a semiconscious state, as though you were in a drunken stupor.

At night, the insects would be on patrol, hunting their victims. The female mosquitoes carrying the parasitic infection were our worst enemy. Their buzzing sound was very loud and disturbing. We were constantly swatting them away, and if you squashed one plenty of blood would squirt out of its little body.

During September and October, S. A. Messina, Al, Shuford, Jonsey, Hilsky, and myself all came down with the fever.[2] Salvatore and I were treated at the Division Field Hospital, which had wooden buildings. The other men in my platoon were taken to an auxiliary tent hospital located about 500 yards east of the field hospital.[3]

In the early days of the war, malaria turned out to be a greater threat than being wounded in battle. In 1942 and 1943, admissions to mobile hospitals in the Pacific area exceeded combat casualties.[4] It was later discovered the 1st Marine Division and supporting troops landed in an area with the highest malarial-infected mosquito rate on the planet.[5] By the second week of September 1942, forty-eight cases of malaria were recorded at the Division Field Hospital.[6] Ten weeks later, 7,667 men had been infected, with a total of 5,415 hospitalized.[7]

Starting on September 10, we were given Atabrine on a daily basis as a precaution against the deadly infection. The dosage was one tablet, twice daily, three times a week.[8] Most of us couldn't be bothered with trying to remember to take the pills. We were too busy scrambling for cover, going out on patrols, and completing our daily tasks. Anti-mosquito equipment (mosquito bars, head nets, nets, and gloves) was also issued, but no one wanted to wear the extra gear. Large nets had also been captured from the Japanese and were used in the field hospitals,[9] and the doctors would prescribe quinine whenever you were hospitalized with the fever.

Mixed in with the Jap supplies we captured were these weird-looking, three-inch gray rings with wicks, designed to drive the mosquitoes away. I don't know what this material was, but after lighting it the smoke emitted a putrid odor. We tried using these rings one night before going to sleep, but when the smoke hit our nostrils, it made us all sick, and the mosquitoes still attacked us. Another Japanese failure!

Aside from malaria, there were many other diseases to contend with. Dysentery also plagued the men. It's caused by unsanitary water containing micro-organisms that damage the lining of the intestines. We were issued halazone tablets to purify contaminated water, but many times the Marines would forget to use them or were just so thirsty from the heat and didn't abide by the rule of waiting a half-hour for the tablets to take effect. As a result, they would end up getting very ill.

Jungle rot, a debilitating tropical skin disease causing intense itching, was another horrible affliction. It would attack your feet (trench foot), armpits, and buttocks. Some men had huge, painful lesions oozing from their feet. It was a miserable condition to have on top of everything else we had to put up with. If a man had a supply of dry socks, he could protect his feet from this infection. But dry socks weren't available, as we didn't have the bare necessities we so badly needed.

Poor sanitary conditions on the island caused many other problems for the Marines. Relentless rain, moist heat, and hordes of insects made it difficult to control diseases in the South Pacific. Many of the men also contracted respiratory tract diseases like the common cold, influenza, and pneumonia.[10]

47. Sunday Mass

One Sunday morning, I attended Mass under the shade of the coconut trees. Our chaplain set up a portable altar where he placed a tin full of sacramental bread (or Eucharist) and chalice of wine, symbolizing Christ's body and blood, for distribution through Communion. This Sunday seemed calm compared to the other days of the week. There was hardly any sniper fire, bombing, or shelling. It was as if God had silenced the impact of war for this one day, so we could worship in peace. I thanked Him every day we had to hold this island in defense, and I never missed one day of praying to spare my life.

Right after Mass, my buddy Yanno suggested we get up a penny ante game. The guys who agreed to play were, Negri, S. A. Messina, Jonesy, Shuford, Johnson, and myself. Gambling was the Marines' favorite pastime, usually poker or dice. It was good for our morale and helped to keep our minds off the war.

About an hour went by, and I was going up and down in my meager winnings. As a new hand was dealt, I began to sweat profusely. Holding my cards, I began to shiver. I didn't know what was happening. Negri looked at me and said, "Old buddy, you better head for regimental sickbay."

"What the hell for?" I replied.

Official USMC Photograph

Kneeling on the sands of tiny Tulagi Island, the Marines receive Holy Communion from Father Fitzgerald, c.1942.

"You just came down with malaria, my friend." The rest of my buddies all agreed with Negri and said I should get to sickbay.

"The hell with it!" I told them. Then Negri jumped up and left in a hurry. I said to the other guys, "Where the hell is he going?" They just shrugged their shoulders.

Five minutes later, Negri showed up with a corpsman who examined me and said, "You better get over to sickbay. You've come down with the fever."

Again, I replied, "The hell with it!"

But then the corpsman raised his voice and demanded that I get over to sickbay immediately. My buddies nudged me to obey, knowing I would go on report. So, I finally got up and followed the corpsman over to sickbay, which was about 100 yards away.

As we walked along, something hit me, and I started staggering. I felt like I was going to fall flat on my face. The malaria fever had found its way into my brain. Negri and the corpsman grabbed my arms and supported me, and when we arrived at field hospital, they helped me onto one of the cots. By this time, I was feeling very sick and dazed with the fever. My head was spinning, and my brain felt like it was on fire. My body became hot, then cold. All my strength was sapped out of me. I was mumbling gibberish and felt like vomiting.

The regimental doctor began shoving quinine into my mouth. He covered me with blankets, but I was sweating so much, I kicked them off. The malarial fever consumed my whole body. I didn't know where I was and drifted into unconsciousness.

About an hour later, Jap bombers came over the island at 40,000 feet. A doctor's voice cried out, "All patients get to the air-raid shelter!"

Slowly, I opened my eyes a little, but my vision was dimmed, and I could only make out shadows. There was a commotion going on in front of me. A voice shouted, "CONDITION RED! JAP BOMBERS DIRECTLY OVERHEAD! TAKE COVER!" This was the last thing I heard before rolling off of my cot. As the bombs exploded, men were frantically making a mad dash for the shelter, but no one noticed me lying on the ground. However, at that particular moment, I was miserably sick and didn't care if I lived or died. My thought was, let the bombs fall!

A short time later, the air raid was over, and the bombs stopped falling. The bombers would be back the next day at noon, and again the day after that. It seemed like it would never end. But this day we had been lucky. None of the bombs hit the field hospital or air-raid shelter.

A major from sickbay found me lying face down on the ground and lifted me back onto the cot. "Why the hell weren't you in the air-raid shelter?" he asked. But I didn't answer. The malaria had left me in a semiconscious state, and the fever was boiling my brain. The major examined me closer and, realizing the fever had taken over, he apologized. He called the corpsman over and reamed his ass out for not helping me get to the shelter. "It was your duty as a medic to help all those who aren't ambulatory to get to the safety!" he barked. "Didn't you see this man was down with the fever?" The corpsman lowered his head. "You're going on report!" the major added. Still,

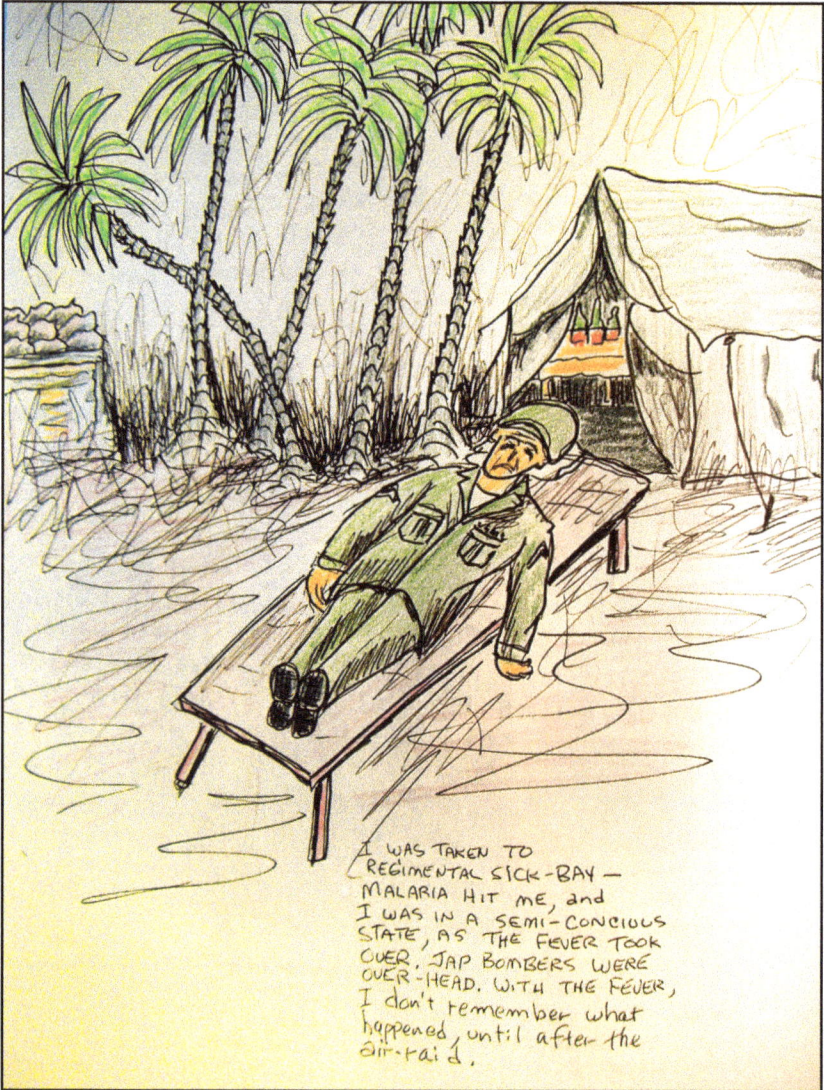

I WAS TAKEN TO
REGIMENTAL SICK-BAY —
MALARIA HIT me, and
I WAS IN A SEMI-CONCIOUS
STATE, AS THE FEVER TOOK
OVER. JAP BOMBERS WERE
OVER-HEAD. WITH THE FEVER,
I don't remember what
happened, until after the
air-raid.

there was no comment from the corpsman; he was only thinking of himself.

Another voice called out, "Chow time!" Someone brought over a food tray and placed it at my side. One look at it and I was ready to vomit. "Take it away," I said. The guy next to me asked if he could have it, and I motioned for him to go ahead. My stomach didn't want anything for two days; I only craved water. They gave me quinine for ten days, the required time to get over malaria.[11] The deadly mosquitoes had done their job well. Despite many men in our division coming down with malaria and other diseases, we still had to defend the island until the Army came to relieve us.

While I was in sickbay, the daily bombardments from the Japs increased. The building shook with each impact. Sometimes the explosions were so close, debris would shower the roof, sounding like large pellets of hail. I didn't like being so close to the airfield. We were scared out of our wits, but there was nothing we could do. If there was enough warning, we'd scramble over to the air-raid shelter, but it was just as dangerous. A direct hit would've killed us all.

My treatment finally came to an end, and I was released to go back to B Company. As soon as the doctor cleared me, I sprang up and got the hell of there. I tried to run but couldn't. Although the malarial fever had worn off, it still left me feeling weak. As I was walking back to camp, a regimental jeep pulled up beside me, and an officer on the passenger side asked where I was going. I told him, and he motioned to the back seat.

"Hop in," he said. "We're headed that way."

48. DOUGHNUTS AND BOMBS

As I jumped off the jeep, my buddy Al rushed up to greet me and welcomed me back with a tight handshake. He wanted to know everything about the malaria treatment. I told him the whole story, then made a suggestion. "Let's take a walk over to the 6th Seabees," I said.

"What for?" he replied.

"I want to see if I can get some sugar, flour, baking powder, and shortening." The Seabees ran the Japanese bakery, along with their regular duties.

Puzzled, he asked, "What are you planning to do, Jim?"

"Make some doughnuts."

Al grinned. "Do you know how to make them?"

I smiled back. "No, but I'm going to ask the cook how."

"Okay," he replied, "let's go!"

The Seabees were happy to help with my idea. I asked the cook for a doughnut recipe, and he obliged, supplying all the ingredients we needed. He asked what we were planning on frying the doughnuts in. I told him I hadn't thought of that.

He laughed, pointing to a large, five-gallon can from the dehydrated potatoes, and said, "That should do the trick."

Al chuckled. "You Seabees sure are clever!"

I told the cook if there was anything we could ever do for him, just let us know. Then we went on our way.

After we arrived back at our bivouac area, some of the guys asked what the big can was for, and we let them in on our plan. The rest of our squad hunted up wood and stones for the base of the fire. We arranged the stones in a circle and placed the large can on top. Stuffing paper and wood beneath, we started the fire. I placed the shortening in the can and waited until it was hot enough for frying. Al and I mixed the other ingredients together, then shaped the dough into medium-sized doughnuts. I plopped six at a time into the hot oil. We managed to make about three dozen.

The aroma of the frying dough filled our nostrils, and we were all licking our chops. Someone suggested we melt the GI bars of chocolate in a coffee can. So, we did and then dunked in the doughnuts into the melted chocolate. One by one, we took them out and placed them on a coconut log to cool down.

There were nine men in our squad, and after the chocolate dried, I passed out three doughnuts to each man. Al and I got to have five each, since we were the cooks. This little scenario was fit for a jungle king. Who would've thought we'd be eating fresh, chocolate-covered doughnuts in the jungle?

As we all enjoyed this tasty treat, Al spoke up. "This was Messina's idea!" he said.

With that, everyone let out a cheer of "Well done!"

Just as the last doughnut was eaten, who appeared on the scene but our infamous Sgt. Breeding. "I need a squad of men to load 500-pound bombs!" he announced. The bombs were for our Douglas SBD Dauntless dive-bombers. Then he turned to Cpl. Podracky, saying, "Get your men, and follow me!" The corporal shrugged his shoulders and signaled the high sign to follow him and Breeding.

We made good use of the captured Japanese trucks, which resembled our own American GMC trucks. Each truck could carry ten 500-pound bombs, and there were two trucks waiting to take us to the ammunition dump, a short distance from Henderson Field. Our squad was assigned to the first truck; a squad from A Company got the other.

Once we arrived, I couldn't believe how many bombs, trench mortars, and gun ammo were piled up under the coconut trees, hidden from view. The people back home were working twenty-four hours a day producing ammunition and supplies for the fighting men in both theaters of war.

The driver parked near a stack of bombs, and we jumped off the truck. It took six of us to load one bomb onto the truck. Three men remained on the truck to help lift and roll the bombs into place. It was very strenuous work, and it showed on our faces. Straining to lift each bomb, I felt sharp pain in my lower back, but I just ignored it. It took the whole day to accomplish this task.

After the trucks were loaded, we headed over to the airfield to unload them. When the last bomb was taken off, we waited for the trucks to take the two squads back to our bivouac. Besides being a soldier, the infantryman was required to do a lot of hard labor. We had to obey every order, or else.

The trucks hauled us back just in time for chow. Today's menu was rice, fish, and hardtack, a half-decent meal. The Japanese soldier lived on one handful of rice a day. The rice we captured from the Japanese was our main supplement. There were hundreds of bags of it stacked up in the makeshift warehouse beneath the coconut trees. I swore, if I ever made it back home, I'd never eat rice again!

49. DUGOUT SUNDAY

During my ten-day stay at sickbay there were other major battles fought on land, air, and sea. Aside from the continuous attacks by the Japanese to retake Henderson Field, another action broke out around the Matanikau River, as the Japs, once again, attempted to infiltrate our perimeter. A few days later, an intense sea battle ensued as a group of our warships clashed with the Imperial Navy. Many ships and aircraft were lost on both sides. It would later be called the Battle of the Santa Cruz Islands.

Larry filled me in on the details of how the Marines, Army, and Navy repulsed these attacks by the Japanese. On October 20, two enemy tanks appeared on the west bank of the Matanikau River. A barrage of artillery was immediately laid down by the Marines. The tanks continued advancing, trying to break through the 3d Battalion, 1st Marine's defense line. One was immediately disabled by our 37mm anti-tank gun, and the Japs quickly retreated.[12] Another attempt was made the next day, this time with more tanks, but they were repelled once again.

Then, at 1800 on October 23, a salvo of mortar and artillery fire rained down on our MLR. At the same time, a company of enemy tanks attempted to cross a sandpit near the mouth of the Matanikau River. This time our 37mm guns disabled nine Japanese tanks.[13] Three battalions (2d, 3d, 5th) of the 11th Marines, and I Battery, 10th Marines, fired back over 6,000 rounds of artillery and mortars between Point Cruz and the Matanikau, killing hundreds of the Jap infantry soldiers advancing behind the tanks.[14] The battle raged on for six hours, ending at midnight.[15]

The following night 700 troops of Puller's 2d Battalion, 7th Marines (2-7), were moved to the southern flank of Sector Three's perimeter near Edson's Ridge.[16] They were supported by the 2d and 3d Battalions, 164th Infantry. Shortly after midnight during a heavy downpour, six battalions of the Imperial Army's Sendai Division waged a massive assault on the southern defense perimeter of the airfield, with repeated attacks throughout the night.[17] The Americans fought back with heavy artillery, mortar, and machine-gun fire, killing about 300 Japs, forcing the remaining troops to withdraw.[18]

The next morning destroyers of the Imperial Navy shelled the perimeter, while the Japanese Army launched a barrage of artillery. Then, starting around mid-morning, twenty-seven Japanese fighters attacked Henderson Field in four separate waves lasting until mid-afternoon. In the final wave, sixteen bombers joined in the assault. Our Cactus Air Force shot down sixteen of the fighters and five bombers.[19] This day would be remembered as "Dugout Sunday," because we spent the whole day scrambling for whatever shelter we could find.

A second Japanese ground attack occurred that night as another barrage of artillery pounded the area. Intense fighting took place on the western and southern defense perimeters. The integrated Army-Marine MLR held strong, beating back the masses of Jap soldiers with 37mm guns, mortars, machine guns, and artillery fire.[20] The remaining force retreated into the jungle. Five days of battle left eighty-six Americans dead and 192 wounded. Japanese estimates were in excess of 2,200 killed.[21] Heavy rain fell during the night, followed in the morning by the hot tropical sun. The quickly decaying bodies had to be hastily bulldozed into mass graves.[22] This failed Japanese counteroffensive would be their last for the remainder of the campaign.[23]

As the Japanese effort to regain control of the airfield was suppressed by the Army-Marines on the ground, a naval showdown was developing near the Santa Cruz Islands, east of the Solomons. The Imperial Navy was under the impression their ground forces had succeeded in recapturing Henderson Field from the Americans. On October 26, our SBDs spotted four Japanese aircraft carriers with 199 aircraft, and forty-three warships positioned to strike.[24] As soon as this information was relayed to Rear Admiral Halsey, his orders were to attack. Two American carrier groups, USS *Hornet* and USS *Enterprise,* carrying 136 aircraft, along with twenty-one warships, engaged with the Imperial Navy. This sea battle was fought solely with carrier- or land-based aircraft.[25] *Enterprise* and two destroyers were heavily impaired, leaving *Hornet* and one destroyer fatally damaged, along with eighty-one aircraft, and killing 266 Americans. Japanese losses were three warships damaged, ninety-seven aircraft destroyed, and between 400 to 500 dead. In the end, both sides claimed victory.[26] After

Guadalcanal, The U.S. Marines in World War II

Japanese Imperial Army soldiers lie dead at the mouth of the Matanikau River after a failed attack on U.S. Marine positions, Guadalcanal, October 1942.

learning the news the Imperial Army's Sendai Division had been defeated on the ground, the Imperial Navy withdrew from the area.[27]

In the days between September 27 and October 26, the Cactus Air Force destroyed a total of 228 Japanese aircraft, while the Americans lost 103.[28] Following the success of the American forces, Roosevelt addressed the Joint Chiefs with a memorandum emphasizing the importance of maintaining control of Guadalcanal. Twenty additional ships were ordered to the Southwest Pacific.[29] With the defeat of the Imperial Army and the news our president was sending more ships to the area, there was a feeling of victory among all the Marines!

50. THE BIG SWEDE

The next morning, I was put on KP duty. Everyone was required to take turns each week. I was assigned to the so-called cook, "Big Swede." He was a son of a bitch to work for, with a bad attitude and no friends. The guy was really big, about six-foot four, with kinky red hair, a very large head, reddish skin, muscles galore, and giant feet. And he sure had a bad temper towards everyone. He was also a chain-smoker, inhaling three to four packs a day. The Swede only spoke when he was forced to do so. No one liked him. I don't even think he liked himself.

The Swede never stopped giving orders. "Hey, Messina!" he barked. "Bring that case of Vienna sausages over here!" There were twelve large cans of sausages in a case. He told me to open all the cans and dump them in the large pot over the open fire. They would be tonight's chow.

As I took the lid off of the wooden crate, I noticed a bunch of ugly, wrinkled maggots crawling all over the cans. Some of the cans had tiny pin holes in them, and if you didn't look closely, you would miss them. I walked over to the Swede as he was putting rice into a large iron kettle perched above the fire and told him about the maggots. "Swede," I said, "this Vienna sausage is no good. It's spoiled."

"What the fuck, you mean spoiled?!"

"There are maggots all over the cans!" I replied.

Then, in his Swedish rage he said, "Wash the cans, open them, and pour the sausages into the pot!"

"Okay," I said, "but I don't like it!"

After pouring them in, I told the Swede I had to go to the head to relieve myself because I was drinking a lot of water in the jungle heat. But I didn't go to the head. Instead, I went over to talk to my buddies and told them not to eat the Vienna sausage. My comrades were glad I told them. I didn't tell the whole company, though, only my buddies. When it came time to eat, my platoon wouldn't eat the sausage. We just had rice, hardtack, and coffee. The rest of our company started through the chow line, not realizing what was about to happen. A little later on, they all got sick with food poisoning. All the men were vomiting their guts out, so to speak.

As soon as Captain McIlhenny got wind of what had happened, he immediately stormed over to the field kitchen and approached Big Swede. "What happened here today, Marine?"

"I don't know what you mean, sir," Big Swede replied.

"What the hell did you feed my men?"

"Vienna sausage and rice, sir."

The captain was fuming. "I want to know about this food poisoning! Where is your mess man?"

The Swede pointed to me and said, "Right there, sir!"

The captain motioned me to his side. "What's your name, Marine?"

"Messina, sir!"

"Tell me what happened."

So, I explained about the crate of sausage having maggots on them, and the Swede telling me to use them anyway.

By the look on our captain's face, I could tell he was boiling mad as I explained the scenario. I felt relieved telling McIlhenny the truth because Big Swede disregarded the welfare of B Company. After I finished, the captain turned to the Big Swede and told him he was demoted from mess sergeant to a PFC, but he would still remain cook for our company. Once McIlhenny left the field kitchen, the Swede told me I was on his shit list, and I would pay for turning him in.

"I told you the sausage had maggots, but you wouldn't dump them!" I wasn't scared of the Swede. If he tried to hurt me in any way, he would be court-martialed. I was glad my KP duty was only for one day.

The next day Negri, Jonsey, and I took a walk down towards the beach. We had to carry our rifles all the time, even when we had to take a crap! We were lucky there weren't any Jap patrols around that day. We walked past the Army's camp that had been established in mid-October, after we'd secured the island. Our nostrils caught the smell of pancakes on a hot grill. Boy, what a wonderful smell for some hungry Marines! My mouth was watering as we stopped a short distance from the Army chow line.

An Army platoon sergeant was standing at the head of the line and noticed us staring at the food. "You gyrenes hungry?" he hollered.

We replied in unison, "You bet, sarge!"

He motioned us to pick up a serving tray and get in line. The Army soldiers eyed us up and down with a look, like, What the hell are these gyrenes doing in our chow line? They were throwing dagger eyes at us, but we didn't care.

The Army sergeant was a stocky, Italian fellow, about five-foot eight inches tall. He looked like a weightlifter. There were five stripes on his shirt, which was soaking wet with sweat. He had rosy-red cheeks and thick, black hair, both on his head and chest. His helmet was too small for his big head, and it looked comical, but we dared not laugh. He seemed like a happy fellow and flashed a big smile when he told us to get in line. When we finished our delicious pancakes, we walked over and thanked him.

"Anytime you're in the neighborhood, you're welcome to share our Army chow!" he replied. Those pancakes were much better than having to eat the Swede's tainted Vienna sausage!

Official USMC Photograph

Four Marines carrying their wounded comrade while under heavy sniper fire, Guadalcanal, c.1942.

51. KOKUMBONA REVISITED

A large Japanese force was suspected to be occupying Kokumbona village, west of the Matanikau River, near the base of Point Cruz. Vandegrift decided to take advantage of the October successes by expanding the defense perimeter further west, seizing Kokumbona and driving the Imperial Army beyond the Poha River. It's at this locale where the coastline curves northwest, stretching to the northern tip of the island. Vandegrift's objective was to force the Japs to land on beaches further up the coast and push the "Pistol Petes" out of firing range from Henderson Field.[1]

The 7th Marines, and 3d Battalion, 1st Marines, needed some rest from all the fighting, and the 164th Infantry was occupied holding an extended frontage on the eastern defense perimeter. My 5th Regiment was considered well-rested and fit for combat but had been greatly reduced in strength.[2] To make up for the shortage of troops, Colonel John M. Arthur's 2d Marines (less the 3d Battalion) were brought over from the island of Tulagi to assist the 5th Marines in the upcoming mission. In addition, we'd have the support of Lieutenant Colonel William J. Whaling's group, composed of the 3d Battalion, 7th Marines, along with the Scout Snipers. There would also be a powerful force of artillery from the 11th Marines and Army, along with assistance from the Cactus Air Force and additional surface naval gunfire.[3]

After a long day's work, fortifying our perimeter, we tried to catch a catnap, but suddenly were awakened by the loud bellow of that rebel Breeding, our well-mannered platoon commander. "Fall out, you shitheads! Fall out!"

We dragged ourselves up and formed a circle around the diehard sergeant. What the hell was so important he had to disturb our hard-earned rest?

"Tomorrow at 0430," he blustered, "the whole 5th Regiment will be moving out to assemble near the mouth of the Matanikau River. Here's the reason, shitheads! One of our patrols spotted Nip positions further west the river. Our orders are to move out and engage with the enemy. We have to secure the perimeter. Any questions?" No one responded. You can't question orders given from Command, only follow them. "Now fall out and get your rations, ammunition, and gear together. Be ready to move out before dawn!"

We smoked, ate pogey-bait, and bullshitted while making up our packs. After we finished packing, Salvatore Messina said, "Well, little brother, this could be it. Do me a favor. If I don't make it back from the Matanikau, I'd appreciate you writing my parents. It would be real nice if my mother received a letter from another Messina." I told him I would, and asked him to do the same, if something should happen to me. We shook hands as we both agreed on this pact.

After chow, everyone tried to get some sleep. It seemed like I'd just closed my eyes when a guard was nudging me with the butt of his rifle to wake up. I strained my eyes trying to see my watch. It was 0400, and everyone was putting on their backpacks. Our marching packs were light, but the ammunition was very heavy to lug. Each man carried a total of 100 rounds of ammo.

Negri was carrying his BAR. This rifle had a lot of firepower. It was the best jungle weapon a man could carry but was twice as heavy as my M1903 Springfield. His bandoliers were also heavier than mine. They held ten large magazines, each with twenty rounds of ammunition. Negri never complained because he knew he had a superb weapon.

At 0430 hours we were ready and waiting for orders to move out. It was twilight, and the sun was just below the horizon, rendering the sky a deep, cobalt blue and casting a dim light around the bivouac area. We could only make out things about twenty feet in front of us. No one uttered a word.

Capt. McIlhenny appeared on the scene with two lieutenants and every sergeant of Baker Company. He then gave a hand signal to move out, taking the lead and looking proud to be a Marine.

As we approached the shore of the Lunga River, the captain signaled us to halt. In whispers, the word was passed on from one Marine to next: "As we enter the jungle, the smoking lamp will be out, and speaking in whispers is forbidden." Sgt. Breeding led us to the river for the long trek to the Matanikau area. We waded across the chest-deep water, holding our rifles high over our heads like before. The whole company pushed across the river in a record fifteen minutes.

After crossing the river, we headed into the jungle. Trudging through the maze of vegetation was a grueling task, and it was very difficult to advance quietly with our heavy marching order. We were feeling our way along, moving very slowly as we stumbled, tripping over vines and undergrowth. We were all nervous, our minds telling us we wouldn't get back alive, constantly expecting something to jump out in front of us.

When dawn broke, hot blades of sunlight sliced through the darkness. At the first hint of light the birds began to chatter, and the whole jungle began to steam. The temperature shot up to eighty degrees in a matter of minutes. The intense heat made our burden even heavier. We sweated profusely under the weight of our loads, and our combat clothes were completely soaked. My steel helmet felt like it weighed thirty pounds. I also felt top-heavy from the load I was carrying on my back. It was very slow progress.

The mosquitoes were our worst enemies. They played havoc around our faces, attacking us at the base of our necks. All the swatting was in vain; they wouldn't let up. It's as if they got their orders came from the Imperial Japanese Command to sting all Marines and give us malaria.

Up ahead, we approached a small opening in the thick vegetation. As we entered, we found two dead Jap soldiers, bloated-up like balloons. Scores of big, black flies were feasting on the decaying bodies. The stench was overpowering, and we quickly covered our noses. One Marine noticed a gold fountainpen set sticking out of the front pocket of the dead Jap. Sgt. Breeding had repeated to us many times in his sermons back at Camp Lejeune not to search or take anything from the enemy's bodies because they might be booby-trapped. But this Marine didn't care. He slowly advanced towards the corpse to retrieve his souvenir. As he inched closer, the rest of us moved back near the safety of the trees, just in case of an explosion. He snatched the pen set and, fortunately, nothing happened. He was lucky this time. At that moment, Sgt. Breeding stormed over to the Marine and, using dramatic hand gestures, silently chewed his ass out. The Marine just nodded his head while inserting the booty in his front pocket. We had another fellow who'd knock the gold teeth out of any dead Jap's mouth that had them.

After our long trek through the sweltering jungle, our regiment silently worked its way to the eastern bank of the Matanikau River, where we assembled for the night.[4] The remainder of our day was spent preparing for the following morning. Everyone kept quiet, communicating only with hand signals. We were all focused on the upcoming battle, double-checking our weapons and ammo. Each man was lost in his own thoughts and the possibility of not making it back home.

At dusk, we hunkered down under a faint moonlight that cast long shadows, making the jungle look even more foreboding. The smoking lamp was on, but I was nervous as hell. Concealed under my wool blanket, I managed to sneak a few cigarettes.

That night I couldn't sleep. In my mind I pictured getting blown up by a trench motor or sprayed with machine-gun fire and dying on the island. God had been watching over me, and I hoped He'd continue to do so. I prayed to Him, yet again, to return me from battle alive and to spare all my buddies. I guess the Japanese soldiers felt the same way. They hoped to live too and make it back to their sweethearts, wives, and families.

While most of the 5th Marines tried to sleep, a few special units were working tirelessly on modifications to help with the morning offensive. In the early hours of November 1, the 1st Engineer Battalion laid three footbridges over the Matanikau River using floating fuel drums. A platoon from, E Company, 2d Battalion, 5th Marines, crossed the river in rubber boats and made their way up the western bank of the river, establishing an outpost to protect the engineers as they worked.[5]

At daybreak we were preparing to cross the Matanikau River when, by field radio, word got back to Capt. McIlhenny our scout planes had spotted a large group of Jap soldiers on the other side of the river, near Point Cruz. The captain ordered our company to halt and sent word to our battalion commander, Major William K. Enright. Artillery was ordered as the 11th Marines and 3d Defense Battalion's five-inch guns began blasting the Jap positions.[6]

Shells were flying overhead, and a few of them exploded in our position. Sadly, some Marines were killed or wounded by our own artillery. This sort of thing happened once in a while, both in the South Pacific and European theater. A slight miscalculation would cause shells to fall short, and men would be killed by friendly fire. Capt. McIlhenny was raving mad! He got back on the radio, swearing and making threats to the men of the artillery unit, telling them there would be court-martials to the ones responsible for this deadly misjudgment.

The next round of shells found their target on the other side of the river. Then, Cactus SBDs and P-39s from Henderson Field roared above us, swooping down strafing and bombing the Japanese artillery positions. The Navy also joined in, shelling the area west of Point Cruz, using the cruisers USS *San Francisco* (CA 38) and USS *Helena* (CL 50), and the destroyer, USS *Sterett* (DD 407). Command also sent B-17s down from Espiritu Santo, dropping 100-pound bombs.[7] The sound of the explosions from the bombardment was thunderous! As soon as the bombing stopped, we were immediately ordered to begin our advance.

Approaching the Matanikau River, we ran into a field of pineapples, which stretched all the way to the river's shore. Suddenly, heavy rain began falling, which lasted about five hours. It was freezing cold and soaked us through to our skin.

52. The Crucible of Combat

At 0630, the 2d Battalion, 5th Marines (2-5), led by Major Lewis Walt, crossed one of the inland footbridges. Major Enright led my 1st Battalion, 5th Marines (1-5) across the bridge closest to the mouth of the river. It took both battalions thirty minutes to get to the other side. Whaling's group crossed the bridge furthest inland. The 3d Battalion, 5th Marines, led by Major Robert O. Bowen, followed behind us and were across by 0800.[8] We also had elements of the 3d Battalion, 1st Marines, and 2d Battalion, 7th Marines positioned along the Matanikau, covering us as we crossed the stream.[9]

Once across, A Company, 1st Battalion advanced right, towards the level beach area, with no opposition. C Company, 1st Battalion moved left along a ridge and ran smack up against the enemy hidden in a ravine. A fierce firefight broke out, and many Marines were killed or wounded. They were quickly ordered to withdraw and scrambled for cover.[10]

My company (B), in regimental reserve, was ordered forward to fill the gap between companies A and C.[11] As we advanced between the coast and a coral ridge, the shit hit the fan! The Japs opened up on us with rifle fire, followed by trench mortars and rapid sprays from machine guns. The cold, pelting rain didn't help as bullets and mortar shells came down on us with fury. Many of us lost our footing struggling through the muck, and we began crawling in the prone position, trying to dodge bullets while artillery erupted around us.

Cpl. Podracky stood up in plain view of the enemy. He was a perfect target but paid no mind, giving orders to our mortar unit to lob shells at the Japanese positions. His calculations were way off as the first round of shells fell short of their target. The next round was a little to the left. One of our scouts shinnied up a coconut tree and began giving hand signals to Podracky, who paid close attention to the scout as he directed the mortars. Then the shells finally found their mark. A direct hit! Our whole squad kept yelling at Cpl. Podracky to get down, but he was too engrossed in commanding the mortar unit. He was a hell of a brave guy and never worried about his own safety. Hilsky managed to pull him down to safety. After that, Podracky gave his orders while lying down on terra firma.

At this point, the Japs had us pinned down under a heavy deluge of weaponry. I managed to take cover in a pineapple patch. My friend Salvatore Messina was in front of me cursing up a storm. "I'll kill every one of you fucking Nips!" he yelled, while firing his rifle.

As I laid there firing back, the bullets were coming in a steady stream from the enemy's .60-caliber machine guns. Keeping my head down, suddenly I noticed someone lying close by on my left. At first, I thought he might be the enemy, and I pointed my rifle directly at him. But then I realized he wasn't. I'd never seen him before, and he didn't look like a Marine officer. I observed him for a moment, wondering who he was. He was a tall, lanky man, with black-rimmed specs and a holster with a forty-five automatic hanging on his hip. There was a patch on his shoulder that read "War Correspondent," and he was jotting down notes in a little black book. Later on, I found out his name was Richard Tregaskis.[12] It turned out, he would be the journalist who wrote the famous novel, *Guadalcanal Diary*. Hollywood would later make a movie of his story.

We didn't exchange any words as I kept firing my rifle at the enemy and he kept scribbling in his book. Then Podracky ordered us to move out. This was the first and last time I ever saw the famed journalist.

At midday, during the chaos of battle, we lost contact with our 2d Battalion.[13] My 1st Battalion was still bogged down in heavy enemy fire. Cpl. Podracky gave a hand signal for us to gather around him. We knew something was up. Our squad was picked for a mission.

"Sgt. Breeding wants to take our squad through this pineapple patch," said Podracky, "over to that high ridge on the left flank. Our orders are to climb up and try to spot Japanese positions, so our artillery can blast them." We all understood and nodded in agreement.

Just as we were about to depart, Salvatore Messina came running towards us, yelling, "Look what they did to your big brother, Jim!" Looking directly at me, he showed me where a Jap's bullet had made a deep crease right down the middle of his helmet. "They're trying to kill your big brother!" he said, panicked.

Meanwhile, the stream of machine gun's bullets kept flying at us. Cpl. Podracky hollered at him, "Get down, Salvatore! Get down, or the Japs will finish you off!" But Salvatore was frozen in fear and didn't realize to take cover. Hilsky yanked him by the arm down to the ground. After Salvatore calmed down, Cpl. Podracky ordered our squad to move out on our mission.

As we started to advance, the Japs opened up on us again. We crouched down in a low posture and made our way to the bottom of the ridge, where there was a narrow jungle stream. Once across, we were in for a steep climb. Scaling our way up was very tiring. Between the humid heat and pouring rain, we were soaked through to the skin in a salty sweat. It began to rain harder, making the climb very slippery and even more difficult. Finally, we arrived at the top of the ridge and had a pretty good view of the enemy's position below.

Sgt. Breeding ordered us to open up with rifle fire, grenades, and trench mortars. The Japs scattered in all directions, returning bursts of machine-gun fire. At the same time, artillery shells began exploding all around us, with shrapnel tearing through everything in its path. The shells were hitting about fifty yards to our right flank. You could hear the metal shards ripping through leaves and bark, slicing small branches off the trees. Everyone scrambled for cover. One of our other artillery crews had spotted us on the ridge and thought we were a company from the Japanese Imperial Army. The shelling turned out to be friendly fire! We had no idea it was our own artillery. No one had passed the word that a platoon from B Company had been ordered up on the ridge to scout for Jap positions. We thought the Japs had spotted us and were firing a barrage of mortars. It was another of many costly mistakes that happened on Guadalcanal.

Between the explosions of our own mortars and the Japs returning gunfire, there was so much confusion that Cpl. Podracky yelled out, "Get the hell off the ridge!"[14] We continued firing at the Japs as we slid down the muddy slope with our heavy equipment and splashed into the stream.

Just then, there was another explosion nearby, and shrapnel flew in all directions. Podracky got hit in the back by shards of hot metal and fell to his knees.[15] Sgt. Breeding immediately rushed towards him through the gunfire. At the same time, Pollock popped up from a tangle of underbrush. Wielding a machine gun, he charged towards the Japs, mowing down five of them before he dove for cover.[16] A bullet struck Breeding's left knee, and he immediately collapsed, rolling on the ground in pain.[17]

The shelling finally stopped, and the Japs quickly retreated. Between the Japs' machine guns and our own artillery, my platoon suffered many casualties. Sgt. Breeding's knee was shattered, and he couldn't stand up.[18] Cpl. Podracky was lying face-down and bleeding badly from multiple shrapnel wounds. Yanno, a short distance away, also had multiple shrapnel wounds on both legs after a shell exploded twenty-five feet from him.[19] Al suffered a concussion and was walking around in a daze. It was a horrible, bloody mess.

The rest of us were frantically trying to help our wounded comrades and yelling for the medics. Two corpsmen dashed onto the scene and headed towards Sgt. Breeding, but he waved them away, pointing to Podracky and Yanno. At that moment, we all realized the true character of our platoon sergeant.

One corpsman attended Cpl. Podracky, while the other rushed over to Yanno. Podracky was unconscious but breathing. Everyone was relieved he was still alive. Yanno was moaning in pain as the other corpsman approached him. They poured powdered iodine on the wounds to stop the bleeding. Shuford and Jonsey helped get Yanno and Prodracky onto stretchers and carried them to a truck a short distance away. Another corpsman ran over to sarge and tied a tourniquet on his thigh. Then he poured iodine over the gash on his knee and wrapped a bandage around it. Larry helped me get Sgt. Breeding on another stretcher. Sarge didn't utter a word as we carried him to the truck, but his expression said it all. As we hurried along, he smiled through his pain, as if to say, "You men are doing a great job!" As we lifted him up on the truck, he turned to me and said, "Thanks, Yankee Messina!" These would be the last words I'd ever hear him speak.

Through this whole ordeal, we didn't realize Austin Pollock was missing. Austin was a brave soldier who always followed orders. We thought maybe the Japs had captured him. Cpl. Hilsky gave the order to fan-out and look for him. I heard Negri call out, "Over here!" We all rushed over. Negri had a blank look on his face as he gazed downward. Austin was draped over a large tree root, lying face down. We rolled him over and he was covered in blood. Austin Pollock was dead.[20]

Tears rolled down our faces as we gently lifted him and carried him back towards the road. Austin was always quiet and kept to himself, but he was a hell of a nice guy and one brave Marine. Later that day Capt. McIlhenny ordered a burial detail. Private Austin Windell Pollock, Jr., was buried 400 yards west of Point Cruz, 600 yards from the sea.[21] One of Austin's close friends wept as he choked out a few words in honor of our fallen comrade.

War makes no sense. You don't realize it until someone close to you loses their life. I kept thinking about Austin's parents receiving a knock on their door, receiving the notification of death from a Marine officer. I prayed for him and his family, and for God to spare my life, so my parents would never have to receive a similar visit.

The pouring rain kept pounding us. We all looked like a bunch of wet rags, and it was playing havoc on our morale. We were soaking wet, hungry, tired, and infuriated with the Japanese for injuring and killing our comrades. We pledged the little Jap bastards would pay dearly with their lives.

Sgt. Breeding, Cpl. Podracky, Yanno, Shuford, Jonsey, Larry, and I rode in an open stake body truck ahead of another truck carrying the rest of our platoon. Once we arrived at the field hospital, our wounded comrades were rushed into triage. We were all pretty shook up from this experience and had to be examined by the doctors, who gave us sedatives to calm us down.

It turned out the shrapnel injuries Prodracky had sustained on his back were only flesh wounds, and he was released from the Division Field Hospital after four days.[22] Yanno's leg wounds were worse. They kept him in sickbay for two weeks. Al would be under observation for his concussion a few days. After he was released, he would never be the same. Sgt. Breeding was evacuated the next day to U. S. N. Mobile Base Hospital No. 2 at Efate, New Hebrides.[23] Our new platoon commander would be Sergeant Albert A. Ward.[24]

After a few hours, they took us back to Headquarters Company, where we received orders to stay put.[25] They needed extra men to help guard the area. After that, we broke out our meager rations and ate our only meal for the day.

Breeding displayed great courage risking his life as he attempted to save one of his men. No one liked him, but he turned out to be a completely different man than we had thought. This was the day we realized Sgt. Breeding was man of great substance. He would always be remembered as a strong leader.

Pvt. Austin Pollock was also fearless as he charged the Japs, trying to protect his comrades and ultimately sacrificing his life. He received the Purple Heart, posthumously, and the award would be presented to his mother the following year.[26]

Both acts of valor are exemplary of what "Semper Fidelis" stands for.

On November 1, 1942, the men of B Company's, 1st Platoon had been tested beyond their limits. In the crucible of combat, our unit persevered, but was forever changed. We were now battle-hardened jungle warriors, instilled with a vengeance and determination to defeat the enemy.

By sundown, we were released back on active duty, and Sgt. Ward led us back to the frontlines. The first day's progress had been very slow.

We'd only advanced about 1,000 yards the whole day. By late afternoon, the rest of my company had dug in for the night near the base of Point Cruz.[27] The fighting died down, but through the night there were spurts of gunfire. I don't think any of us slept a wink.

In the meantime, Companies I and K of the 3d Battalion (3-5) advanced and filled the gap between the 1st Battalion (1-5) and the beach, east of the enemy. My battalion was situated near the enemy's southern front, parallel to the coastline.[28]

The next day, the inland advance of the 2d Battalion (2-5) turned north towards the coast, circling back, and closing in west of the Japanese force. Our three battalions encircled the Japs, and now they were surrounded.[29] The only place for them to retreat was into the sea. As the fighting intensified, they knew their fate was creeping up on them.

By November 3, the three battalions of the 5th Regiment had reduced the Japanese force down to a scant resistance. At midday, my 1st Battalion (1-5) was ordered to withdraw and maintain defensive positions at Sector Two of the perimeter.[30] Sgt. Ward ordered us to fall in. We all formed up, single file, for the trek through the jungle and back to our bivouac area fifteen miles away. Baker Company moved out as our last battle of the Matanikau River was coming to an end.

As we were making our way back through the jungle, there was a fellow by the name of Miller who hailed from New Jersey. He had kinky-brown hair and a pimply round face that was always red as a beet. He was average height and had a funny walk, waddling side to side like a penguin. He also had a girlfriend named Sue, and he was forever whistling the song "Sweet Sue." Miller was always cracking jokes and was good for our morale.

As we trudged along, he quipped, "Boy, when we were back there in battle, and pinned down by machine-gun fire, I was so scared I crawled up into my helmet and looked back and saw my feet sticking out. Boy, did I pull them in in a hurry!" A roar of laughter broke out. Miller was one funny guy. He made a few more jokes, then silence took over the troops for the remainder of the hike back.

Suddenly, a shot rang out. It sounded like Japanese .25-caliber rifle fire. We all hit the deck, ready for the enemy. A runner appeared and gave the news. There were some Marines up ahead burning a native bamboo village. As the bamboo burned, it cracked and sounded like rifle fire. They burned the village so the Japs couldn't use the huts for shelter. The burnt bamboo really stunk, and as we passed the native village, all that was left were piles of black ashes smoldering.

After my battalion had been ordered to withdraw, the 2d and 3d Battalions, 5th Marines, and 1st Battalion, 164th Infantry, would mop-up the remaining Japanese pocket.[31] By November 4, the final annihilation took place with three bayonet assaults against the enemy.[32] We were told later a few surviving Japs fled into the water, trying to swim for their lives. I Company, 3d Battalion, 5th Marines, stood on the shoreline firing at bobbing heads in the water.[33] After four days of intense combat, nearly 350 Japs were killed.[34]

Also in this skirmish, another brave Marine would go down in the WWII annals—a hero of the fabled 1st Marine Division. During close combat, Corporal Anthony Casamento, a machine-gun squad leader of the 1st Battalion, 5th Marines, faced the enemy after all the men in his unit were killed. Being severely wounded himself, he continued firing at the enemy, holding them back and protecting his comrades in the other companies. Thirty-eight years later, on September 12, 1980, President Jimmy Carter would present him with the Medal of Honor.[35]

We had won it for 'Old Glory.' Remember Pearl Harbor! There would be so many lives sacrificed on both sides before WWII was over. The Japanese would fight to the last man, so as not to lose face for their country.

53. Condition Yellow!

Sgt. Ward's voice broke the stillness of the early morning hour. "All right men, fall in! I said fall in—now!"

Baker Company had been picked to go out on patrol. I jumped up quickly, being a very light sleeper. Our new sergeant picked right up where Breeding had left off. He was the typical, gung-ho Marine commander, always barking out orders.

Ward shouted, "Listen up! I want every man to gear up right now. If we encounter the enemy there will be no shots fired unless they spot us. Then, and only then, we will defend ourselves. There will be no bullshitting on the trail. I want complete silence! Hand signals only. Clear?"

"CLEAR!" we responded in unison.

We all knew the rules for being out on patrol. They pounded it into our heads back at New River, North Carolina. We tried to move stealthily through the jungle, just like the natives.

The final words from Ward were, "Fall in and prepare to move out!" Just then a runner showed up with orders from Capt. McIlhenny. Our patrol was cancelled until the next morning, for some reason.

After we got back to the bivouac and unloaded our heavy gear, Al said, "Whadda you say we hike out to Henderson Field?"

"What for?" I asked.

"To talk to the pilots."

I was all for it, so we headed out towards Henderson.

As we strolled down the dirt road through the coconut trees, there was a very loud explosion, causing us to hit the deck. We thought the Japs were lobbing artillery shells at us again. Then there was a second explosion, so we took off running in the opposite direction.

We heard someone shout, "Our 155mm howitzers are opening up on the Japs!" Al and I suddenly realized what the big explosions were all about. They were *our* big guns! We went to check them out.

The 155s had been initially left behind back in New Zealand, due to a shortage of cargo space.[36] Later, once we found out the Army wasn't coming to relieve us, Command ordered the guns shipped to Guadalcanal ASAP. It ended up taking three months for them to arrive. After they finally arrived on November 4,[37] a cable snapped, and we lost one of them to the bottom of the Sealark Channel.

We followed the loud kabooms, working our way up a ravine until the 155mm gun positions came into view. Stopping short at about 500 feet, we stood there in silence and watched the gun crews operate this

Official USMC Photograph

155mm cannon discharges its missile toward the Japanese lines, Guadalcanal, c.1942.

beautiful weapon. There were five men in each gun crew, and they all had wads of cotton stuffed in their ears. Four men would load the gun and cock it. Another Marine, holding a long rope tied to the firing pin, would pull the rope, and send the big shell was on its way. There was a terrific, thundering boom that came from this gun—like a big explosion from ten sticks of dynamite. These huge cannons could fire shells up to nine miles.[38]

The crew had the gun pointing west, where it was suspected the Japs positioned their big cannons. Around this location, high up on a mountain, the Japs had two Type 92 10 cm cannons set up in a cave.[39] These huge guns were mounted on rails. They would roll them out of concealment, fire a few shells, then push them back into the cave. They were a very effective weapon for the Japs, with a range of over eleven miles,[40] wreaking havoc on the airfield and the perimeter. Our bombers constantly searched for these huge guns but could never find them. Now, our 155s were giving the Japs a taste of their own medicine. We watched them fire two more rounds, then we decided to get back on the road to Henderson Field.

As we arrived at the airfield, we noticed a few Navy fighter pilots lounging around their bivouac area of pyramid tents. One pilot was sitting on an ammo box with his back leaning against a coconut tree, sipping on a bottle of cherry pop. Approaching him, we asked if he was busy.

"Not right now," he replied. "What can I do for you boys?"

I said, "We wanted to let you know what a swell job you fighter pilots are doing, sir."

The pilot's name was John, and he was in his late twenties. He had a light complexion and black hair and sported a handlebar mustache. John hailed from Boston, Massachusetts, and was a hell of a nice guy. He flew a Grumman Wildcat, a plane that was used in dogfights against the Jap Zeros. Our Marine pilots flew the same type of aircraft, and we watched these air battles play out many times over the island. On the side of his plane were twelve markers indicating the number Jap planes he had shot down.

John asked about ground actions the Marines had been fighting. We told him how all the battles against the Japs were tough, but Bloody Ridge was the worst. We lost many men there, but the Japs lost twice as much.

"The young Marines are doing a hell of a good job keeping up with the traditions of the United States Marine Corps," he replied.

We talked for about an hour, when suddenly, a voice rang out: "CONDITION YELLOW!" The Jap bombers were on their way. John immediately sprang up, waved good-bye, and jumped aboard his aircraft. He and many other pilots started their engines to try and intercept the incoming enemy bombers.

Al and I took off in a big hurry. We wanted to get as far away from Henderson as possible. We sprinted down the dirt road and didn't slow down until we were about a half-mile away.

Just then, a jeep came to a sliding stop, and the driver asked, "Where you guys headed?"

In unison, Al and I responded, "Baker Company." We were in luck. The driver was heading in the same direction.

"Hop in," he said, and took off like a bat outta hell. We held on for

Official USMC Photograph

Seabees laying down Marston Matting on Henderson Field, Guadalcanal, c.1942.

dear life, bouncing around in the jeep. It was the wildest ride I ever had in a military vehicle.

About two minutes later, another voice blared out from under the coconut trees: "CONDITION RED! JAP BOMBERS DIRECTLY OVERHEAD!" Suddenly, the driver slammed on the brakes, coming to an abrupt stop. We were practically thrown out of the jeep as we ran for cover under the trees. We were fortunate to find a vacant bomb shelter made of sandbags and logs, and we quickly dove into a big hole. Twenty-six Jap bombers thundered overhead. Their engines made a weird, droning sound, like they were straining to stay aloft under the heavy load of bombs. Next, came that terrifying, ripping-canvas noise as the bombs fell, raining down all around on us. The boom of each impact caused a shock wave, sending tremors through the ground, and loosening the logs above us.

The airstrip and the planes parked around it were always the bombers' main target. After the air raid, the runway would be one big mess. It was no sweat, however, for our 6th Seabees to remove the tangled mess and install new portable plates, which interlocked together. Afterwards, the bulldozers would smooth out the runway. These men would have it operational in no time at all. Sometimes they'd have the runway completely repaired in twenty to thirty minutes.

The Seabees were a great bunch of hard-working sailors. They labored endlessly and never complained about anything. Their problem was the Navy didn't issue the Seabees any weapons. As the intense fighting continued on the island, they had nothing to protect themselves with against the Japanese ground assaults.

They were always asking the infantry men if we had any weapons to give them. We obliged by giving them rifles from our fallen comrades. In exchange, they'd give us ice cream they made from GI chocolate at the Jap icehouse. The Marines renamed it "Tojo's Ice Company, Under New Management."[41]

The little Jap bastards thought of everything to give themselves the comforts of home. We were glad they had built a bakery and icehouse. Our Marine cooks baked fresh bread anytime they had a chance, between the bombing of aircraft, shelling from ships, and ground fighting. They would bake late in the evening so the Jap planes couldn't spot smoke rising from the oven. We didn't get bread too often, but when we did, you'd have thought someone gave us a lobster dinner!

The air raid lasted about five minutes as the enemy dropped their massive bombs, and, boy, were we scared. Many men lost their lives and were buried alive in shelters. You never knew whether you should run or stay put in your foxhole. Eventually the bombers would disappear and repeat their performance again the next day. Twenty-six bombers always showed up at noon, like clockwork.

We were soaked with sweat as we scrambled out of the bomb shelter and climbed back on the jeep. The driver, a corporal from A Company of our 1st battalion, was Captain Kaempfer's personal driver. He'd been running an errand to the hospital when he picked us up. As we jumped out, he flashed a big smile, as if to say, "We made it back alive!" We saluted him, and he was on his way.

54. Unfit for Combat

In the aftermath of the battle at Matanikau River, the 1st Marine Division was weak and battered. It was bad enough we had to put up with poor nutrition, unsanitary conditions, endless labor, around-the-clock patrols, constant bombings, sleepless nights, and combat fatigue. There was another war being waged against us, and that enemy was winning. The culprit: malaria. A division report stated a secondary anemia had resulted from the disease, causing the condition of the troops to rapidly deteriorate. Every Marine had been completely drained of his strength and stamina, and the corpsman were administering twenty grams of quinine to each man, daily.[42]

Many of the men in B Company, including myself, had already been fighting this menace. During November and December, Captain McIlhenny, Jonsey, and Al succumbed to the malaria fever, and were admitted to sickbay.[43] The number of malaria cases reported by the 1st Marine Division from August to December totaled 5,599.[44]

On November 8, Admiral Halsey flew to Guadalcanal and toured the operation. After talking to many Marines and observing their poor condition, Vandegrift suspected the admiral had decided to replace the 1st Marine Division as soon as possible.[45] By mid-November it was determined the division was beaten down so badly, no man was fit for the front lines.[46]

Although we were taken off offensive operations, the month of November went by quickly for my platoon, with our busy daily routine of patrols and work details. After the final battle, our orders were to occupy and defend Sector Two of the perimeter, a duty we shared with the 7th Marines.[47] Each battalion alternated patrolling jungle trails and sections of the beach, day and night.[48]

Prior to our arrival on the island, many narrow trails had been cut by the natives, and the British had cleared costal roads for their coconut and banana plantations. The East-West trail, situated inland and parallel from the beach, spanned the northern shoreline. This trail would be the focus of our daily patrols throughout most of November. Our daytime patrols were usually to reconnoiter south and east. Sometimes we'd follow this trail past the base of Mount Austen and across the Matanikau River, west to the high coral ridges. Our night patrols were along the beach, mostly between the Tenaru River and Ilu River (Alligator Creek).[49]

No one liked patrolling at night. It was very scary because you never knew what was gonna jump out in front of you. If there was a full moon, your eyes would adjust to the dim light, and you could see a little better. On nights when it was overcast, the island was pitch black. You'd have to feel your way, moving your rifle back and forth in front of you, like a blind person uses a cane. The beach was a little bit easier. You didn't have to worry about stepping into a booby trap or tripping over vines. The bad part about being on the beach is you were a sitting duck for snipers.

Despite the fact we'd defeated the enemy in our last battle, there were still Japs lurking about in the vegetation. The snipers never let up— they were a deadly pain in the ass, and they managed to knock-off a few Marines unexpectedly. Each time this happened, we'd hunt them down and leave them dangling in the trees once we killed them.

Ever since the November 1 battle, Al hadn't been himself. He was always wondering off alone, but never while we were on patrol. One day, while my platoon was on patrol, Al told us he needed to take a leak. After five minutes he didn't return. We called out for him in loud whispers, but there was no answer. Thinking he might have been captured by the enemy, we reported him missing. A search unit was sent out but came back empty. It turned out he went AWOL for almost eight hours.

Around 2000 hours, he turned up in the camp, and Sergeant Ward really chewed him out. Two days later, Al was sent to sickbay to get checked out. The doctor said he was suffering from combat fatigue. Sgt. Ward issued a Summary Court-Martial (SCM) and assigned him extra punitive duties (EPD) at the Division Field Hospital.[50] His pay was also docked to $15.00 a month for six months. He would only make $90.00 for half a year's service.[51] I felt real bad for Al and tried to stop by sickbay often and cheer him up.

The following day, we celebrated the 167th birthday of the United States Marine Corps.[52] After our day patrol, we cracked open bottles of warm Japanese beer, and saluted all the brave men who had come before us. After everything we had endured on Hell Island, we still felt proud to be a part of this tradition.

A few days later, the 1st Battalion was ordered to begin organizing the Regimental Reserve Line (RRL) between the Tenaru and Lunga Rivers. We concentrated our fortifications along the western shore of Alligator Creek.[53] We also had to keep an eye out for another danger: giant saltwater crocodiles. These large reptiles could grow up to twenty feet long and weigh as much as 2,000 pounds.[54] Most had been spooked from all the constant explosions, so we didn't see them too often. Surprisingly, I never heard of anyone being attacked by these huge monsters.

Around this same time, the Seabees started laying down a bridge over the Tenaru River in the 1st Battalion's area. An outpost was established, and units were rotated around the clock to guard the bridge during its construction and after it was completed.[55] This was the easiest duty we had. We usually just stood around smoking and bullshitting.

The Seabees gave names to all the bridges they built on the island. This one was named, Trainer Bridge, after Chief Ship Fitter Trainer, who supervised the construction. It spanned the river 209 feet and had a twenty-foot-wide roadway. The Seabees utilized Jap supplies including twelve-inch diameter telephone poles, I-beams, and other lumber. These guys worked their butts off, twenty-four hours a day, seven days a week. The bridge was ready for traffic by December 5. Before this construction, they had laid down bridges over small streams and one over the Lunga River (Douglas Bridge). They also constructed and maintained many coral roads. Once the coral was crushed down it was almost as good as a cement highway.[56]

On November 26, my platoon was posted at Trainer Bridge. At 1630, we were relieved by the 1st Battalion, 8th Marines.[57] This was a welcome break from the nonstop work during the day and nerve-racking patrolling at night. Command moved us over to Division Reserve, where we bivouacked. Each of our three battalions would then be rotated to be on alert for tactical employment.[58] From November 26 to December 4, there was an air raid just about every night.[59]

55. THE BANANA CAPER

This one day, we didn't have any patrols or working details. All we did was stay close to our tents and wait for orders. We sat in a circle bullshitting about the civilian lives we left behind to join the Marine Corps.

Hennigan and I were talking to each other when we noticed three Marine trucks pass by carrying a native working party. Some of them were sitting on the in-gate with their legs dangling over the edge. The natives had many bunches of nice, ripe bananas—at least ten inches long! One of them dropped two large bunches along the road and motioned for us to pick them up. We both waved to thank them as we ran over and grabbed the bananas, which we gladly shared with the rest of our platoon.

As I began eating mine, I said, "Hey, Henny, let's go look for more bananas. Okay?"

Hennigan looked at me sheepishly and groaned. "Where the fuck are you going to find more bananas?"

"Well, I'll tell you where," I replied. "I was talking to a truck driver right after he delivered supplies to our company, and he told me there were banana groves east past Koli Point.

"That's too gawd-damn far, Messina!"

"What the hell! How many twenty-mile hikes have we already trekked?"

"You're crazy!" he shouted. "Go by yourself!"

The men around us started laughing. Then, Cpl. Podracky said to Hennigan, "Are you afraid to go? You think there might be some leftover Imperial Japanese soldiers wondering around there?"

Hennigan was mad as a hornet. "Fuck you, Podracky! Why don't you go with him?"

"Messina didn't ask me," Pod retorted.

"Fuck you!" snapped Hennigan.

I stood up and put my cartridge belt on, picked up my rifle, and started walking east. About thirteen miles down the beach the Seabee's had just built a new Naval camp at Koli Point.[60] If there had been any recent Japanese landings, they would've radioed it in by now. Besides, the coastwatchers would have notified us of any enemy activity. And I was craving more bananas!

BANANAS
The Marine Corps
trucks were going
by with a native
working party.
One of the
natives tossed a
couple bunches to
the ground for
us, and motioned
us to come and
get them. They
were large ripe
bananas.

1942
John Messina

Cpl. Podracky and the men began to chant, "Hennigan is yellow! Hennigan is yellow!"

Hennigan just laughed, holding his crotch. "I got your yellow, right here!" They kept chanting and Hennigan got even madder. The veins on his neck bulged out, and his face was beet red. "My fucking buddies," he grumbled, as he slowly picked up his rifle and cartridge belt and came running after me.

As he came up behind me, I didn't say anything. I just looked at him with a smile on my face.

He responded by saying, "Fuck you, Messina!"

The best part of the whole thing was we were good friends. I was head-scout, and he was my assistant. We really got to know each other when Sgt. Breeding first put us together as scouts back at Camp Lejeune. Hennigan was very slow in his ways, and he constantly bitched about everything. He hated the snakes, iguanas, mosquitoes, spiders, land crabs, Japs, malaria—you name it. I liked Hennigan, and he liked me, but he showed it in his own stupid way. If Hennigan didn't swear at you, you knew he didn't like you.

Hennigan thought his hometown of Grand Rapids, Michigan, was the best city in the United States, and he constantly bragged about it. He came from a poor family like I did, and we had a lot in common in the way we grew up. Both our parents struggled to put food on the table. We also both worked after school every day for a quarter, which we happily handed over to our parents. Back then, a quarter could buy two and a half pounds of pork chops.

Sometimes we argued over stupid things, but we never fought. As we walked along the beach, Hennigan asked me, "Do you know exactly where the bananas are?"

"Yeah, I know. The truck driver told me."

"Where?"

"It's a little bit past the new Naval camp," I replied. "Up the beach."

"The Navy camp!" he replied. "That's fifteen miles down the beach!"

"I know!"

A mother-f——g spiders, land crabs, Iguana's, mosquitos, snakes, Japs, and malaria on this island !!!! Hennigan was always complaining about anything and everything!

Jim Dasma

"That's a long way to carry a heavy stock of bananas, you stupid dago!"

"Quit your bitchin'!" I said. "We'll take turns, or we'll carry it together!"

We hiked about six miles along the beach, when suddenly there was a foul odor in the air. The stench was so bad we both started gagging. We were in the Tenaru area, where the Japanese had been buried after the battle back in August. Our bulldozers pushed hundreds of dead bodies into craters made by bombs. They were buried deep beneath the earth, but their rotting funk still seeped up through the sand. In the jungle heat, the corpses begin to decay in a matter of hours. I think this is the worst smell that can come into anyone's nostrils. It's so putrid it makes you want to vomit. Hennigan and I held our hankies pressed tightly to our noses and ran as fast as we could until we were past the mass graves.

After we slowed down to a walk, red-eyed Hennigan cursed, "You fucking dago! If I knew it was going to be like this, I would've never come!"

"Quit your bitchin', Hennigan," I responded. "I'm putting up with it too!"

"Yeah, yeah, Messina. Fuck you!"

The next mile we walked along without talking, listening intently for any unfamiliar sounds. It felt as though eyes were peering at us through the vegetation, and I had a tingling feeling running down my spine. I thought to myself, what if there are a few Japs in this area? I think Hennigan was thinking the same thing, because he was pointing his rifle into the jungle, scanning from the treetops to the thick undergrowth.

Eventually, we arrived at the Naval camp and noticed many tents pitched along the sandy beach. The 14th NCB had recently arrived from Aola Bay, forty miles east of the Lunga perimeter, where they had just attempted to build an airfield.[61] The area was all swamplands, so the project was moved to this location where construction would begin in a few days.[62]

We stopped to talk to the sailor on guard duty—a puny-looking guy in Navy dungarees. This kid looked like he was about sixteen years old. His white sailor cap was cocked forward and perched on his nose, and he had two upside-down stripes on the bottom cuff of his left sleeve.

"Hey, gyrenes," he asked, "what you guys doin' in this neck of the

we took our rifles with us.
we carried our ponchos
— to put the fruit in —
We had to walk about a
mile past the Navy outpost to
get to the banana groves.
We first came upon a pineapple
patch before reaching the bananas.
Henni gan stopped to pick pineapples.
I went on alone to get a whole
stock of green bananas.

DRAWN
(1994)
Jim Messena

woods? Can't you see the Navy has the situation well in hand?" He was a cocky little guy, too!

Hennigan fired back. "What the hell you talkin' about, swabby?"

"I said we don't need any help around this area from you gyrenes."

Hennigan started after the young sailor with clenched fists, and I quickly inserted my finger in his back belt loop, stopping his advance. "Don't pay any attention to the swab jockey, Henny," I said. "The last thing we need is a court-martial, right now. He's just another one of those little smart-ass bastards! Let's go look for bananas, like we planned."

Hennigan threw him the finger and cussed out the whole damned Navy. The sailor had a shit-eatin' grin on his face as we walked away.

I remembered the truck driver telling me we would find the banana trees about a quarter mile past the Naval camp. So, we continued and stumbled upon a pineapple patch. Guadalcanal pineapples were long and narrow, about 10 inches long. The natives had taught us how to pick the ripe ones. You tug on the top leaves, and if one comes out easily, the pineapple is ready to eat. Hennigan immediately began pulling out pineapples and loading his sack.

"What the fuck are you doing!" I said. "I thought we came for bananas?"

"Go ahead," he muttered. "I'll catch up with you."

About 1,000 yards from the pineapple patch, I spotted the banana trees, which were about twelve feet tall. Looking up, I was amazed at one particular stock of green bananas. Each banana was at least a foot long. I whipped out my pocketknife and shinnied up the tree.

Once I reached the stock, I braced myself between two branches and began cutting the huge stem. The wood was very stringy and tough, so I had to hack at it a little at a time. It took me at least twenty minutes to cut through.

Next, I lowered the bananas to the ground, and climbed down the tree. Once I was on the ground, I remembered something I'd heard about giant banana spiders lurking in between the fruit. I immediately began to worry, thinking about the bite I'd endured from the little spider.

Examining the stock closely, I was relieved there were no arachnids inside.

After taking a short rest, I hoisted the stock over my shoulders, grunting from the heavy weight. My rigorous military training helped me bear the burden of the load. As I approached the pineapple patch, I lowered my stock to the ground and looked in all directions, but Hennigan was nowhere to be found!

I whispered loudly, "Hennigan! Hey Hennigan, where the hell are you?" There was no answer. I tried one more time. Still no answer. I felt an uneasiness being there all alone and didn't want to call out again, so I quickly put my load back on my shoulder and headed towards the Naval camp.

Reaching the camp, the little sailor spotted me. There were a few more sailors on duty with him this time. I stopped a few feet in front of them and was about to ask a question when the little smart-ass spoke up.

"Your buddy went by here about a half-hour ago with a sack full of pineapples," he said.

"Yeah," I replied. "Go on."

"He wouldn't even give us one measly pineapple. Nice guy, your buddy!"

The bananas seemed to get heavier as I was standing there. The sailor was now expecting a bunch of bananas, but he didn't get any. I just smiled and walked away. I didn't look back, but I could hear them cussing out the Marine Corps.

There were a lot of trucks passing me on the road, but no one stopped, even though I had my hitchhiking thumb out. After walking about two miles down the road, a jeep finally stopped, and the driver told me to hop in. We both held our noses as the jeep passed through the burial site of the dead Japanese soldiers.

As we entered the bivouac area, the jeep skidded to a stop. I jumped out and ripped off a bunch of the bananas, handing them to the driver. He flashed a big grin and sped away. I turned around, and the first thing I saw was my buddy Hennigan sitting on a log, slobbering on a pineapple. He was spinning it around in his mouth like an ear of corn and gobbled it so fast the juice gushed off his chin, drenching his shirt. The rest of my platoon was there dribbling juice down the front of their shirts, too.

"You son of a bitch!" I said, walking up to Hennigan. "Where the hell did you disappear to?"

"Whata you mean?" he replied, slobbering.

"I called your name over and over, but you were nowhere in sight!"

"You dumb bastard, the banana trees were too far from the pineapple patch. I wasn't gonna stay out there alone and be a target for a sniper. So, I left!"

By this time, I was really irritated. "Thanks a lot, Hennigan! That's the last time I suggest anything to you!"

"Fuck you!"

We didn't stay mad at each other, though, and it blew over real quick. We had a lot of laughs together. He still was my friend, foul mouth and all.

My bananas were green, so I needed to find a place to hide them until they were ripe. So, I put them at the base of a coconut tree a good distance from the camp. A whole week passed by, and when I checked them, they were still green! No one told me they should've been buried in the ground to ripen quickly. All my efforts to acquire those bananas was in vain. It was a lesson well learned. After that, I never hiked so many miles for this jungle treat again. All my future bananas would come from our friendly natives.

56. Turning Point

In remaining days of November, while the 5th Regiment had been removed from offensive operations, the Allied Forces and the Armed Forces of the Empire of Japan faced off in a number of ground actions, air assaults, and two major air-naval battles. Both sides were feverishly trying to get additional reinforcements onto the island, as the situation on Guadalcanal had reached a critical moment.

From October 23 to 25, General Vandegrift had met with other military leaders at Nouméa and expressed the poor condition of his 1st Marine Division, making it clear he could hold the island only if more reinforcements and support were delivered. The newly appointed commander of the South Pacific area, Admiral William F. Halsey, Jr., assured our general he would receive the support he requested.[63]

Prints & Photographs Division, Library of Congress

Sailing with their sterns to the rising sun, ships of an American convoy set out for the Southwest Pacific, c.1940-46.

On October 24, 1942, President Roosevelt sent a message to the Joints Chiefs of Staff that Guadalcanal must be reinforced.[64] Once these orders were given, a significant buildup of forces on land and sea quickly followed. The new battleship USS *Indiana* (BB 58) and its task force, along with the repaired aircraft carrier USS *Enterprise*, were sent to the South Pacific area.[65]

By November 4-5 additional Army-Marine forces, 500 Seabees, and two batteries of 155mm guns, arrived on the island.[66] After three long months without adequate food, supplies, or reinforcements, the Marines would finally get the help they so desperately needed to defeat the enemy once and for all.

The Japanese, determined to take back the island, were also trying to bring in more reinforcements. Little did they know the Americans weren't going to let that happen. Having fresh troops on the ground and additional air and sea support, the Allied forces increased pressure on the enemy, and the fighting intensified.

After defeating the enemy at Point Cruz, Vandegrift suspended the offensive in the Matanikau area and concentrated on a new eastern threat.[67] An action began on November 3, with five Japanese destroyers arriving to unload cargo and 300 Imperial Army troops. In the meantime, a sizable force of Jap troops was marching east, retreating from the aftermath from the Battle of Henderson Field.[68]

While the battle in the eastern sector was fought, on November 5, an air raid of twenty-seven Bettys and twenty-four Zeros thundered over the perimeter, hidden by an overcast sky. By nightfall seventeen ships of the Tokyo Express followed—ten going to Tassafaronga and six to Cape Esperance, delivering more Japanese reinforcements.[69]

By November 9, Army-Marine forces surrounded the enemy at Gavaga Creek, east of the Metapona River. Around 3,000 soldiers, part of the 17th Imperial Army, managed to escape through a pocket by means of a swampy creek on the southern side of the American lines. This gap was closed on November 11, and by the 12th the remaining Japanese soldiers were killed, leaving 450 dead. The Americans lost forty men, with 120 wounded.[70]

One fine example of raw jungle fighting by the Marines involved Lieutenant Colonel Evans F. Carlson's 2d Raider Battalion, also known as "Carlson's Raiders." After the 3,000 enemy soldiers escaped into the jungle, Carlson organized his Raiders to pursue the enemy as his marines struggled through the treacherous terrain. After a series of twelve guerrilla actions from November 11 to December 4, they killed over 488 enemy soldiers. The Raiders only lost sixteen men, with eighteen wounded.[71]

Another violent clash between the Allied naval forces (aided by Cactus Air Force) and the Imperial Navy, took place from November 12-15 during the Naval Battle of Guadalcanal. Although, there were significant losses on both sides, the U. S. came out victorious, preventing most of the Japanese troops and supplies from reaching the island, and averting more shelling of Henderson Field from their battleships.[72]

The night of November 12-13, we heard loud booms far offshore, and everyone rushed down to the beach to watch the spectacular air-naval conflict. Star shells rose and burst, illuminating the night sky, and bright orange lines cut huge arcs through the darkness from giant tracers.[73] We witnessed the breathtaking display in awe, but knew the aftermath would be grim.

Two days later, in a desperate attempt to land their troops, four remaining transports of the Japanese reinforcement group ran aground at Tassafaronga. As a result of the "Buzzard Patrol" (planes from Henderson and Espiritu Santo that joined forces with ground artillery and Naval shelling), the Japanese transports were left empty, burning hulls. Most of the men escaped, and the Japs managed to deliver 10,000 new troops, but American air and sea actions would prevent the Tokyo Express from delivering further supplies or reinforcements.[74]

This battle was a victory for the Americans and would be a major turning point.[75] Our Navy lost two outstanding commanders, Rear Admiral's Daniel J. Callaghan, and Norman Scott. Both of these brave seamen were posthumously awarded the Medal of Honor. At the end of the four-day air-naval conflict, American losses totaled ten ships, thirty-six aircraft, and 1,732 men killed. The Japanese lost seventeen ships, sixty-four aircraft, and 1,900 men.[76]

Scores of sailors lost their lives or were severely injured during this epic conflict. One of the most tragic stories, however, involved the five Sullivan brothers, all of whom were assigned aboard the light cruiser, USS *Juneau* (CL 52).[77] The 6,000-ton cruiser, which was already damaged from an earlier hit on the morning of November 13, was struck again by a torpedo fired from a Japanese submarine. It immediately exploded, erupting into a massive gush of water and dark smoke before sinking. Of the 700 sailors aboard the ship, only about 120 men survived. Their fate would turn out to be a heart-wrenching effort to stay alive. In a swirling whirlpool of thick oil, the lone surviving Sullivan brother, George, called out for his four siblings, but there was no answer. Albert, Francis, Joseph, and Madison had all perished along with countless others.[78]

Sadly, two other damaged cruisers nearby, USS *San Francisco* and USS *Helena*, did not attempt to rescue the survivors, fearing additional casualties.

The remaining sailors tied together three rafts and seven life nets, and began rowing towards San Cristobal Island, far off in the distance. After three days, they ran out of food, and rain became their only source of drinking water. Aside from exhaustion, starvation, and, in most cases, delirium, their scanty armada began attracting sharks. These dire circumstances ended in gruesome and agonizing deaths for many of the sailors. George Sullivan lost his life on the fifth night.[79] In the end, the total number of men killed from the sinking of USS *Juneau* would total 687.[80]

As a result of this unimaginable loss for the Sullivan family, the U. S. War Department adopted the Sole Survivor Policy. Enacted in 1948, the law was designed to protect family members from the draft or combat duty if other members of the family were lost in military service.[81] The list of tributes honoring the five Sullivan brother's legacy is long, including a museum, two Navy destroyers named after them, a movie, and many other accolades.[82]

After this decisive sea battle, Vandegrift turned his attention west again, determined to extend the western perimeter beyond the Poha River. The Last Action of the Matanikau, involving elements of the 164th and l82nd Army Infantries and 8th Marines, took place November 18-23.[83]

On November 18, our engineers installed a footbridge across the Matanikau River. Over the next three days, four units of the American forces advanced west, securing a 1,700-yard line of attack stretching south from Point Cruz. The Japanese had a concentration of forces at Kokumbona and further inland on the western bank of the Poha River. The enemy resisted strongly, and the attack was halted. On November 23, our troops were ordered to dig in north of Point Cruz. The battle, which lasted for six weeks, ended in a stalemate. We ended up losing 134 Army-Marine soldiers, but the number of Japanese losses was never confirmed.[84]

During last two weeks of November, after the Tokyo Express had been disrupted, the Japs tried getting supplies to their ground troops using submarines, which proved to be unsuccessful. Following this failure, they came up with another plan. They used empty oil drums and filled them with food and supplies, stringing them together with ropes. As Jap destroyers passed by Guadalcanal, the drums would be launched towards the island, and a small boat or swimmer would pull the supplies ashore.[85]

Their first attempt of this new method occurred on November 30. In a final blow by our Navy, another engagement took place on this night called the Battle of Tassafaronga. A U.S. force of five cruisers and four destroyers attacked eight Japanese destroyers attempting to deliver supplies and ground forces to Guadalcanal. Our Navy lost one cruiser, with three destroyers heavily damaged, and 395 sailors killed. Japanese losses were one destroyer sunk and 349 killed.[86]

57. Leaving Hell Island

In the last days of November, we received word the 25th Army Division was coming in to relieve us.[87] This was the best news we'd heard in four months. No one knew where Command would send us, but we all cheered anyway. All we knew for sure was we were finally getting off "Hell Island," with all its infestations and other annoyances!

On December 7, we started moving equipment to the beach near the Lunga lagoon area. There was another air-raid alarm that day, and everyone scattered, but no enemy planes were spotted.[88] This same day, General Vandegrift issued his final division letter on Guadalcanal to his troops. This is an excerpt of what he wrote:

> In relinquishing command in the Cactus Area, I hope I can convey to you my feeling of pride in your magnificent accomplishments and my thanks for the unbounded loyalty, limitless self-sacrifice and high courage which have those accomplishments possible… To the soldiers and Marines who have faced the enemy in the fierceness of night combat… I say that at all times you have faced without flinching the worst that the enemy could do to us and have thrown back the best that he could send against us…[89]

Vandegrift was one hell of a commander, and we were just as proud to serve under his leadership.

The next day at dawn, a convoy of three transports, USS *Crescent*

City (AP-40), USS *President Jackson* (AP-37), and USS *President Adams* (AP-38), along with a destroyer escort, arrived in the harbor and anchored 1,500 yards off Lunga Point.[90] USS *President Jackson* started unloading troops and equipment of the Army's 132d Infantry.[91] Boy, were we happy to see them! I don't think anyone actually believed we were being relieved until we saw them face to face. We worked all morning into the early afternoon moving our equipment to the beach.[92]

The day of our departure from Guadalcanal came on December 9, 1942. Reveille blew at 0300, and chow was served at 0400.[93] At daybreak there was much excitement as we packed our gear, and there were happy faces all around. As we marched to the beach, the 7th Marines were there to see us off. They hated to see us leave and said farewell with a salute of *"Semper Fi."* A small group of landing boats were waiting near the shore to take us to the ships anchored in the channel.

Waving goodbye to the 7th Marines, we boarded the Higgins boats. After the first eight were loaded, the coxswains guided their boats off Lunga Point out to the transport ships. We were lucky to leave Guadalcanal alive.

Most of us struggled, clambering up the cargo net to get to the top deck. Some Marines were too weak to climb and had to be hoisted up by the sailors.

The 1st Marine Division arrived at Guadalcanal looking snappy, well-fed, and physically fit. But on the day of our departure, we were worn out and frail, and our uniforms were dirty and tattered. Almost every man had dropped about twenty pounds.[94]

At 1200, the 1st Battalion, 5th Marines, embarked the USS *Crescent City*.[95] A Company was the first to climb up the cargo net and onto the deck of the ship. The second bunch of men to board was our outfit, B Company. As I stepped onto the deck, I turned my head towards the stern and saluted the flag. This was always the Navy's rule, whenever you came aboard any ship. Next, I saluted the OOD and asked, "Permission to come aboard, sir?"

He saluted back and replied, "Permission granted." There are no words to describe the feeling I had at that very moment, as I took in a big breath of the fresh sea air. For the rest of my life, I will be forever grateful to God for sparing my life on Hell Island.

When the time came for us to leave Guadalcanal, General Vandegrift handed over his command to Major General Alexander M. Patch of the U.S. Army.[96] The 1st Marine Division would be relieved by the 2nd Marine Division, and the Army's 25th Infantry.[97] Later, additional reinforcements would be sent to Guadalcanal, and the Japanese would be driven off the island by February 9, 1943.[98]

By the time it was all over, the Allied Forces would lose twenty-nine ships, while the Japanese lost thirty-two, along with six submarines.[99] Among the downed aircraft, 615 were American and 683 were Japanese.[100] After the conflict ended, the twenty-mile stretch of Sealark Channel between Savo Island, Florida Island, and Guadalcanal would become known as "Iron Bottom Sound," for the many aircraft and ships lying on the sea floor. The combined total losses of life of the U.S. and Allied forces for land, sea, and air amounted to 7,400 men; the total Japanese dead was 30,343.[101]

In the Guadalcanal campaign, which lasted over four months, we would experience many sad moments. The day before our departure, my platoon visited the island's cemetery, where we saw 650 white crosses for the fallen comrades of our 1st Marine Division.[102]

President Franklin D. Roosevelt awarded General Vandegrift the Medal of Honor for his leadership of the American forces, calling it an "Outstanding and heroic accomplishment." Also, the entire 1st Marine Division (Reinforced) was awarded the Presidential Unit Citation for "Outstanding gallantry."[103]

There was a national sigh of relief when the Japs were knocked off that island, a radio news commentator has said, and the name Guadalcanal has passed into history bearing the magical qualities of such other American battlefields as Valley Forge, Gettysburg, and Belleau Wood.[104]

Official USMC Photographs

Top: Coconut palm leaves cover the graves on Guadalcanal, last resting place for the gallant Marines killed in action avenging Japanese tyranny; Bottom: A Higgins boat takes aboard a load of Marines to take them to waiting transports for transfer to another South Pacific base, c.1942.

GLOSSARY AND GUIDE TO ABBREVIATIONS

1st Lt. First Lieutenant

2nd Lt. Second Lieutenant

6th Seabees construction battalion of the Civil Engineering Corps of the US Navy

Able call letter for Company "A"

Adm. Admiral

AF store ship

AK cargo ship

Atabrine synthesized quinine, it's the common trade name for the malaria impotence and the fact that it would turn the skin bright yellow

AP transport

APA troop-carrying assault transport

ammo ammunition

Aotearoa Maori native's name for the country of New Zealand, its literal translation is "land of the long white cloud"

APD high-speed transport (converted destroyers)

AWOL absent without official leave

Baker call letter for Company "B"

bandolier pocketed shoulder-belt used for carrying individual cartridges/bullets

banzai shortened term for "Long live the Emperor" Japanese battle cry during the Pacific War

BAR Browning Automatic Rifle

battalion a large body of troops consisting of four to six companies; can include up to about 1,000 soldiers

BB battleship

BSIPD British Solomon Island Protectorate Defense Force

Betty Japanese Mitsubishi G4M, or Mitsubishi Navy Type 1 attack bomber

boondocks remote wooded areas

boot a Marine fresh out of boot camp, or no experience in actual combat

BTO (Big Time Operator) someone who is always looking for a way to make money, usually by selling items that not available at many times the cost

CA heavy cruiser

Cactus code name for the island of Guadalcanal

cadence a rhythmic flow or sequence of sounds or words; the beat, rate, or measure of any rhythmic movement

Capt. Captain

CCC Civilian Conservation Corps

cheval-de-frise a wooden frame covered with spikes or barbed wire, used by the military to block enemy advancement

chit official slip of paper issued by the military to be redeemed for food or lodging during the 1940s

chow food

CL light cruiser

CO Commanding Officer or Commissioned Officer

coastwatchers Allied military intelligence operatives stationed throughout Australia and the South Pacific during WWII to observe enemy movements

Col. Colonel

combat fatigue also known as shell shock, it's a type of post-traumatic stress disorder caused by wartime conditions

company smallest body of troops that functions as a complete administrative and tactical unit

COMSOPAC Commander South Pacific Area and South Pacific Force (WWII era)

corpsman the Marine equivalent of an army medic

Cosmoline the trademark for a military generic class of rust preventives

CP command post

Cpl. Corporal

CPO Chief Petty Officer

C-Ration an individual canned, pre-cooked, and prepared wet ration

dago an ethnic slur referring to Italians

DD destroyer

depth charge an antisubmarine weapon that is dropped near a target and descends to a predetermined depth where it explodes; also called a depth bomb

DI drill instructor

Division Reserve a group of military personnel or units not committed to a battle so that it remains available to address unforeseen situations

dope truth or real story

doped out investigated by intelligence

drink ocean

dumdum a bullet with the tip snipped off

echelon a subdivision of a military or naval force

entrenching tool small shovel with a folding handle

EPD Extra Punitive Duties; punishment assigned where the individual is required to perform cleaning duties after working hours (on his or her liberty time)

fourragère a military award in the form of a braided cord, distinguishing military units as a whole

FMF Fleet Marine Force

Gen. General

GI Government Issue or General Issue

goldbricker a member of the military who feigns illness to avoid duty

greenback a dollar bill

gung-ho unthinkingly enthusiastic and eager, especially about taking part in fighting or warfare

gyrene low-ranking Marine; combination of GI and Marine

head any marine bathroom aboard a boat or ship

Headquarters Company military unit supplying the necessary specialist personnel for headquarters of a battalion or higher unit

heavy marching order term for when troops are fully equipped for field service

hitch one term of service in the military: usually four years

Hollywood Marines Parris Island Marines term for West Coast Marines

Joe Army soldier

jungle rot any cutaneous disease or condition caused or induced by a tropical climate

King Shit someone with an overly inflated self-opinion

KP kitchen police

LCP(L) Landing Craft Personnel (Large)

LCVP Landing Craft, Vehicle and Personnel

leatherneck seasoned Marine

longhair music classical music

lorry (plural lorries) a large, heavy motor vehicle for transporting goods or troops; a truck

Lt. Lieutenant

Lt. Col. Lieutenant Colonel

Lt. Gen. Lieutenant General

Mac Marine

Maggie's drawers a total miss at the shooting range

Maj. Major

Maj. Gen. Major General

Māori a member of the aboriginal people of New Zealand

MLR main line of resistance

MP Military Police

MI903 US-built Springfield .30-caliber bolt-action rifle

NCB Naval Construction Battalion

NCO Non-Commissioned Officer

ninety-day wonder WWII nickname for college graduates who were commissioned as second lieutenants after a brief ninety-day officer-training course.

Nip an ethnic slur for the Japanese enemy

Nippon bridge the first crossing above the Matanikau River mouth, a small footbridge about 2,000 yards inland

oblique a naval movement during close-order drill where the entire formation pivots diagonally at a forty-five-degree angle

OD officer of the day

OIC officer in charge

old salt a seasoned sailor, especially one who is hardy and forthright in manner

OOD officer of the deck

OP outpost

P-39 Bell Air Cobra fighter (Army Air Force)

PBY US Navy Consolidated Catalina twin-engine patrol bomber

penny ante low stakes poker game

PFC Private First Class

Pistol Pete Marine's nickname for a Japanese long-range field artillery piece that lobbed random shells into the Marine-held sector on Guadalcanal

platoon a military unit normally consisting of two or more squads or sections

pogey bait old term for candy or sweets

police up to pick up items (such as litter or expended ammunition casings)

prone position laying on your stomach while firing a rifle at a range of five-hundred feet

PTSD post-traumatic stress disorder

pulling butts to mark and score targets on a shooting range from behind a berm

Pvt. Private

PX Post Exchange; a store at a US military base selling food, clothing, and other items

quinine antimalarial drug derived from the bark of the cinchona tree

Raggedy-Ass Marines West Coast Marine's term for Parris Island Marines

regiment a military unit normally consisting of a number of battalions

RRL regimental reserve line

salty experienced or well-worn person or object, from the salt that would accumulate after long-term exposure to salt water.

SBD US Navy/Marine Douglas Dauntless dive-bomber

scuttlebutt gossip and/or rumors

seabag Marine khaki barracks bag

Seabees name given to US Navy construction engineers and their work crews

Seagoing Bellhop derogatory term for Marines

Semper Fi shortened version of "*Semper Fidelis,*" motto of the Corps, Latin for "always faithful"

Sgt. Sergeant

Sgt. Maj. Sergeant Major

shit on a shingle chipped or creamed beef on toast

SIC Sergeant in Charge

smoking lamp phrase used figuratively in the military for restrictions concerning smoking cigarettes, cigars, or a pipe

smoke stacking to tell a lie

S.O.I. the locals' moniker for the Order Sons of Italy in America hall in West Aliquippa, Pennsylvania, the largest and oldest Italian American fraternal organization in the United States

squad a US Marine Corps unit consists of a squad leader and three fireteams (four men each) in a rifle squad, a total of thirteen men, or three to eight men in a crew-served weapons squad

SS steamship

swab jockey (swabby) anyone in the US Navy below the rank of Vice Admiral

The Slot the name given to New Georgia Sound and Indispensable Strait by the Allies during the WWII to describe the central geographic area between the two chains of Solomon Islands

tin can Navy destroyer

U-boat German submarine

USMC US Marine Corps

USN US Navy

USS United States ship—used in the names of US naval vessels

V. Adm. Vice Admiral

Wildcat US Navy/Marine F4F Wildcat Fighter plane

YP (Yippie) former San Diego tuna boats sent to the Solomons by the US Navy for duty as supply ships in the Pacific theater during WWII

Zero Japanese Mitsubishi fighter

NOTES

CHAPTER 3

1. https://pearlharbor.org/man-who-planned-the-attacks/, retrieved: June 2021.

CHAPTER 4

1. https://en.wikipedia.org/wiki/John_A._Lejeune, updated: 5 December 2018.
2. Official Military Personnel File of Robert James Johnson, National Archives at St. Louis.
3. William L. Hawkins, Division of Press Intelligence, 14 September 1942, *News-Times*, Danbury, Connecticut
4. Cosimo Angelo Negri, Casualty Card, Historical Reference Branch, USMC History Division.
5. Official Military Personnel File of Andrew John Yanno, National Archives at St. Louis.
6. ibid., Salvatore Anthony Messina.
7. ibid., Davie Warren Shuford.
8. ibid., George Felton Jones.
9. ibid., Gerrit Edward Heidema.
10. ibid., Robert Julius Johnson.
11. ibid., Robert Joseph Hilsky.
12. ibid., Austin Windell Pollock, Jr.
13. Lawrence Ray Cokley, Casualty Card, Historical Reference Branch, USMC History Division.
14. Official Military Personnel File of Eugene Breeding, National Archives at St. Louis.
15. *The Old Breed*, George McMillan, p. 2.
16. Official Military Personnel File of Albert Steve Podracky, National Archives at St. Louis.

CHAPTER 5

1. *The Old Breed*, George McMillan, pp. 8-9.
2. ibid., p.14.
3. http://www.1stmardiv.marines.mil/About/History, retrieved: June 2017.
4. *The Old Breed*, George McMillan, p. 11.
5. *The 1st Marine Division and its Regiments,* Danny J. Crawford, Robert V. Aquilina, Anne A. Ferrante, and Shelia P. Gramblin, Reference Section, Historical Branch, p. 1.
6. *The Old Breed*, George McMillan, p. 12.
7. *Once a Marine*, A. A. Vandegrift, as told to Robert B. Asprey, p. 98.
8. https://www.ibiblio.org/hyperwar//USCG/V2-Transports/index.html, page 1, retrieved: July 2017.
9. *Once a Marine*, A. A. Vandegrift, as told to Robert B. Asprey, p. 100.
10. https://www.ibiblio.org/hyperwar//USCG/V2-Transports/index.html, page 1, retrieved: July 2017.
11. https://dmna.ny.gov/historic/veterans/transcriptions/Murphy_Francis_Gregory_Diary.pdf, retrieved: August 2017.
12. ibid.
13. https://www.ibiblio.org/hyperwar//USCG/V2-Transports/index.html, page 1, retrieved: July 2017.
14. https://dmna.ny.gov/historic/veterans/transcriptions/Murphy_Francis_Gregory_Diary.pdf, retrieved: August 2017.
15. *Guadalcanal: The Definitive Account of the Landmark Battle,* Richard B. Frank, p. 48.
16. https://dmna.ny.gov/historic/veterans/transcriptions/Murphy_Francis_Gregory_Diary.pdf,

retrieved: August 2017.

17. http://nzshipmarine.com/nodes/view/27, retrieved: October 2017.
18. *Once a Marine*, A. A. Vandegrift, as told to Robert B. Asprey, p. 100.
19. *Guadalcanal: Starvation Island*, Eric Hammel, p. 30.
20. https://dmna.ny.gov/historic/veterans/transcriptions/Murphy_Francis_Gregory_Diary.pdf, retrieved: August 2017.

CHAPTER 6

1. Official Military Personnel File of James J. Messina, National Archives at St. Louis.
2. https://www.nationalww2museum.org/students-teachers/student-resources/research-starters/research-starters-us-military-numbers, retrieved: October 2017.
3. http://nzshipmarine.com/nodes/view/27, retrieved: October 2017.
4. *The Old Breed*, George McMillan, p. 17.
5. ibid., p. 18.
6. ibid., p. 20.
7. Official Military Personnel File of James J. Messina, National Archives at St. Louis.
8. Final Report on Guadalcanal, United States Marine Corps, 1st Marine Division, Phase I, p. 6.
9. *A Narrative History of the 1st Battalion, 11th Marines During the Early History and Deployment of the 1st Marine Division, 1940-43*, James C. Rill, p. 46.
10. http://nzshipmarine.com/nodes/view/27, retrieved: October 2017.
11. *Once a Marine*, A. A. Vandegrift, as told to Robert B. Asprey, p. 112.
12. Final Report on Guadalcanal, United States Marine Corps, 1st Marine Division, Phase I, p. 7.
13. ibid.

CHAPTER 7

1. *Guadalcanal: The Definitive Account of the Landmark Battle,* Richard B. Frank, p. 35.
2. *Combat Narratives: Solomon Islands Campaign: I The Landing in the Solomons,* Naval History and Heritage Command, pp. 5-8.
3. *The Old Breed,* George McMillan, p. 22.
4. *Once a Marine*, A. A. Vandegrift, as told to Robert B. Asprey, p. 118.
5. *Combat Narratives: Solomon Islands Campaign: I The Landing in the Solomons,* Naval History and Heritage Command, pp. 5-8.
6. *The Old Breed,* George McMillan, p. 23.
7. *First Offensive: The Marine Campaign for Guadalcanal,* Henry I. Shaw, Jr., p. 6.
8. *The Old Breed,* George McMillan, p. 19.
9. *Once a Marine*, A. A. Vandegrift, as told to Robert B. Asprey, p. 113.
10. https://en.wikipedia.org/wiki/South_Pacific_Mandate, retrieved: February 2018.
11. *The Old Breed,* George McMillan, p. 22.
12. Final Report on Guadalcanal, United States Marine Corps, 1st Marine Division, Phase I, Annex P, p. 2.
13. ibid., p. 9.
14. *The Old Breed,* George McMillan, p. 31.
15. Muster Roll, Company B, 1st Battalion, 5th Marines, 1st Marine Division, September 1942, p. 1.
16. *The Old Breed,* George McMillan, p. 23.
17. Final Report on Guadalcanal, United States Marine Corps, 1st Marine Division, Phase II, p. 1.
18. Final Report on Guadalcanal, United States Marine Corps, 1st Marine Division, Phase II, Annex L, p. 1.
19. Final Report on Guadalcanal, United States Marine Corps, 1st Marine Division, Phase II, p. 1.
20. T*he Old Breed,* George McMillan, p. 30.

21. *Guadalcanal: The First Offensive,* John Miller, Jr., p. 69.
22. *The Old Breed,* George McMillan, p. 33.
23. Final Report on Guadalcanal, United States Marine Corps, 1st Marine Division, Phase II, Annex L, p. 1.
24. ibid., p. 1.
25. *Guadalcanal: The First Offensive,* John Miller, Jr., p. 70.
26. *Guadalcanal: The Definitive Account of the Landmark Battle,* Richard B. Frank, p. 50.
27. Final Report on Guadalcanal, United States Marine Corps, 1st Marine Division, Phase II, Annex G, p. 7.
28. http://www.battleforaustralia.org/Theyalsoserved/Coastwatchers/Coastwatchers_Guadalcanal.html, 13 January 2011.
29. *Guadalcanal: The Definitive Account of the Landmark Battle,* Richard B. Frank, p. 67.
30. Final Report on Guadalcanal, United States Marine Corps, 1st Marine Division, Phase II, p. 10.
31. https://en.wikipedia.org/wiki/Martin_Clemens, updated: 15 January 2018.
32. *Guadalcanal: The Definitive Account of the Landmark Battle,* Richard B. Frank, p. 70.
33. ibid., p. 72.
34. ibid., p. 70.
35. Final Report on Guadalcanal, United States Marine Corps, 1st Marine Division, Phase II, Annex L, p. 2.
36. *Guadalcanal: The Definitive Account of the Landmark Battle,* Richard B. Frank, p. 80.
37. ibid., p. 102.
38. ibid., p. 105.
39. *First Offensive: The Marine Campaign for Guadalcanal*, Henry I. Shaw, Jr., p. 12.
40. *Guadalcanal: The Definitive Account of the Landmark Battle,* Richard B. Frank, p. 116.
41. *The Old Breed,* George McMillan, p. 42.
42. *Guadalcanal: The Definitive Account of the Landmark Battle,* Richard B. Frank, p. 121.
43. ibid., p. 117.
44. *Guadalcanal: The Definitive Account of the Landmark Battle,* Richard B. Frank, pa.120.
45. **a.** https://en.wikipedia.org/wiki/Battle_of_the_Coral_Sea, updated: 1 March 2018;
    b. https://en.wikipedia.org/wiki/Battle_of_Midway, updated: 27 February 2018.
46. *First Offensive: The Marine Campaign for Guadalcanal*, Henry I. Shaw, Jr., p. 13.
47. *Guadalcanal: The Definitive Account of the Landmark Battle,* Richard B. Frank, p. 125.
48. *The Old Breed,* George McMillan, p 45.
49. Final Report on Guadalcanal, United States Marine Corps, 1st Marine Division, Phase II, Annex L, p. 3.
50. https://en.wikipedia.org/wiki/Al_Schmid, updated: 20 September 2017.
51. http://www.historynet.com/marine-sergeant-al-schmid-september-96-world-war-ii-feature.htm, updated: 8/19/1996.
52. *Guadalcanal: The Definitive Account of the Landmark Battle,* Richard B. Frank, p. 128.

CHAPTER 8

1. ibid., p. 130.
2. *The Old Breed,* George McMillan, p. 52.
3. https://en.wikipedia.org/wiki/Frank_Goettge, updated: 20 December 2017.
4. *Guadalcanal: The Definitive Account of the Landmark Battle,* Richard B. Frank, p. 130.
5. *The Old Breed,* George McMillan, pp. 52-55.
6. *Guadalcanal: The Definitive Account of the Landmark Battle,* Richard B. Frank, p. 130.
7. Final Report on Guadalcanal, United States Marine Corps, 1st Marine Division, Phase III, Annex J, p. 2.
8. *Once a Marine*, A. A. Vandegrift, as told to Robert B. Asprey, p. 137.
9. Final Report on Guadalcanal, United States Marine Corps, 1st Marine Division, Phase III,

      Annex J, p. 4.
10. ibid., p. 4.
11. ibid., p. 4.
12. ibid., p. 4.
13. ibid., p. 4.
14. ibid., p. 4.
15. *Guadalcanal: The Definitive Account of the Landmark Battle,* Richard B. Frank, p. 133.
16. Final Report on Guadalcanal, United States Marine Corps, 1st Marine Division, Phase III, Annex J, pp. 4-5.
17. ibid.
18. Muster Roll, Company B, 1st Battalion, 5th Marines, 1st Marine Division, September 1942, p. 2.
19. Navy Medical Units on Guadalcanal, 1942-1945, Reference Document (unpublished), Andre B. Sobocinski, BUMED Archives.
20. *Once a Marine,* A. A. Vandegrift, as told to Robert B. Asprey, p. 138.
21. http://www.aviation-history.com/grumman/f4f.html, updated: 19 February 2014.
22. *The Old Breed,* George McMillan, pp. 67-68.
23. *First Offensive: The Marine Campaign for Guadalcanal,* Henry I. Shaw, Jr., p. 16.
24. *Guadalcanal Diary,* Richard Tregaskis, p. 198.
25. *The Old Breed,* George McMillan, p. 46.
26. "Guadalcanal," U. S. Navy Medical Department Administrative History, 1941-1945, Volume One (unpublished), BUMED Archives, p.12.

CHAPTER 9

1. *Guadalcanal: The Definitive Account of the Landmark Battle,* Richard B. Frank, p. 153.
2. ibid., p. 154.
3. *The Old Breed,* George McMillan, Chapter 6, Section II, p. 61.
4. *Guadalcanal: The Definitive Account of the Landmark Battle,* Richard B. Frank, p. 154.
5. https://en.wikipedia.org/wiki/Jacob_C._Vouza, updated: 31 January 2018.
6. https://en.wikipedia.org/wiki/Battle_of_the_Tenaru, updated: 12 October 2019.
7. *Guadalcanal: The Definitive Account of the Landmark Battle,* Richard B. Frank, p. 150.
8. ibid., p. 145.
9. ibid., p. 152.
10. Final Report on Guadalcanal, United States Marine Corps, 1st Marine Division, Phase IV, Annex F, p. 1.
11. ibid.
12. *Once a Marine,* A. A. Vandegrift, as told to Robert B. Asprey, p. 141.
13. *Guadalcanal: The Definitive Account of the Landmark Battle,* Richard B. Frank, p. 152.
14. *Once a Marine,* A. A. Vandegrift, as told to Robert B. Asprey, p. 142.
15. ibid.
16. *Guadalcanal: The Definitive Account of the Landmark Battle,* Richard B. Frank, p. 156.
17. *The Old Breed,* George McMillan, p. 64.
18. *Guadalcanal: The Definitive Account of the Landmark Battle,* Richard B. Frank, p. 156.
19. Final Report on Guadalcanal, United States Marine Corps, 1st Marine Division, Phase IV, Annex F, p. 1.
20. https://en.wikipedia.org/wiki/Battle_of_the_Eastern_Solomons, updated: 17 April 2018.
21. *First Offensive: The Marine Campaign for Guadalcanal,* Henry I. Shaw, Jr., p. 21.
22. Final Report on Guadalcanal, United States Marine Corps, 1st Marine Division, Phase IV, Annex F, p. 2.
23. ibid.
24. *Guadalcanal: The Definitive Account of the Landmark Battle,* Richard B. Frank, p. 195.
25. ibid.

26. http://ibiblio.org/hyperwar/USMC/Guadalcanal/index.html, chapter V, page 78, updated: 9 July 1998.
27. ibid.
28. ibid.
29. *Guadalcanal: The Definitive Account of the Landmark Battle*, Richard B. Frank, p. 196.
30. Official Military Personnel File of Robert Joseph Hilsky, National Archives at St. Louis.
31. Muster Roll, Company B, 1st Battalion, 5th Marines, 1st Marine Division, August 1942, pp. 3-4.
32. ibid., *August*, page 6.
33. ibid., *August*, page 5.
34. ibid., *September*, page 5.
35. History of Mobile Hospital No. 6/Fleet Hospital 106 (Wellington, New Zealand), History of Naval Hospitals (Unpublished) 1970, W. K. Patton, BUMED Archives.
36. Muster Roll, Company B, 1st Battalion, 5th Marines, 1st Marine Division, August 1942, p. 4.
37. ibid., *September*, p. 2.
38. Muster Roll, Company A, 1st Battalion, 5th Marines, 1st Marine Division, August 1942.
39. *On the Canal, The Marines of L-3-5 on Guadalcanal, 1942*, Ore J. Marion with Thomas and Edward Cuddihy, p. 99.
40. *Guadalcanal: The Definitive Account of the Landmark Battle,* Richard B. Frank, p. 197.
41. Final Report on Guadalcanal, United States Marine Corps, 1st Marine Division, Phase IV, Annex F, p. 3.

CHAPTER 10

1. Final Report on Guadalcanal, United States Marine Corps, 1st Marine Division, Phase IV, Annex F, p. 5.
2. *Guadalcanal: The Definitive Account of the Landmark Battle,* Richard B. Frank, p. 205.
3. https://history.army.mil/books/wwii/GuadC/gc-05.htm, Page 113-114, updated: 6 November 2000.
4. Guadalcanal: The Definitive Account of the Landmark Battle, Richard B. Frank, p. 220.
5. ibid., p. 221.
6. *Once a Marine,* A. A. Vandegrift, as told to Robert B. Asprey, p. 151.
7. *Guadalcanal: The Definitive Account of the Landmark Battle,* Richard B. Frank, p. 222.
8. http://www.davidbruhn.com/Chapter1BattleStars.pdf, retrieved: October 2019.
9. https://ebird.org/species/buhcou1?siteLanguage=en_US, retrieved: April 2018.
10. *The Guadalcanal Campaign,* Naval History and Heritage Command, Major John L. Zimmerman, p. 72.
11. https://www.aapc.com/blog/26557-wwii-military-health-in-the-pacific/, retrieved: April 2018.
12. *Guadalcanal: The Definitive Account of the Landmark Battle,* Richard B. Frank, p. 127.
13. https://en.wikipedia.org/wiki/Lofton_R._Henderson, retrieved: April 2018.
14. https://www.history.navy.mil/content/dam/museums/Seabee/UnitListPages/NCB/006%20NCB.pdf, retrieved: May 2018.
15. http://pwencycl.kgbudge.com/M/a/Marston_Mat.htmPage, retrieved: May 2018.
16. *Guadalcanal: The Definitive Account of the Landmark Battle,* Richard B. Frank, p. 127.
17. https://en.wikipedia.org/wiki/Cactus_Air_Force, retrieved: October 2018.
18. *Once a Marine,* A. A. Vandegrift, as told to Robert B. Asprey, p. 138.
19. *Guadalcanal: The Definitive Account of the Landmark Battle,* Richard B. Frank, p. 223.
20. ibid., p. 222.
21. *Once a Marine,* A. A. Vandegrift, as told to Robert B. Asprey, p. 151.
22. ibid.
23. ibid., p. 99.
24. https://en.wikipedia.org/wiki/Marine_Raiders, retrieved: October 2019.
25. *Guadalcanal: The Definitive Account of the Landmark Battle,* Richard B. Frank, p. 226.

26. *Once a Marine,* A. A. Vandegrift, as told to Robert B. Asprey, p. 153.
27. *Guadalcanal: The Definitive Account of the Landmark Battle,* Richard B. Frank, p. 228.
28. ibid.
29. *Once a Marine,* A. A. Vandegrift, as told to Robert B. Asprey, p. 154.
30. *Guadalcanal: The Definitive Account of the Landmark Battle,* Richard B. Frank, p. 235.
31. https://en.wikipedia.org/wiki/Battle_of_Edson's_Ridge, retrieved: October 2019.
32. *Guadalcanal: The Definitive Account of the Landmark Battle,* Richard B. Frank, p. 245.
33. *Battle for Guadalcanal,* Samuel B. Griffith, p. 144.
34. Final Report on Guadalcanal, United States Marine Corps, 1st Marine Division, Phase IV, Annex F, page 6
35. ibid., pp. 6-7.
36. https://en.wikipedia.org/wiki/Cheval_de_frise, retrieved: October 2019.
37. https://en.wikipedia.org/wiki/Walter_Stauffer_McIlhenny, retrieved: October 2019.
38. *First Offensive: The Marine Campaign for Guadalcanal,* Henry I. Shaw, Jr., p. 28.
39. *Once a Marine,* A. A. Vandegrift, as told to Robert B. Asprey, p. 153.
40. https://www.ibiblio.org/hyperwar/USMC/I/USMC-I-VI-6.html, chapter VI, page 310, retrieved: October 2019.
41. http://pwencycl.kgbudge.com/E/s/Espiritu_Santo.htm, retrieved: October 2019.
42. *Guadalcanal: The Definitive Account of the Landmark Battle,* Richard B. Frank, pp. 251-52.
43. ibid., pp. 248-50.
44. ibid., pp. 251-52.
45. Final Report on Guadalcanal, United States Marine Corps, 1st Marine Division, Phase V, Annex P, p. 1.
46. *Once a Marine,* A. A. Vandegrift, as told to Robert B. Asprey, p. 161.
47. Final Report on Guadalcanal, United States Marine Corps, 1st Marine Division, Phase V, Annex A, pp. 1-3.
48. *Guadalcanal: The Definitive Account of the Landmark Battle,* Richard B. Frank, p. 261.
49. Final Report on Guadalcanal, United States Marine Corps, 1st Marine Division, Phase V, Annex A, p. 1.
50. ibid., *Annex P,* p. 1.
51. ibid.
52. ibid.
53. *Guadalcanal: The Definitive Account of the Landmark Battle,* Richard B. Frank, p. 270.
54. http://sb.geoview.info/mount_austen,2109687, retrieved: October 2019.
55. *First Offensive: The Marine Campaign for Guadalcanal,* Henry I. Shaw, Jr., p. 28.
56. ibid., pp. 28-29.
57. Final Report on Guadalcanal, United States Marine Corps, 1st Marine Division, Phase V, Annex P, p. 2.
58. *Guadalcanal: The Definitive Account of the Landmark Battle,* Richard B. Frank, p. 274.
59. Final Report on Guadalcanal, United States Marine Corps, 1st Marine Division, Phase V, Annex P, p. 3.
60. Muster Roll, Company B, 1st Battalion, 5th Marines, 1st Marine Division, October 1942, p. 5.
61. ibid.
62. *Guadalcanal: The Definitive Account of the Landmark Battle,* Richard B. Frank, p. 283.
63. Final Report on Guadalcanal, United States Marine Corps, 1st Marine Division, Phase V, Annex P, p. 4.
64. *Guadalcanal: The Definitive Account of the Landmark Battle,* Richard B. Frank, p. 285.
65. *First Offensive: The Marine Campaign for Guadalcanal,* Henry I. Shaw, Jr., page 31
66. *Guadalcanal: The Definitive Account of the Landmark Battle,* Richard B. Frank, p. 289.
67. ibid., pp. 309-10.
68. Final Report on Guadalcanal, United States Marine Corps, 1st Marine Division, Phase V, p. 16.
69. *Guadalcanal: The Definitive Account of the Landmark Battle,* Richard B. Frank, p. 313.
70. *First Offensive: The Marine Campaign for Guadalcanal,* Henry I. Shaw, Jr., p. 33.

71. Final Report on Guadalcanal, United States Marine Corps, 1st Marine Division, Phase V, p. 15.
72. ibid., Annex G, p. 2.
73. **a.** Muster Roll, Company B, 1st Battalion, 5th Marines, 1st Marine Division, October 1942, p. 5;

    b. Navy Medical Units on Guadalcanal, 1942-1945, Reference Document (unpublished), Andre B. Sobocinski, BUMED Archives.
74. *The Old Breed,* George McMillan, p. 101.
75. ibid., pp. 102-3.
76. *Guadalcanal: The Definitive Account of the Landmark Battle,* Richard B. Frank, p. 319.
77. Final Report on Guadalcanal, United States Marine Corps, 1st Marine Division, Phase V, p. 16.
78. ibid.
79. http://ibiblio.org/hyperwar/USMC/USMC-Chron1935-1946/index.html#1942, page 32, retrieved: October 2019.
80. Final Report on Guadalcanal, United States Marine Corps, 1st Marine Division, Phase V, p. 16.
81. *Guadalcanal: The Definitive Account of the Landmark Battle,* Richard B. Frank, p. 327.
82. ibid., p. 338.
83. Final Report on Guadalcanal, United States Marine Corps, 1st Marine Division, Phase V, Annex P, p. 7.
84. Final Report on Guadalcanal, United States Marine Corps, 1st Marine Division, Phase V, p. 14.
85. ibid, Annex P, p. 6.

CHAPTER 11

1. Final Report on Guadalcanal, United States Marine Corps, 1st Marine Division, Phase V, p. 17.
2. Muster Rolls, Company B, 1st Battalion, 5th Marines, 1st Marine Division, September-October 1942.
3. *Navy Medical Units on Guadalcanal,* 1942-1945, A.B. Sobocinski.
4. ibid.
5. Guadalcanal, U. S. Navy Medical Department Administrative History, 1941-1945, BUMED History Division, p. 26.
6. ibid., p. 15.
7. ibid., p. 25.
8. ibid., p. 28.
9. ibid., p. 27.
10. Guadalcanal, U. S. Navy Medical Department Administrative History, 1941-1945, BUMED History Division, p. 16.
11. *Don't Strip Tease for Anopheles: A History of Malaria Protocols during World War II*, Rachel Elise Wacks, page 16.
12. *First Offensive: The Marine Campaign for Guadalcanal*, Henry I. Shaw, Jr., p. 36.
13. ibid.
14. *Guadalcanal: The Definitive Account of the Landmark Battle,* Richard B. Frank, pp. 350-51.
15. Final Report on Guadalcanal, United States Marine Corps, 1st Marine Division, Phase V, p. 22.
16. https://en.wikipedia.org/wiki/Battle_for_Henderson_Field, retrieved: October 2019.
17. Final Report on Guadalcanal, United States Marine Corps, 1st Marine Division, Phase V, p. 24.
18. *Guadalcanal: The Definitive Account of the Landmark Battle,* Richard B. Frank, pp. 354-56.
19. *The Defense of Henderson Field, Guadalcanal*, Brian A. Filler, Major, p. 21.
20. *First Offensive: The Marine Campaign for Guadalcanal*, Henry I. Shaw, Jr., p. 38.
21. *Guadalcanal: The Definitive Account of the Landmark Battle,* Richard B. Frank, pp. 362-67.
22. *Once a Marine,* A. A. Vandegrift, as told to Robert B. Asprey, p. 187.
23. *First Offensive: The Marine Campaign for Guadalcanal*, Henry I. Shaw, Jr., p. 38.
24. *Guadalcanal: The Definitive Account of the Landmark Battle,* Richard B. Frank, p. 371.
25. https://en.wikipedia.org/wiki/Battle_of_the_Santa_Cruz_Islands, updated: 16 October 2019.

26. ibid.
27. *First Offensive: The Marine Campaign for Guadalcanal*, Henry I. Shaw, Jr., p. 40.
28. *Guadalcanal: The Definitive Account of the Landmark Battle*, Richard B. Frank, p. 366.
29. ibid., pp. 404-5.

CHAPTER 12

1. *Once a Marine*, A. A. Vandegrift, as told to Robert B. Asprey, p. 192.
2. Final Report on Guadalcanal, United States Marine Corps, 1st Marine Division, Phase V, p. 27.
3. *Guadalcanal: The Definitive Account of the Landmark Battle*, Richard B. Frank, p. 411.
4. Final Report on Guadalcanal, United States Marine Corps, 1st Marine Division, Phase V, Annex P, pp. 8-9.
5. https://www.ibiblio.org/hyperwar/USMC/USMC-M-Guadalcanal/USMC-M-Guadalcanal-8.html, p. 131.
6. *United States Army in World War II, The War in the Pacific, Guadalcanal: The First Offensive*, John Miller, Jr., p. 192.
7. ibid.
8. *Guadalcanal: The Definitive Account of the Landmark Battle*, Richard B. Frank, p. 412.
9. *United States Army in World War II, The War in the Pacific, Guadalcanal: The First Offensive*, John Miller, Jr., p. 192.
10. *Marines in World War II, The Guadalcanal Campaign*, Major John L. Zimmerman, p. 132.
11. ibid.
12. *Guadalcanal: The Definitive Account of the Landmark Battle*, Richard B. Frank, p. 332.
13. https://www.ibiblio.org/hyperwar/USMC/I/USMC-I-VI-8.html, p. 344, retrieved: October 2019.
14. *Marines in World War II, The Guadalcanal Campaign*, Major John L. Zimmerman, p. 132.
15. Muster Roll, Company B, 1st Battalion, 5th Marines, 1st Marine Division, November 1942, p. 2.
16. https://www.newspapers.com/clip/7602471/austin_windell_pollock/, retrieved: April 2018.
17. Muster Roll, Company B, 1st Battalion, 5th Marines, 1st Marine Division, November 1942, p. 10.
18. ibid., p. 2.
19. Official Military Personnel File of Andrew John Yanno, National Archives at St. Louis.
20. Muster Roll, Company B, 1st Battalion, 5th Marines, 1st Marine Division, November 1942, p. 8.
21. ibid., p. 6.
22. ibid., p. 2.
23. ibid.
24. ibid.
25. Muster Roll, Company B, 1st Battalion, 5th Marines, 1st Marine Division, December 1942.
26. https://www.newspapers.com/clip/7602471/austin_windell_pollock/, retrieved: April 2018.
27. *United States Army in World War II, The War in the Pacific, Guadalcanal: The First Offensive*, John Miller, Jr., p. 194.
28. *Guadalcanal: The Definitive Account of the Landmark Battle*, Richard B. Frank, pp. 412-13
29. ibid.
30. *The Guadalcanal Campaign*, Naval History and Heritage Command, Major John L. Zimmerman, p. 133.
31. ibid.
32. Final Report on Guadalcanal, United States Marine Corps, 1st Marine Division, Phase V, p. 28.
33. *On the Canal, The Marines of L-3-5 on Guadalcanal, 1942*, Ore J. Marion with Thomas and Edward Cuddihy, p. 191.
34. *Once a Marine*, A. A. Vandegrift, as told to Robert B. Asprey, p. 192.
35. *First Offensive: The Marine Campaign for Guadalcanal*, Henry I. Shaw, Jr., p. 41.

36. ibid., p. 6.
37. https://www.ibiblio.org/hyperwar/USMC/I/USMC-I-VI-8.html, p. 342.
38. http://pwencycl.kgbudge.com/A/r/Artillery.htm, retrieved: September 2018.
39. **a.** https://www.nettally.com/jrube/@guadaug.html, retrieved: September 2018.

   b. https://en.wikipedia.org/wiki/Type_92_10_cm_cannon, updated: 2 June 2019.
40. https://en.wikipedia.org/wiki/Type_92_10_cm_cannon, updated: 2 June 2019
41. *World War II in the Pacific*, William A. Renzi and Mark D. Roehrs, p. 109.
42. *The Old Breed*, George McMillan, p. 135.
43. Muster Roll, Company B, 1st Battalion, 5th Marines, 1st Marine Division, November-December 1942.
44. Final Report on Guadalcanal, United States Marine Corps, 1st Marine Division, Phase V, Annex T, p. 7.
45. *Once a Marine*, A. A. Vandegrift, as told to Robert B. Asprey, p. 195.
46. *The Old Breed*, George McMillan, p. 134.
47. Final Report on Guadalcanal, United States Marine Corps, 1st Marine Division, Phase V, Annex P, p. 10.
48. ibid., pp. 9-15.
49. ibid., pp. 10-14.
50. Muster Roll, Company B, 1st Battalion, 5th Marines, 1st Marine Division, November 1942, p. 5.
51. ibid., December 1942, p. 5.
52. Final Report on Guadalcanal, United States Marine Corps, 1st Marine Division, Phase V, Annex P, p. 11.
53. ibid., p. 12.
54. https://www.inaturalist.org/check_lists/15988-Guadalcanal-Check-List?page=1&view=plain, retrieved: October 2019.
55. Final Report on Guadalcanal, United States Marine Corps, 1st Marine Division, Phase V, Annex P, pp. 11-14.
56. https://www.history.navy.mil/content/dam/museums/Seabee/UnitListPages/NCB/006%20NCB.pdf, pp. 33-36
57. Final Report on Guadalcanal, United States Marine Corps, 1st Marine Division, Phase V, Annex P, p. 14.
58. ibid., pp. 14-15.
59. ibid.
60. https://www.history.navy.mil/content/dam/museums/Seabee/UnitListPages/NCB/014%20NCB.pdf, p. 18.
61. *Navy Seabees on Guadalcanal,* Captain Larry G. DeVries, CEC, USNR, Retired.
62. *Guadalcanal: The Definitive Account of the Landmark Battle,* Richard B. Frank, pp. 420-21.
63. https://www.ibiblio.org/hyperwar/USMC/I/USMC-I-VI-8.html, p. 341
64. ibid.
65. ibid., p. 342.
66. ibid.
67. https://en.wikipedia.org/wiki/Guadalcanal_campaign, retrieved: October 2019.
68. https://en.wikipedia.org/wiki/Koli_Point_action, retrieved: October 2019.
69. *Guadalcanal: The Definitive Account of the Landmark Battle,* Richard B. Frank, p. 421.
70. ibid., p. 423.
71. ibid., p. 423-24.
72. https://en.wikipedia.org/wiki/Naval_Battle_of_Guadalcanal, l retrieved: October 2019.
73. *Guadalcanal: The Definitive Account of the Landmark Battle,* Richard B. Frank, p. 451.
74. ttps://www.ibiblio.org/hyperwar/USMC/I/USMC-I-VI-8.html, pp. 356-57.
75. *Guadalcanal: The Definitive Account of the Landmark Battle,* Richard B. Frank, p. 491.
76. https://en.wikipedia.org/wiki/Naval_Battle_of_Guadalcanal, retrieved: October 2019.

77. https://en.wikipedia.org/wiki/Sullivan_brothers, retrieved: October 2019.
78. *Guadalcanal: The Definitive Account of the Landmark Battle,* Richard B. Frank, p. 457.
79. ibid., p. 456-58.
80. https://en.wikipedia.org/wiki/USS_Juneau_(CL-52), retrieved: October 2019.
81. https://en.wikipedia.org/wiki/Sole_Survivor_Policy, retrieved: October 2019.
82. https://en.wikipedia.org/wiki/Sullivan_brothers, retrieved: October 2019.
83. *Guadalcanal: The Definitive Account of the Landmark Battle,* Richard B. Frank, pp. 493-94.
84. ibid., p. 494-97.
85. https://en.wikipedia.org/wiki/Battle_of_Tassafaronga, retrieved: October 2019.
86. ibid.
87. *The Guadalcanal Campaign,* Naval History and Heritage Command, Major John L. Zimmerman, p. 152.
88. Final Report on Guadalcanal, United States Marine Corps, 1st Marine Division, Phase V, Annex P, p. 15.
89. *Once a Marine,* A. A. Vandegrift, as told to Robert B. Asprey, p. 203.
90. USS Crescent City, War Diary, Notes, December 9-14, Part of Task Unit 62.4.8, p. 13.
91. https://www.ozatwar.com/usmc/1stmarinedivision.htm, updated: 08 September 2018.
92. Final Report on Guadalcanal, United States Marine Corps, 1st Marine Division, Phase V, Annex P, p. 15.
93. ibid., p. 16.
94. *Guadalcanal: The Definitive Account of the Landmark Battle,* Richard B. Frank, p. 522.
95. Final Report on Guadalcanal, United States Marine Corps, 1st Marine Division, Phase V, Annex P, p. 16.
96. *Guadalcanal: The Definitive Account of the Landmark Battle,* Richard B. Frank, p. 521.
97. https://en.wikipedia.org/wiki/Alexander_Patch, retrieved: October 2019.
98. *First Offensive: The Marine Campaign for Guadalcanal,* Henry I. Shaw, Jr., p. 51.
99. *Guadalcanal: The Definitive Account of the Landmark Battle,* Richard B. Frank, p. 601.
100. ibid., p. 611.
101. ibid., p. 614.
102. ibid., p. 522.
103. *First Offensive: The Marine Campaign for Guadalcanal,* Henry I. Shaw, Jr., p. 52.
104. *The Old Breed,* George McMillan, p. 27.

BIBLIOGRAPHY

Bartsch, William H. *Victory Fever on Guadalcanal: Japan's First Land Defeat of World War II.* Texas A&M University Press, 2014.

Budge, Kent G. *Guadalcanal.* The Pacific War Online Encyclopedia, © 2007-2010, 2012-2014, pwencycl.kgbudge.com/G/u/Guadalcanal.htm.

DeVries, Larry D., Captain, CEC, USNR (Retired), *Navy Seabees on Guadalcanal,* Seabee History, 1992, www.seabeecook.com/history/canal/cactus.htm.

Domagalski, John J. *Lost at Guadalcanal: The Final Battles of the Astoria and Chicago as described by survivors and in official Reports.* McFarland & Company, Inc, 1969.

Dunn, Peter, *1st Marine Division," The Old Breed", United States Marine Corps (USMC) in Australia During WW2.* Australia @ War, 2003, www.ozatwar.com/usmc/1stmarinedivision.htm.

Frank, Richard B. *Guadalcanal.* Penguin Books, 1992.

Friedman, Kenneth I. *Morning of the Rising Sun.* Booksurge Publishing, 2007.

Griffith, Samuel B. *The Battle for Guadalcanal.* Lippincott, 1963.

Hammel, Eric M. *Guadalcanal: Starvation Island.* Crown Publishers, 1987.

Hammel, Eric. *Guadalcanal, The U.S. Marines in World War II, A Pictorial Tribute.* Zenith Press, 2007.

Haywood, Jacob A. *War Diary for Company B, 1st Battalion, 5th Marines, 1st Marine Division, FMF during the Guadalcanal Campaign , World War II* (These records are part of Record Group 127, Entry A1 1051, Series: Records Relating to United States Marine Corps Operations in World War II, Box 43, Textual Reference Operations, National Archives at College Park, MD).

Hough, Frank O., Lieutenant, USMCR, et al. *U.S. Marine Corps, History of U.S. Marine Corps Operations in World War II, HyperWar: Pearl Harbor to Guadalcanal, Volume I.* The Public's Library and Digital Archive: Historical Branch, G-3 Division, Headquarters, HyperWar Foundation, 2011, www.ibiblio.org/hyperwar/USMC/I/index.html.

Lane, Kerry. *Guadalcanal Marine.* University Press of Mississippi, 2004.

Marion, Ore J., and Thomas and Edward Cuddihy. *On the Canal, The Marines of L-3-5 on Guadalcanal, 1942.* Stockpole Books, 2004.

McMillan, George. *The Old Breed, A History of the First Marine Division in World War ll.* Infantry Journal Press, 1949.

Miller, John, Jr. *United States Army in World War II, The War in the Pacific, Guadalcanal: The First Offensive.* Center of Military History, United States Army, 1995, Library of Congress Catalog Card Number: 50-13988, First Printed 1949-CMH Pub 5-3, history.army.mil/books/wwii/GuadC/GC-fm.htm.

Millett, Allan R. *In Many a Strife: General Gerald C. Thomas and the U. S. Marine Corps, 1917-1956.* Naval Institute Press, 1993.

Naval History and Heritage Command, Publications Branch, Office of Naval Intelligence - United States Navy, 1943. *Combat Narratives : Solomon Islands Campaign : I The Landing in the Solomons, 7-8 August 1942, Confidential [declassified].* 2 November 2017, www.history.navy.mil/research/library/online-reading-room/title-list-alphabetically/s/solomon-islands-campaign-i-the-landing-in-the-solomons.html.

Naval History and Heritage Command, Publications Branch, Office of Naval Intelligence - United States Navy, 1943. *The Solomons Campaign: Guadalcanal, August 1942–February 1943.* November 2020, www.history.navy.mil/browse-by-topic/wars-conflicts-and-operations/world-war-ii/1942/guadalcanal.html.

Naval History and Heritage Command, The Navy Department Library. *Building the Navy's Bases in World War II: History of the Bureau of Yards and Docks and the Civil Engineer Corps, 1940-1946.* U. S. Govt. Print Office, 1947, catalog.hathitrust.org/Record/000810658.

Quantock, David E., Lieutenant-Colonel, Compiled and formatted by Alan Clark & Patrick Clancey. *Disaster at Savo Island, 1942.* United States Army, U.S. Army War College, Carlisle Barracks, PA: HyperWar Foundation, 2002, www.ibiblio.org/hyperwar/USN/rep/Savo/Quantock/.

Renzi, William A., and Mark D. Roehrs. *World War II in the Pacific.* Routledge, 2004.

Santelli, James S. *A Brief History of the 7th Marines.* History and Museums Division Headquarters, United States Marine Corps, 1980.

Shaw, Henry I., Jr. *First Offensive: The Marine Campaign for Guadalcanal, Marines in World War ll, Commemorative Series.* History and Museums Division, Headquarters, U.S. Marine Corps, 1992.

Tregaskis, Richard. *Guadalcanal Diary.* Random House, 1943.

USMC History Division, Historical Reference Branch. *News-Times* [Danbury, Connecticut], "Danbury Marine Landed by Superiors in The Solomons." 14 September 1942.

USMC History Division, Historical Reference Branch. *The Bridgeport Post* [Bridgeport, Connecticut], "Home from The Wars." 29 August 1943.

Vandegrift, A. A., as told by Robert B. Asprey. *Once a Marine.* Ballantine Books, 1964.

Zimmerman, John L., Major. *The Guadalcanal Campaign.* Naval History and Heritage Command, USMCR Historical Section, Division of Public Information, Headquarters, U.S. Marine Corps, 1949.

WORKS CITED

Alexander Turnbull Library, 70 Molesworth Street, Thorndon, Wellington 6011, New Zealand.
Page 103 - PAColl-6075-32.

Critical Past LLC. 12100 Sunrise Valley Drive, Box E-230-16, Reston, Virginia 20191.
Cover photo - 65675060330_001012-HR.
Page 113 - 65675067283_000690. 65675021761_001363. 65675067283_000736. 65675067283_000598.
Page 114 - 65675021761_001450. 65675021761_001624. 65675021761_001740. 65675067764_001196.
Page 132 - 65675060320_005382.
Page 154 - 65675021761_005249.

Hammel, Eric. *Guadalcanal, The U.S. Marines in World War II, A Pictorial Tribute.* Zenith Press, 2007.
Page 208 - "Dead Japanese soldiers on beach." Official USMC Photograph, p. 129.

Library of Congress, 101 Independence Ave SE, Washington, DC 20540.
Page 1 - LC-USW33-000138-ZE.
Page 9 - LC-USF34-043247-D.
Page 38 - LC-USW3-022994-C.
Page 57 - LC-USF346-026485-D [P&P].
Page 58 - LC-USF34-043197-D [P&P].
Page 242 - LC-USE6- D-008871 [P&P].

McMillan, George. *The Old Breed, A History of the First Marine Division in World War II.* Infantry Journal Press, 1949.
Page XXX - (Map) "The Solomon Islands." p. 26.
Page 50 - "Platoon marching." p. 9.
Page 89 - "Marines boarding train." p. 16.
Page 159 - "Marines in landing craft." p. 274.

Miller, John, Jr, *Guadalcanal: The First Offensive,* Center of Military History, United States Army, Washington, D. C., 1995, Card Number: 50-13988, First Printed 1949- CMH Pub 5-3.
Page XXXII - (Maps) "Mantanikau Action." p. 90. "Push Toward Kokumbona." p. 193.

National Archives at College Park, 3301 Metzerott Rd, College Park, Maryland 20740.
Page XXIX - (Poster) "U.S. Marines, on Land, at Sea, in the Air." World War II Posters, 1942 - 1945, ARC Identifier: 515111.
Page 47 - Department of the Navy. 80-G-16871. ARC Identifier: 520590.

Page 103 - Official U.S. Navy Photograph. 80-G-10760.
Page 104 - Official U.S. Navy Photograph. 80-G-13455.
Page 105 - Official U.S. Navy Photograph. 80-G-K-554.
Page 113 - "Marines descending net ladder." 208-AA-76U-9.
Page 114 - Top Right: Official U.S. Navy Photograph. 80-G-10151.
Page 125 - Official U.S. Navy Photograph. 80-G-17066.
Page 176 - Official USMC Photograph. ARC Identifier: 5891308.
Page 185 - Official USMC Photograph. ARC Identifier: 74250474.

National Personal Records Center, 1 Archives Dr, St. Louis, Missouri 63138.
Official Military Personnel Files of the U. S. Marine Corps, Records Group 127,
Records of the National Archives and Records Administration.
Page 8 - Service Record: PFC James Joseph Messina.
Page 15 - Service Record Portrait: Pvt. Albert Donald Palermo.
Pages 64 - Service Record Portraits: PFC Gerrit Edward Heidema. PFC Robert Joseph Hilsky. PFC Robert James Johnson. PFC Robert Julius Johnson. PFC George Felton Jones. PFC Salvatore Anthony Messina. PFC Davie Warren Shuford. PFC Andrew John Yanno.
Page 66 - Service Record Portraits: Sgt Eugene Breeding. Cpl. Albert Steve Podracky.

Naval History and Heritage Command, Washington Navy Yard, 736 Sicard St SE,
Washington, DC 20374.
Zimmerman, Major John L., USMCR, Historical Section, Division of Public
Information, Headquarters, U.S. Marine Corps, 1949.
Page XXX - (Map) "*The Guadalcanal Campaign*. Guadalcanal - Tulagi Objective Area, 7 August 1942." pg. 26.
Page 75 - L45-298.06.01.
Page 81 - 80-G-466191.
Page 93 - NH 81447.
Page 106 - NH 92699.
Page 113 - NH 91509.
Page 114 - Mid Right: NH 97484. Bottom Right: NH 97740.
Page 125 - NH 69114.
Page 145 - USN 42969.

Photos and Documents from the Estate of James J. Messina.
Page XV - (crop) Official USMC Photograph, Company B, 5th Regiment, 1st Battalion, 1st Marine Division, F.M.F.
Pages 78-79 - Official USMC Photograph, Company B, 5th Regiment, 1st Battalion, 1st Marine Division, F.M.F.
Page 96 - Shellback certificate for crossing the Equator.
Page 97 - Archives New Zealand, Postcard, c.1942.

San Diego Air and Space Museum, 2001 Pan American Plaza, San Diego, California, 92101.
Page 93 - SHIPS00442.

Shaw, Henry, I., Jr., *First Offensive: The Marine Campaign For Guadalcanal, Marines in World War II, Commemorative Series,* **Marine Corps Historical Center, 1992.**
Page XXXI - (Maps) "Guadalcanal, Tulagi-Gavutu, and Florida Islands," p. 4. "Landing on Guadalcanal and Capture of the Airfield, 7-8 August 1942," p. 8.

USMC Archives and Special Collections, Gray Research Center, Quantico, Virginia, 22134.
Page 89 - Alexander A. Vandegrift Collection (COLL/3166).
Page 152 - Sir Jacob Charles Vouza (Marine Corps).
Page 169 - Defense Dept Photo (Marine Corps), Headquarters, No: 52928.
Page 185 - Marines firing machine gun (Marine Corps) 51340.
Page 197 - Defense Dept Photo (Marine Corps), Headquarters, No: 72695.
Page 228 - Defense Dept Photo (Marine Corps), Headquarters, No: 76324.
Page 249 - Top: File No: W-FU-26-40565. Bottom: Defense Dept Photo (Marine Corps), 52978.

USMC History Division, Archives Branch, flickr.com.
Page 108 - Thayer Soule Collection (COLL/2266).
Page 117 - Julian Smith Collection (COLL/202).
Page 120 - (2) Thayer Soule Collection (COLL/2266).
Page 154 - Thayer Soule Collection (COLL/2266).
Page 172 - Thayer Soule Collection (COLL/2266).
Page 190 - Thayer Soule Collection (COLL/2266).
Page 200 - Thayer Soule Collection (COLL/2266).
Page 212 - Thayer Soule Collection (COLL/2266).
Page 226 - Thayer Soule Collection (COLL/2266).

COAUTHOR'S FINAL THOUGHT

Celebrating James and Kathrine's 40th wedding anniversary at Le Mont restaurant, Pittsburgh, Pennsylvania, 1986.

There isn't one day that goes by that I don't think of you, and I am grateful for this incredible gift you have given me.

Semper Fi

www.ingramcontent.com/pod-product-compliance
Lightning Source LLC
Chambersburg PA
CBHW041827090426
42811CB00010B/1135